HYPATIA

SPECIAL ISSUE
Lesbian Philosophy

edited by
Claudia Card

VOL. 7, NO.4
FALL 1992

A Journal of Feminist Philosophy

Hypatia (Hy-pay-sha) was an Egyptian woman philosopher, mathematician, and astronomer who lived in Alexandria from her birth in about 370 A.D. until her death in 415. She was the leader of the Neoplatonic School in Alexandria and was famous as an eloquent and inspiring teacher. The journal *Hypatia* is named in honor of this foresister. Her name reminds us that although many of us are the first women philosophers in our schools, we are not, after all, the first in history.

Hypatia has its roots in the Society for Women in Philosophy, many of whose members have for years envisioned a regular publication devoted to feminist philosophy. *Hypatia* is the realization of that vision; it is intended to encourage and communicate many different kinds of feminist philosophy.

Hypatia (ISSN 0887–5367) is owned by Hypatia, Inc., a not for profit corporation, and published by Indiana University Press, which assume no responsibility for statements expressed by authors. *Hypatia* is published four times a year. Subscription rates, in U.S. funds, for 1992–93 are: institutions, $50/yr; individuals, $32.50/yr. Foreign subscribers add $12.50/yr surface post. Single copies are: institutions, $20; individuals, $10.00. A discount is available on bulk orders for classroom use or bookstore sales.

Address all subscriptions and business correspondence to the Journals Manager, Indiana University Press, 601 North Morton Street, Bloomington, IN 47404. Notice of nonreceipt of an issue must be sent within four weeks after receipt of subsequent issue. Please notify the Press of any change in address; the Post Office does not forward third class mail. Manuscripts and other editorial correspondence should be addressed to: Linda Lopez McAlister, Editor, *Hypatia*, University of South Florida, SOC 107, Tampa, FL 33620-8100/ (813) 974-5531. FAX (813) 974-2668. Bitnet: DLLAFAA@CFRVM. Internet: DLLAFAA@ CFRVM. CFR. USF. EDU.

Hypatia is indexed in the on-line and CD-ROM index, *Academic Index*, as well as in the *Alternative Press Index*, *Studies on Women Abstracts*, *Women's Studies Abstracts*, *Sociological Abstracts*, *The Philosopher's Index*, *Women's Studies Index* and in *The Philosopher's Index* database, file 57 of DIALOG.

Hypatia was published in 1983, 1984, and 1985 as special annual issues of *Women's Studies International Forum*. Articles which appeared in those issues are available in book form in *Hypatia Reborn*, (Indiana University Press, 1990).

Hypatia

Sharon Bishop, *California State University, Los Angeles*
Judith Butler, *Johns Hopkins University*
Claudia Card, *University of Wisconsin, Madison*
Lorraine Code, *York University*
Elizabeth Eames, *Southern Illinois University at Carbondale*
Ann Ferguson, *University of Massachusetts, Amherst*
Jane Flax, *Howard University*
Nancy Fraser, *Northwestern University*
Marilyn Friedman, *Washington University*
Marilyn Frye, *Michigan State University*
Carol Gould, *Stevens Institute of Technology*
Susan Griffin, *Berkeley, California*
Donna Haraway, *University of California, Santa Cruz*
Nancy Hartsock, *Johns Hopkins University*
Hilde Hein, *College of the Holy Cross*
Sarah Lucia Hoagland, *Northeastern Illinois University*
Helen Bequaert Holmes, *University of Massachusetts*
Alison Jaggar, *University of Colorado*
Elizabeth Janeway, *New York*
Evelyn Fox Keller, *University of California, Berkeley*
Eva Feder Kittay, *State University of New York, Stony Brook*
Carolyn Korsmeyer, *State University of New York, Buffalo*
Rhoda Kotzin, *Michigan State University*
Lynda Lange, *University of Toronto-Scarborough*
María Lugones, *Carleton College*
Mary B. Mahowald, *University of Chicago*
Patricia Mann, *City College of New York*
Andree Nichola-McLaughlin, *Medgar Evars College*
Linda Nicholson, *State University of New York, Albany*
Andrea Nye, *University of Wisconsin, Whitewater*
Susan Ray Peterson, *Nassau Community College, New York*
Christine Pierce, *North Carolina State University*
Connie Crank Price, *Tuskegee Institute*
Laura M. Purdy, *Wells College*
Blanche Radford-Curry, *Eckerd College*
Sara Ruddick, *New School of Social Research*
Betty Safford, *California State University, Fullerton*
Naomi Scheman, *University of Minnesota*
Elizabeth V. Spelman, *Smith College*
Nancy Tuana, *University of Texas at Dallas*
Karen Warren, *Macalester College*
Caroline Whitbeck, *Massachusetts Institute of Technology*
Iris Young, *University of Pittsburgh*
Jacquelyn Zita, *University of Minnesota*

Contents

LESBIAN COMMUNITY AND RESPONSIBILITY

Introduction

CLAUDIA CARD

In *Lesbian Ethics: Toward New Value*, Sarah Hoagland (1988) declined to define "lesbian."[1] Nor did I, in issuing a call for papers for this special issue of *Hypatia*, attempt to define either "lesbian" or "lesbian philosophy," although these concepts are neither clear nor univocal. One could say that the meanings of "lesbian" and "lesbian philosophy," for purposes of this issue, are a function of what was submitted and what I chose to include. That is true; but there is also more to say. Theorists in this area exhibit diverse understandings of lesbian philosophy. Some construe it broadly as philosophy *by* lesbians, taking it that lesbian perspectives on all kinds of things emerge from lesbian histories and identities. Others, more interested in focusing *on* lesbians, take it to be philosophy not only *by* but also *about* lesbians. Still others, interested in the changing concepts of "lesbian" that emerge from interaction in lesbian community and relationships, take it to be about what lesbians reflect on in such contexts, i.e., philosophy *by* lesbians interacting *with* lesbians.

My own approach is not quite identical with any of the above. I treat "lesbian" as first of all an adjective, a modifier, a qualifier of experiences, relationships, dreams, imaginings, practices, communities, philosophy—and secondarily as a noun naming an identity, usually political and voluntarily embraced. In this respect, I find myself allied with Adrienne Rich (1979a, 1979b, 1980) and to a certain extent with recent historians who maintain that lesbian *identities* are a relatively recent phenomenon, though lesbian behavior and relationships are as old as humanity, and same-sex bonding, no doubt much older. Moreover, my approach to philosophy is Socratic in a very particular respect: I think of philosophy as fundamentally a kind of self-knowledge. So understood, lesbian philosophy can include reflections on lesbian experience, relationships, and possibilities by women who regard these experiences, relationships, and possibilities as their own but have not—often for political reasons—chosen to embrace a lesbian identity. In my view, lesbian experience, embracing many forms of erotic interaction between women, is a subversive part of most women's lives, though its pervasiveness and manifestations in individual lives vary with the circumstances and commitments of the individual. It is also my view that most women know this, on some level or during some moments, though we don't all or always choose the term "lesbian" to describe what we know. If I am right, (almost) any woman reflecting on lesbian possibilities is bound to confront some that are hers. The papers in this issue exemplify the search for wisdom in and about lesbian activity, choices, relationships, communities, perspectives, and ideals by writers who evidently take such things seriously and treat them respectfully and with good humor. Yet the reader should not take it that a particular contributor identifies herself as a lesbian, or identifies herself under any other sexual or erotic orientation label, unless she says so.

Lesbian philosophy, in the sense delineated above, is being done today by thinkers with differing political allegiances, affiliations, and backgrounds. One set of such thinkers doing major creative work is a small but dynamic group of academic philosophers in the Midwest Society of Women in Philosophy (SWIP) who have publicly identified as lesbian for many years. Lesbian philosophies have been growing in Midwest SWIP for more than a decade and a half, stimulated by the gynocentric highs of semiannual, increasingly multicultural, weekend conferences. Not all who have a part in this development currently live in midwestern states; participants travel to meetings regularly from both coasts. Influential works—many discussed in this issue—by writers in the Midwest SWIP group include Marilyn Frye's *The Politics of Reality* (1983) and other essays (1980, 1988, 1990c, reprinted in her new *Willful Virgin*, 1992); María Lugones's "Playfulness, 'World'-Travelling, and Loving Perception" (this journal, 1987), Sarah Hoagland's *Lesbian Ethics: Toward New Value* (1988); essays by Joyce Trebilcot (1979; 1984b; 1986; this journal 1988b and 1990), and Jeffner Allen's *Lesbian Philosophy: Explorations* (1986) and essays collected in her anthology *Lesbian Philosophies and Cultures* (1990). These philosophers share a concern with creative alternatives for living and with extralegal modes of resistance to oppression. For some, gynocentric contexts of inspiration are also provided by the writings of thinkers who work in literature rather than philosophy, notably by poets Audre Lorde, Susan Griffin, Adrienne Rich, and Gloria Anzaldúa. Support for lesbian philosophy has been generated and maintained over the years also by SWIPpers who do not identify as lesbian and some who do not claim lesbian experience—support ranging from the provision of welcoming spaces (physically on campuses and intellectually on conference programs) to thoughtful and constructive audience responses, spontaneous and written comments, engagement with lesbian philosophy in their own writings, and networking. Lesbian philosophy emerging from Midwest SWIP has been typically tended by socialist midwives. It shares a commitment to antiracism and to addressing issues of class, body size, able-bodiedness, and, more recently, able-mindedness.[2] This is the context of lesbian philosophy that I know best. My own philosophical thought has been nourished here for the past fifteen years.

Still others work in, or find their thought nourished by, mixed-gender contexts of thinkers who identify as gay, lesbian, or bisexual and are often allied with organizations descended from what began as predominantly men's gay rights groups of the early 1970s. These groups have been concerned fundamentally with justice and legal change. They have attended increasingly to issues of gender, race, class, and disability. It was here that my lesbian pride found early support from the early to the mid-1970s, and here I found also a context for my philosophical interests in the area of justice.

Yet others come to lesbian philosophy in religious contexts or from theological backgrounds, as Mary Daly, Janice Raymond, Carter Heyward, and Martha Saunders (this issue) have done. Mary Daly's *Gyn/Ecology: The Metaethics of Radical Feminism* (1978) energized lesbian readers worldwide and transformed the general consciousness of the global extent of misogyny and its histories.

There are surely many groups not known to me with histories of support for lesbian thought, working quietly, sheltered from mainstream publicity. And some lesbian thinkers, not allied with particular organizations or identified with backgrounds I have mentioned, write from their own histories, read widely and eclectically, and develop their own syntheses and innovations, while many others are yet in hiding, fearful for their lives and livelihoods. There is overlap of concerns and some reciprocal influence among writers who work in or are working out of various of these contexts, more in some cases than in others. Dyke philosophers of Midwest SWIP, for example, have been avid readers of Mary Daly and Janice Raymond. Yet a salient aspect of being lesbian or doing lesbian work has been isolation from each other. Acutely aware of limits of our knowledge, we aim to facilitate lesbian connections. One thing that makes this issue special is not that it represents all our voices—it doesn't—but that its very publicity furthers the aim of connection and, thereby, of self-knowledge.

While essays in this issue come from several of the backgrounds mentioned, a more interesting way to approach them is by theme. They exhibit several overlapping themes. Four that stand out are (1) creativity and experiments in wisdom-seeking, often coupled with critiques of traditional philosophy, especially its dualisms and methods; (2) the "sex wars," contested sexual attitudes and activities; (3) constructing the meaning of "lesbian"—what goes in and what stays out?—and (4) lesbian community and responsibility.

Creativity emerges in a variety of ways. In a vein of protest preparing the way for her ongoing experimentation with alternatives, Joyce Trebilcot continues her critique of patriarchal ideals of inquiry, coupling it this time with a critique of "lesbian" as too suggestive of sexuality to describe accurately the locus of concerns of some of those who, like herself, will be drawn to this special issue of *Hypatia*, hoping to find some likeminded thinkers therein.[3] It is interesting to read her essay following upon Jacqueline Zita's portrait of Jeffner Allen, the short essays and songs by Tangren Alexander, and María Lugones's interpretive essay on Gloria Anzaldúa's *Borderlands/La Frontera*, as Jeffner Allen and Tangren Alexander push at the boundaries of philosophy and eros, integrating emotion and intellect, and María Lugones takes seriously Gloria Anzaldúa's observation that in the "borderlands" resisting multiple oppressions requires developing a tolerance for contradiction and ambiguity. Creativity at a very mundane, practical level emerges in María Lugones's continued articulation of the "multiplicitous self" that develops in the "borderlands," a self she distinguishes from the hyphenated selves (such as "Mexican-American") imperialistically imposed by a culture that regards other cultures as ornamental, exploitable, less real.[4]

The second theme, "sex wars," takes us to contested sexual attitudes and activities, especially sadomasochism. Gynocentric lesbianfeminists and sexual-liberationist lesbians (some identifying also as gay and feminist) have clashed politically over stances regarding pornography and prostitution (often called "sex industries") and over stances regarding "consensual sadomasochism." Concerning these "sexuality debates," Bat-Ami Bar On argues that, however painful, keeping them alive is crucial to a radical feminist critique of personal life and preferable to the "normalizing" of lesbianism that has come to characterize contemporary standpoint feminism. In the spirit of keeping such debates alive, Lorena Saxe, focusing on an aspect of the sadomasochism issues, takes up the question what admissions policies, if any, feminist events such as music festivals should have, especially regarding the *sadist* partners of "sadomasochist contracts": whether it is justifiable to exclude them, whether it is justifiable not to, and what values are at stake in trying to answer these questions. There are also some remarks on "sex wars" in Ruth Ginzberg's essay, and, in the essay by Kathleen Martindale and Martha Saunders, there is a discussion of Carter Heyward's observations on sadomasochism, pondering the implications of its pervasiveness among lesbians generally in patriarchal society.

On the third theme, constructing (what it means to be) "lesbian," Ruth Ginzberg offers a nonessentialist interpretation of Audre Lorde's conception of eros and suggests that María Lugones's " 'world'-travelling" offers a way to move beyond debates about who is and who isn't lesbian. These lines of thought raise new issues explored by Elisabeth Däumer and Jacqueline Zita. Presenting "queer ethics" as developing some ideas motivating Sarah Hoagland's *Lesbian Ethics: Toward New Value*, Elisabeth Däumer raises the question (mentioned also by Ruth Ginzberg) whether a political understanding of "lesbian" makes possible *male lesbians*. Several of us who teach radicalesbian feminist philosophy have encountered men in our classes who wanted to be lesbians and some who insisted that they were. Jacqueline Zita takes that question seriously, exploring critically her resistance to acknowledging the possibility of male lesbians, and setting the inquiry in the context of postmodernism.

The fourth theme, lesbian community and responsibility, comes to the fore in essays by Barbara Houston and by Kathleen Martindale and Martha

Saunders, who take issue with positions supported recently in the lesbian ethics of Sarah Hoagland and in the journal *Lesbian Ethics*. Barbara Houston argues, contrary to Sarah Hoagland, that blaming is an important moral response for lesbians to retain for the development of agency in oppressive contexts. Kathleen Martindale and Martha Saunders, founders and editors of the *Canadian Journal of Feminist Ethics* (1986-89), argue for a conception of lesbian ethics oriented toward justice, and they recommend the work of theologian Carter Heyward on eros, justice, and spirituality. Partial background to some of these issues is provided by Sarah Hoagland in her overview and discussion of motivations for writing *Lesbian Ethics: Toward New Value* (1988), as well as in this editor's review of the journal *Lesbian Ethics* (1984-present). (Attorney) Ruthann Robson, taking the justice system seriously, explores dangers of domestication facing lesbians who confront U.S. legal systems around issues of motherhood. Naomi Scheman, in a self-reflective review essay, explores elements of history and spirituality in Jewish identity and how these elements have connected with lesbian choices in recent writings by Jewish lesbians.

I have compiled for this issue and placed at the end a bibliography of reference works, periodicals (past and present), anthologies, books, and articles (chapters, etc.) in lesbian philosophy and culture, based largely on what I have found valuable in teaching lesbian feminist philosophy since 1977 and lesbian culture in women's studies since 1981 at the University of Wisconsin and on what I have learned working in this area for twenty years. This bibliography does not include all references from essays in this special issue; it does include many items not mentioned elsewhere in the issue.

Thanks to Linda Lopez McAlister, general editor of *Hypatia*, for suggesting the idea of this issue to me; to those who wrote special review essays; and to the many who reviewed and commented extensively on submissions, some on more than one occasion.

NOTES

1. Works referred to in this introduction can be found in the "Selected Bibliography of Lesbian and Related Works" at the end of this issue.

2. On able-mindedness, see Carol Van Kirk (1990).

3. For earlier criticism of patriarchal methods of philosophy and a presentation of alternatives, see especially Joyce Trebilcot (1988B and 1990).

4. On the "multiplicitous self," see María Lugones (1990b and 1990c).

Jeffner Allen: A Lesbian Portrait

JACQUELYN N. ZITA

This review essay covers the lesbian writing of philosopher Jeffner Allen, contrast-
ing her fiercely separatist earlier work with her more recent experimental writing. A
quest for a separate ontic space—defining difference qua Lesbian and consistently
characterized by Allen as "the open"—links her earlier work with her more recent
atonalities richly coded with ritual, myth, memory, and play.

> Not enough theory? The end of
> discipline? What if a field were to
> burst into bloom mountains become
> deserts washed by oceans?
> — Jeffner Allen (1989a, 27)

In the cold of January in Minnesota, I am walking across our campus, preoccupied with a hostile wind and sharp blustering snow, my eyes cast to the ground as I carefully traverse icy pathways that promise what seems an interminable journey. My body heat is condensed beneath heavy layers of clothing, yet with fierce persistence the environment cuts through to me, not at all friendly. I counsel: Don't fall! Don't lose consciousness! Be aware! At some point, the *lesbian symbols* on the wall jump out at me. I read this vandalism oddly, running through the lecture I will someday give on the politics of graffiti, the writings of powerlessness, large and obtrusive in the public domain. I also feel old, judgmental, too established, and distanced from the hands that defaced a university wall and from the anarchy of enthusiasm I imagine there. My head full of the writings of Jeffner Allen, I focus again. Something is different. I see something warm and friendly, struggling for life in "syllables nestled in bones," in syllables that "continue to speak themselves out of the need to be heard" (Courtot 1977, 8). A nostalgia for that Difference we as Lesbians can call our own sweeps through me, along with a desire to exit this established order of things within which we were most certainly not invited

Hypatia vol. 7, no. 4 (Fall 1992) © by Jacquelyn N. Zita

to exist and against which we transgress to write against the wall. I retire to the library with Jeffner in hand.

As I review Allen's lesbian writings, I recall a recent conversation with a female graduate student, who described how when she came to the University of Minnesota she met postmodernism and now finds herself without a vocabulary to speak and write as a feminist. This peculiar silence within postmodernist aphasia still hints of a memory, traces of a different lifeworld, where bold words were not considered out of place, wrongly said, symptoms of essentialism, but forceful signs inspiring defiance and political action. In *Lesbian Philosophy: Explorations* (Allen 1986a), Allen refreshes our memories of such writing. She gives us conduit to a different way of naming and inhabiting the body marked "Lesbian," a lifeworld that is at once local, personal, and not co-optable, anchored by ancient myth and in the aqueous boundarylessness of the lesbian body.

Lesbian Philosophy: Explorations challenges women to do the "unthinkable"—hate men, consider violence, "evacuate" motherhood, touch women, remember and invent, a marshaling of practical energies that draws reference to the "indecent" militancy of seventies' radical lesbianism. These "unthinkable" and "unnatural" acts make possible not only the corporeal deconstruction of "woman" (characterized by Allen as an object of male sexual entitlement, essentially "empenised") but also a lifeworld of lesbian friendship and effective survival. A new self is constructed in "the actions that form my body as lived" and greeted by Allen, as a "freely chosen subjectivity," with genuine wholeness, harmony, exuberance, and well-being, "keeping free" a spontaneous subjectivity as an end-in-itself.

In contrast, the survival of women in the world of patriarchy requires a constant vigilance, strategies for defending the boundaries of our bodies while "looking at our blood," a metaphor Allen employs for seeing "the reality and possibility of Amazonian harmony and strength" (Allen 1986a, 35). This blood that pulses through Amazonian body and its lineage of shameless militancy is contrasted with the blood of rape. "Rape is that moment when a woman's life blood stops. My body is occupied and used by a man. My life is not my own. I become bloodless" (Allen 1986a, 47). In one of the most controversial sections of *Lesbian Philosophy: Explorations*, Allen describes in detail her own rape experience. In the mid-1980's this descriptive fidelity to a rape experience marks a new form of testimonial writing reflecting women's knowledge and experience of male violence. Allen's descriptions, contextualized by the complexities of an interracial rape, are tangibly painful and dangerous, speaking her truth against the psychologizing charges of racism and pathologized man-hating. Allen describes her own reasons for including these passages:

Descriptive fidelity to the primary moments of a particular rape is a way of being true to the self which survives the change. Reflective description of the "how" of one particular rape forms the basis for a narrative that responds to men's terrorism of women. . . . In surviving rape, I exercise a radical choice to negate terror, to retain a blood, life, body, apart from the world of the rapist. In part due to the reprieve by the rapist, in part because of radical choices acted upon, I am still alive. I remember how I fought back and how I cared for my life. (Allen 1986a, 47-48)

Allen counsels on the importance of remembering how we have survived a world hostile to women: recount the terror "made visible by the unfreedom of my body" (Allen 1986a, 47) and recover the body. For Allen, who came close to getting killed in the rape of her body, "he cannot be found, and I must kill him and his world of terrorism—with the pen" (Allen 1986a, 54). As readers we are asked to remember the act, not the apologies. We are asked to focus on the details of the rape, feeling the pain and tactility of her terror as she redescribes her experience. We are asked to recall how we can survive these violations, recollecting our power. We are asked not to invert misogyny but to experience the ferocity of man-hating as a profound "grief at an injustice, a deep bereavement and caring" (Allen 1986a, 23). Allen writes: "My hatred of men is, rather, my experience of the loss of myself and others as autonomous subjects. My man-hating is grief of myself and other women at the loss of our bodies and memories and history" (Allen 1986a, 23). For her, to hate is to care. Her body becomes a conduit, "anew the fabric into which objects and words are woven" (Allen 1986a, 92) in the "unending surprise of bodily presence" (Allen 1986a, 90) as she returns to her lesbian world, where "slowly, my body is touched, traced, and retraced, as I revive" (Allen 1986a, 55). In that world of touch, tongue, aqueous celebrations, and the creation of forbidden meanings and pleasures, "woman" becomes Lesbian. Allen's writing is stark and unsettling—a jolt within the established order of things. We are stopped in our tracks, reminded of inspired anger and the treacheries of remembering our survivals.

Allen's articulations of lesbian ontology and a metaphysics of touch move us beyond the seductive commonplaces of reproductive motherhood, androgyny, nonviolence, and the virtues of feminine passivity. Also left behind is the world of male logocentrism, defined by principles of identity and hegemony of the Same, a metaphysics of vision, an ethics of domination, and epistemologies of propriety and correspondence. Allen's ontological rupture is splendid in its release, returning us to our bodies as sources for the felt emergence of new meanings. In return, this body demands access to food, literacy, energy supplies, and resources—a concrete and global political agenda required for women's effective and autonomous survival. Allen locates the materialism of women's oppression under patriarchy in these body-centered oppressions, held in place by sexual terrorism and by keeping women hungry, illiterate, and cut off from energy resources and weapons. She works on her analysis of these material conditions in two other essays, "Woman and Food" (Allen 1984a) and "Lesbian Economics" (Allen 1986c), where she explores the use and abuse of female bodies in patriarchal economies. Consistent with Allen's other lesbian writing, these essays also pursue "a way out" (marked as "Lesbian") of these harsh economies of exchange that consume, dislocate, starve, and impoverish the female body. "Woman" is both constructed and obstructed by these conditions that work hard to block the creation of Difference, the mark of Lesbian as a signifier for elsewhere, for "the open."

This personal and intellectual preoccupation with deliverance from the Same and a desire for an "Otherness" that truly evades the grasp of power is a distinguishing characteristic of Allen's lesbian writing. She longs for a separation in philosophy, word, and deed and a separatism in politics that will be final and total against the co-optations of a totalizing power. Her prolific work of the late 1980s articulates this radical otherness through the body—through the pores of sensual perception and returning memory that create a self in "the form of a body as lived," in the immediacy of the present, in all its mundane, daily, and local transactions. The vicissitudes of this body enter multiple economies and pluralities of difference, defying easy categorization, as touch, tongue, fluidity, and *jouissance* traverse the unruly routes and pleasures of lesbian existence. Because of an epistemic investment in lesbian invisiblity and a disdain for the mundane, these undisciplined journeys have escaped the gaze of more traditional philosophy. Even male philosophers of "the body," such as Foucault, Merleau-Ponty, and Barthe, Allen criticizes for their overriding commitment to a metaphysics of the Same, which obscures the possibility of a "plurality of ideas and values which are transacted in local currencies, and which often have no exchange value elsewhere" (Allen 1988a, 304). For Allen these new ideas and values are not simple negations or reactive attacks on the Same, which would maintain the ambivalence of the dominant paradigm and the ruse of androgyny in all its forms; rather they constitute a "breaking out" into "the open," signifying *the end* of hegemonic economies of exchange that violate women and *the beginning* of our communication with another culture that "we are already on the way to constituting" (Allen, 1986b, 241).

Deliverance from the Same is not univocal. As Jeffner comments, "How I speak myself as lesbian or feminist, or as both, is specific to how I experience myselves, is multiple in meaning, resists normative classification" (Allen 1988b, 108). The violence of lesbian and feminist writing makes this possible:

Lesbian and feminist writing makes actual—logically and materially—worlds in which females choose freely the course of our lives. The startling repercussions of these textual worlds take by surprise, and devastate, patriarchal institutions which would control the distribution of meaning, value, and physical goods against the self-defined interests of each woman. (Allen 1988c, 108)

Commitment to "living in the plural" as the mark of Lesbian appears again in Allen's recent anthology *Lesbian Philosophies and Cultures* (1990), where her introductory comments encourage us not to expect a singular lesbian stand-point but a collection of "irreducible pluralities of shifting continuities and discontinuities" defying a "single point of convergence" (Allen 1990, 2). Lesbian theorizing is for Allen overtly plural and political, aimed at challeng-ing and dismantling positions of privilege while not defining itself monolith-ically or solely in relation to, or in contrast to patriarchy or heterosexuality. The utility, positivity, and irreducibility of such theorizing is, for Allen, once again found in attention to daily life, to "how each lesbian, including oneself, inhabits the cultures where she lives" (Allen 1990, 2). This is a pluralism grounded in real bodies, not the fictional positionalities of postmodernism.

While some readers may find the essays anthologized by Allen of different qualities and asundered directions, Allen valorizes this as a polyphonic explo-ration. She describes her process of editing as a matter of listening to the essays as they arrived day by day in her mailbox.

Slowly, ever so slowly, I began to hear chorusing

tones	*different tones*		*and then rhythms*
several rhythms at once		*rhythms changing*	
songs	*several songs at once*		*voices*
	some voices taking up when others were fading out		
	some insistent		*some more tenuous*
others not distinguishable	*as yet*		*by me*

(Allen 1990, 3)

In Allen's latest writing—and in particular in "On the Seashore: A Writing of Abundance" (Allen 1990)—included as the last essay in *Lesbian Philosophies and Cultures* we begin to see a new Allen-in-writing: mythopoetic and philo-sophical, breaking away from linearity and coherencies of printed medium and traditional philosophical form. We witness an activity of apparant disintegra-tion as she writes her way into "the open"—toward personal wholeness and integration. Allen draws on the memory of "wimmin" writing, a memory of abundance before there was war, scarcity, and domination by the Same and where "woman," "the word which has betokened the constriction of female existence as womb and wife of man, dissolves in myraid currents: womon, womyn, wommin" (Allen 1990, 390). Memory's sturdiness, which helps reinvent the present, washes up like beach rubble—"what will not assimilate is expelled" (Allen 1990, 395)—on the shore where writing *is* abundance, "flowing with the waves and without bounds" (Allen 1990, 390), an inexhaustible plenitude.

> I emerge with writing: a nebular I.
> The I of authority, disciplinary I that would judge writing from a distance, transparent I for whom writing must be to become legible for everyone even if indecipherable for oneself, loses hold before an I of shifting densities, darknesses, florescence. (Allen 1990, 392)

> It is a matter of significance that clitoral currents are lesbian: warm billowing, radiant.

> Sensual and scriptural configurations are at play when writing is cyprine. (Allen 1990, 392)

In this more recent work, Allen's lesbian writing moves toward evocation and creative solitude, casting out from a seashore where land and sea divide and cleaving a new self in surrender to writing, a "coming to be of a writing as she *is*" (Allen 1990, 391), a conception of self through "parthenogynesis." "On the shore, amid rubble washed by the sea, I live" (Allen 1990, 393). This self-in-writing rejoins ancient myth and present rituals that relocate the body beyond the Same and the tyranny of its scarcity. "My memory travels with a writing before which the dissolution of patriarchy is a matter of fact." (Allen 1990, 393).

This new writing surprises the reader by its less militant tone as compared to Allen's previous work and by its utter indifference toward the proper standards of philosophical writing. Pleasures suggested at the end of *Lesbian Philosophy: Explorations* (Allen 1986a) circulate in "the excitement of the open, a writing of cultures of womyn on the lost coast, llamas, red hummingbirds, wild berries, sea gulls" (Allen 1990, 401). While Allen has a remarkably prodigious publication and translation record on Edmund Husserl's phenomenology (e.g., Allen 1977, 1979; Husserl 1981, 1990) for which she is renowned, her new sensual writing strikingly contrasts with the institutionalized and disciplined writing of her Husserl scholarship, adapted to the economies of competition and canonical conformity. Allen contrasts these voices:

> At my job, I circulate among languages, none of them my own, and when I write I am told, "not philosophy," "poetry," ". . . using language as it was not intended."

> I partake in migrations not sought, but taken on, to be to myself a writing companion and for economic sustenance, to

> make real a world that enlivens my senses, to be with friends.
> (Allen 1990, 400-01)

Perhaps Allen's latest writing begins the activity that she has fought for and promised to herself in her earlier work. It arrives in a new form, difficult for us to recognize as "the open" placed in the context of philosophy. Are her latest endeavors—philosophy, poetry, mythopoetics, phenomenological feminism, performance art—a becoming, an event? Whoever dares to care about this question will meet those academics who claim her as "not the ideal woman we had in our minds" (Allen 1990, 401) and "the others" who claim her as a wayward lesbian traveler resting from war in the refuge of her own inner abundance and love of wisdom. In her most recent writing, we are carried away, far away, out of earshot and eyesight of harmful weaponry and in communion with another culture. Out there, Allen is far from lonely.

I return to my own here and now, a small cell in the library system. Institutional Sameness Everywhere. I return to the lesbian graffiti scrawled on the wall, a writing that has now become plain and beautiful. Screaming in its silence. Honest in its criminality. Desperate in its presence. I think of Jeffner on the shoreline. "Hermes, communications technology satellite, circles the earth, while wild mares frolic on the shore" (Allen 1990, 397).

REFERENCES

Allen, Jeffner. 1977. Husserl's philosophical anthropology. *Philosophy Today* 21: 347-55.
———. 1979. What is Husserl's first philosophy? *Proceedings of the Husserl Circle*, 25-45. New Orleans: Tulane University.
———. 1984a. Women and food. *Journal of Social Philosophy* 15(2): 34-41.
———. 1986a. *Lesbian philosophy: Explorations*. Palo Alto, CA: Institute of Lesbian Studies.
———. 1986b. Through the wild region: An essay in phenomenological feminism. *Review of Existential Psychology and Psychiatry* 18: 241-56.
———. 1986c. Lesbian economics. *Trivia* 8: 37-53.
———. 1988a. The economy of the body in a post-Nietzschean era. In *The collegium phaenomenologicum: The first decade*, ed. J. Sallis, G. Moneta, and J. Taminiaux. The Hague: Kluwer.
———. 1988(b). Poetic politics: How Amazons took the acropolis. *Hypatia* 3(2): 107-22.
———. 1989(a). Passions in the gardens of delight. *Woman of Power* 13: 26-27.
———. 1990. *Lesbian philosophies and cultures*, ed. Jeffner Allen. Albany: State University of New York Press.
Courtot, Martha. 1977. *Journey*. Tucson: Up Press.
Husserl, Edmund. 1981. *Renewal: Its problem and method*, trans. Jeffner Allen. In *Shorter works*, ed. Peter McCormick and Frederick Elliston. Notre Dame, IN: University of Notre Dame Press.
———. 1990. *First philosophy (1923/24): First part: Critical history of ideas (Husserliana VII)*, trans. Jeffner Allen. The Hague: Martinus Nijhoff.

BIBLIOGRAPHY OF JEFFNER ALLEN'S LESBIAN WRITINGS

1980. Doing gender: Gender: An ethnomethodological approach. *Human Studies* 3: 107-15.

1982. An introduction to patriarchal existentialism: Accompanied by a proposal for a way out of existential patriarchy. *Philosophy and Social Criticism* 9: 450-65. Reprinted in an expanded version in *The thinking muse: Feminism and recent French thought*, ed. Jeffner Allen and Iris Marion Young. Bloomington: Indiana University Press. 1989. Also reprinted in *Feminism and philosophy*, ed. Rosemarie Tong and Nancy Tuana. New York: Paragon House. Forthcoming.

1984a. Women and food. *Journal of Social Philosophy* 15(2): 34-41.

1984b. Motherhood: The annihilation of women. In *Mothering: Essays in feminist theory* ed. Joyce Trebilcot. Totowa, NJ: Littlefield, Adams. Reprinted in *Women and values: Readings in recent feminist philosophy*, ed. Marilyn Pearsall. Belmont, CA: Wadsoworth.

1984c. Looking at our blood: A lesbian response to men's terrorization of women. *Trivia* 4: 11-38.

1984d. Regard sur notre sang. Trans. D. Vielleux, *Amazones d'Hier* 3 (2): 80-96.

1984e. *Remembering*. Berkeley: Acacia Press.

1985. Une economie lesbienne. *Amazones d'Hier* 4: 16-27.

1986a. *Lesbian philosophy: Explorations*. Palo Alto, CA: Institute of Lesbian Studies.

1986b. Through the wild region: An essay in phenomenological feminism. *Review of Existential Psychology and Psychiatry* 18: 241-56.

1986c. Lesbian economics. *Trivia* 8: 37-53. Reprinted in *Theorizing lesbian existence*, ed. Marlene Wildeman. Toronto: Toronto Women's Press, forthcoming.

1987. Women who beget women must thwart major sophisms. *Philosophy and Social Criticism* 13(4): 315-25. Reprinted in an expanded version in *Women, knowledge, and reality*, ed. Ann Garry and Marilyn Pearsall. New York: Unwin and Hyman, 1989. Reprinted in *Wisdom in the bones: Autobiographical literary criticism*, ed. Freedman and Zauhar. Durham: Duke University Press, 1991.

1988a. The economy of the body in a post-Nietzschean era. In *The collegium phaenomenologicum: The first decade*, ed. J. Sallis, G. Moneta, and J. Taminiaux, 289-308. The Hague: Kluwer.

1988b. *La maternité: Annihilation des femmes*, trans. D. Vielleux. *Amazones d'Hier* 2: 65-87, 173-93.

1988c. Poetic politics: How Amazons took the acropolis. *Hypatia* 3(2): 107-22.

1989a. Passion in the gardens of delight. *Woman of Power* 13: 26-27. Reprinted in *Sexualities*, ed. Judith Barrington. Portland, OR: Eighth Mountain Press, 1991.

1989b. *The thinking muse: Feminism and recent French thought*, ed. Jeffner Allen and Iris Young. Bloomington: Indiana University Press.

1990. *Lesbian philosophies and cultures*, ed. Jeffner Allen, Albany: State University of New York Press.

1991a. Julie Velton Fauve. In *A history of women in philosophy* 3, ed. Mary Ellen Waithe. The Hague: Kluwer.

1991b. Clarisse Gauthier Coignet. In *A history of women in philosophy* 3, ed. Mary Ellen Waithe. The Hague: Kluwer. A short version of this essay was published in *RFR: DRF. Resources for Feminist Research: Documentation sur la recherche feministe* 16: 62-63.

TANGREN ALEXANDER

LESBIAN SLIP

We were relaxing after supper, my daughter, who was ten, and my ninety-six-year-old grandmother, and I. Marcella had long known that I was a lesbian, and in her simple child's way understood perfectly. Grandma was another matter; I would have to wait for her to die before I could be open in the family about who I was. She could never be told. I loved her; there seemed no reason to distress her, who kept herself so deliberately innocent about the facts of life, let alone their infinite variety.

Over coffee and dessert, our talk turned to words; perhaps we had been playing anagrams, as we often did. I found myself speaking about how words can shape our perceptions, and started to illustrate my point with the fact that the Eskimos have twenty-eight or so words for snow, whereas we have only one.

"For instance," I began, "the Lesbian word for snow . . ." There it was, spilled out on the table. "I mean the Eskimo word . . ." I recovered, without missing a beat, and went on with my point. I don't know what Grandma thought, if she noticed it at all, or if she noticed but obediently promptly forgot. Marcella, for whom the word lesbian carried no particular charge, had not marked my slip.

And I, as I talked on, giving other examples, was thinking ". . . Hmmm, now why did I do that?" Lesbian, Eskimo. . . . Both, three-syllabled, similarly accented words, to be sure. My mind had groped, and grabbed the wrong one. . . . But why was Lesbian filed there right next to Eskimo? As if it were the name of a language. "Lesbian spoken here." . . . As if one might perhaps find words here for all the variations, the subtleties, the possibilities, and distinctions in things—concepts our old language never noticed. Worlds we never imagined, to be found right under our noses.

Hypatia vol. 7, no. 4 (Fall 1992) © by Tangren Alexander

2:00 AM, VALENTINE'S MORNING

This is a journal entry written in 1980.

. . . And then, on top of all that, this is the week we are talking about "homosexuality" in ethics class.

Yesterday morning I showed the film *Word Is Out.*[1] The afternoon class had already seen it, had laughed a lot, had picked up on what the gay people said. But the morning class . . . just sat there.

"Well," I thought, "at least I know it's not just *me* having a hard time moving them, getting through to them."

(Once, Seaweed Sapphofire told me how she'd camped for a whole summer on women's land. Her home was out in the open, under an oak tree high on a hill. From one branch she hung a banner made from a skirt she used to wear when she was a college professor.)

I came home between classes—to touch in with this place, and the play of light inside, while outside the bushes peacefully followed the light through the day. "Look," I told myself, "your life is so much more than this current dilemma."

Yet there is the current dilemma to be faced. Now. I still do not know whether to come out in class the next hour. The morning class feels impossible; but this is sometimes a kind and caring group. And, much furthermore, there are three lesbians in the class, all of whom plan to say so in the discussion. So for the first time I know I would not be alone.

And a part of me wants so much to do it. I feel such schizophrenia maintaining the personality I need to deal with college reality, keeping my mind within reach of my students.

The pain it creates, trying to find my way back to the self that knows everything that I, with my unique life, do know. It really is a kind of split personality; some of my selves know things that others of my selves don't know at all. . . . If only I didn't get lost in those selves, but I do. It takes days to thread my way back through "college professor" to "mommy" to "economic self" to "friend" to anyone who can write. Or pray.

. . . So on the one hand I really wanted to come out, just for the healing it might promise, to be able to speak who I am and what I know. . . . But I felt so weak and uncentered; would I be able to know what I know? . . . And even if I tell them I'm a lesbian, I still can't come out as Pearl Time'sChild, lesbian erotic writer. Even though that has everything to do with all this.

. . . *In* the class, someone said, "About the film. Well, it's all fine to say 'They're just people like the rest of us' and all that. But you have to think about the parts the movie doesn't show. You have to think about what they actually *do* with each other."

. . . I remember first learning about "intercourse." I was fourteen, sitting on the high school lawn, under a tree, in the spring sunshine, in a pink-and-white checkered dress, reading a borrowed book, Evelyn Mills Duval's *The Facts of Life and Love for Teenagers*. I knew vaguely about intercourse, about what went where; but many of the details were new to me: how the penis gets full of blood and stands up stiff. . . . I wish I had the book now; it said something like "Intercourse is completed by an in-and-out motion of the penis. This continues until . . ." followed by some description of ejaculation.

. . . It sounded ghastly. I closed my eyes. "Deborah Kerr *does* that," I made myself think. "My *mother* does that!" That night I wrote, "I feel as if a veil has come between me and all married women."

Now my point in telling you this is that I did get beyond my initial shock at what people actually did, as described so baldly—*because* I had the whole force of society and culture helping me. My imagination was fed not only by that meagre description. Every time a man and woman kissed on the screen, humbled themselves, opened themselves to one another, to trembling strains of music, I knew that this, too, was part of it, of sexual love. . . . And there was so much more. My mother, it could not be denied, had engaged in intercourse, and my grandmothers, too.

And there were those fierce new longings to be filled that I was feeling. And in the untouchableness of teenagerhood, the simple longing just to touch. All these, I knew, were part of it, too. All these I had to go on, to know that some man and I, too, could create around that in-and-out act something complex, loving, rewarding.

And we did.

. . . Though in a way, a part of me still sees "intercourse" as a little ridiculous and undignified. For one thing, it does look pretty funny, I've got to admit. But I know too, now, that that's all part of the fun. To be that vulnerable. To share those funny, raw, red, hairy parts of ourselves. To trust that much. . . .

To return to the point. The culture imagined heterosexuality for me, to me, as something both attractive and inevitable. I saw Deborah Kerr sparkle before Cary Grant, with fire and challenge and sexuality. And I saw her give herself in kindliest compassion to John Kerr, who loved her so hopelessly. I was never shown a woman loving a woman.

". . . But you've got to remember what it is they actually do with each other." And I know his images of "what we actually do" are on the level of Evelyn Mills Duval.

. . . Can I begin to tell him what it is we actually do? Can I even know it, here?

Could they imagine what it's like to live in this culture as a lesbian or a gay man? To walk down the street where only the others can touch. Where the movie romances are always man and woman. Where the question "But why don't those two men. . . ?" or "Why don't the women notice each other?" will never even be raised. Never to see anything like your life in a play or a book.

. . . I did hear of a new movie about gays. A lurid gay underground, to be exact, and a series of gory close-up murders, very violent murders of gay people.

. . . Switch to a young woman in class: "I knew a man who was murdered, actually murdered, just because he was gay, just because he loved another man." She passes on the orange,[2] and cradles her head on her desk.

. . . Switch to San Francisco: It is Harvey Milk's birthday. Meg Christian and Holly Near and thousands of people are singing, "We are a gentle, angry people. And we are singing, singing for our lives."[3]

. . . Sometimes I imagine things getting worse as backlash flourishes. I imagine the weathering boards of my house spray-painted in purple, LEZZIE, and my father finding out that way. I imagine the carefully loved interior of this house vandalized. . . . I try not to imagine these things. And yet, how do I know who I'm talking to in a class? And what they'll hear? And whether it *is* safe to say these things? I feel so exposed up there before them.

. . . And then there are questions about my job. I would be the first teacher to come out in a class on this campus. . . . And questions about losing the students' trust, of losing credibility with them. A "homosexual" is so often seen as an unfortunate, someone with something wrong with them. I need all the trust I can muster in that class. . . . And yet, how am I to feel my own strength, when I am not allowed to know who I am, in there?

. . . The night before I was to show *Word Is Out*, I had a dream:

I went to the class, passed out the rest of the journals, and announced when the journals were due again. Then I sat down to try and recollect today's topic. No, it wasn't "relationships," we did that last time. And, no, it's not "sexuality," that's next. Oh, it's the one in between. Oh, "homosexuality." . . . Oh. But, uh, today we see the film. But, oh, I've forgotten to bring it. I send the class on over to the media center and hurry back to my office for the film.

But on the way, I meet someone who wants to return some books to me, and some clothes. The books are large and unwieldy. (One is a big art book; another is the shape of a music book.) With my hands full, I climb the rickety staircase outside the building, stepping around my long skirt.

When I get to the top, I have to put the things down to find my keys; but there's really no room. I balance the books beside me, but some slacks slide off and down into the mud below. Finally I get the door open. The threshold is about a foot high. So, balancing my books, I manage the step, and hurry down the hall to my office, then back down the steps to retrieve the clothes—when it hits me—the class is up there waiting, and I still don't have the film!

. . . Well, the first thing I notice about that dream is how when I dream about teaching these days the college buildings are always dilapidated and poorly planned. Certainly I am telling myself something with these images, perhaps that the setting is making life very difficult.

. . . So maybe I ought to come out in class. If I lose students, I lose them. If I lose my job, I lose it. Maybe I don't want it on these terms.

Yet it's so much to give up—for something which is, after all, only one week's topic, out of a whole year of teaching. And it's such a good job; and I've worked for it for so long. And I do do some good at my post.

* * *

Listening to the tape of that afternoon class, I sound so much stronger than I remember feeling. Wryly pulling the books one at a time from a "plain brown wrapper" paper bag. *Gay American History* (Katz 1976). I pass it around. Then, for the more artistically inclined, Elsa Gidlow (1982). Pulling out one more, presenting *Country Lesbians* (Sue et al. 1976). You can't hear it on the tape, but I remember faltering trying to describe the book. Losing it, I decide to risk no more extemporizing, and dive into the text: Billie's classic coming-out letter to her parents. I ask them to imagine getting this letter from a daughter, from a sister, (from a mother), from a friend. "Or," I add, "writing it."

. . . Reading the simple words, I feel them so deeply. I cannot help but see how each and every word applies to me, and to this situation right now. I cannot help but mean the words as I say them; and yet as I say them I think, "But I am sitting here in front of my class, a teacher at this college! How can I suddenly be saying these words here?"

Afterwards, I don't trust myself to say anything more. I invite them to reflect on the film, on the letter, or anything else. I toss the orange, forgetting to comment that it's not from Florida, that it's many-segmented, that it's a fitting symbol today for the fruit of the knowledge of good and evil. Unable to speak, or even to remember this, I toss the orange.

The first man catches it. He's "willing to let these people do what they want," but "the idea of it is damaging to the family," and he thinks they ought to allow it, "but not accept it ideologically." "If that's possible," he adds.

The second orange-holder, a woman, says: "Well, I'm pretty close-minded on this subject. I think it's wrong; and I wouldn't really care to hear the other side. I don't know what happens to these people; I guess something just snaps in them, like happens with murderers. It upsets me that people are that way. I think people *should* be allowed to do what they want—but they shouldn't publicize it."

The whole north row are rather grim. Most are against the more unfair kinds of discrimination, but yet . . . The question is asked, "Can they help it? Is it a choice?" "No," someone answers, "some of them really didn't have a choice. They just always were that way."

. . . Did I have a choice? Was I always this way?

Once I wrote: "I have been a college professor for two years, a mother for eight, a wife for fifteen, and a lesbian, somewhere in my minds, somewhere in my overlapping worlds, a lesbian since before I was born. At any rate, I'm sure that my birth, my mother's glad rush of joy that I, her firstborn, was woman-

same, and that the embroidered dresses were not in vain, settled the matter once and for all."

"Were you always that way?"

I remember *Little Women*, that family of sisters sharing a life. Jo, in the attic, writing, and Beth, only looking in to ask, "Does genius burn?" I remember Pearl, my magic grandmother, reading this story to me, and how happy we were sharing those lovely visions together.

And when I remember this, then I would answer, "Always."

Yet I married, and for years thought of lesbians as "other," strange and dangerous. Somewhere in my heart, I knew of something else, another possibility, not this weird "lesbian" stuff, but. . . . But I seemed to be the only one who had ever noticed this possibility. And so it was best forgotten. . . . Was it a choice? Yes. If to choose to be who you deeply are is a choice.

Did I have a choice? Yes. An agonizing choice. I was in a good marriage with a man I loved. With our daughter we were a family, with a long past of knowing each other, and cherished Christmas ornaments. As a family, we had a good life. And with a shade of difference I could be there still.[4] But someone was dying there. A woman who was a writer. A woman who loved women.

"Homosexuals—I think that some of them must have been hurt by the opposite sex a lot, or something," someone says. . . . How can I know? when she says that—how can I even remember? that, for me, well, sex with a man has been full, and fun, opening, and satisfying, and a true making of love.

But with a woman, sometimes, it has been . . . tenderness mirrored, a doubled surrender, opening into worlds of worship. A falling together to a place of Oneness, not just an image, now, but known, felt, experienced, real.

Some heterosexuals find Oneness, too, I'm sure of it. But, for me, it happens because of the knowing there can be between two same-ones, two women.

Did I have a choice? Yes. And I chose. In fear and trembling, in joy and bravery, prayerfully, I chose to walk the path with a heart.[5]

Could I say that? Know that? No! I could barely manage to write down "choice?" on my notepad. In pencil!

Postscript, 1992: No one came out in class that day. The orange didn't even make it around to the lesbians. But things were different the next meeting. The lesbians had had time to recoup, and spoke out clear and strong. When my turn came, I said, "I'd like to read you one more piece of writing by a gay person," and read them the above journal entry. One man did walk out; but the rest of the students returned me respect, gratitude, and, well, love. Since then I've come out in one way or another in almost every class I teach. So far I still have my job, my house has never been vandalized; and by now my father knows anyway. On the other hand, the Oregon Citizens' Alliance, after objecting to my 1990 course "The Lesbian Experience," is at work to change the Oregon constitution to, among other things, make it illegal for anyone at a state institution to teach anything other than that homosexuality is perverse and unnatural. . . . Myself, I've never regretted that first coming out at school; and my different selves know each other much better today.

EST ET NON: THE DREAM BODY

Sometimes I wonder if I could be the world's last living dualist. . . . And then sometimes I wonder if I am one. . . . But I have a feeling in my gut that simply won't let me let go of dualism and Cartesian doubting. So this paper is an attempt to take some of these ideas—mind, body, doubt, and dreaming—and throw them up into the air, and see if I can get them to fall down in a new pattern.

William Harvey had found valves and such in the human heart, the circulation of the blood. Galileo had so lately been lucid about machines. In such things Descartes saw a possibility for explaining how the body might work. He was much taken by the fountains found in the fashionable houses and palaces of the time, with their elaborate hidden systems of valves and plumbing. There was a fountain he had seen in whose waters bathed a marble statue of Diana; when anyone approached, the visitor's footstep set off a system of valves that caused the statue to retreat and hide among the rosebushes. Perhaps he saw in such elaborate plumbing a way to understand the body, glimpsed the tremendous power explanations along these lines would prove to have.

Maybe this was part of the illumination he had in his stove, or in his bed above the stove, or in his stove-heated room, whichever translation you prefer. Shut in by snow, or resolution, for three days, inside a small, warm place, with nothing to do but to be a thinking being, he had a revelation. All in a flash there came to him the fundamental principles, he said, of a wonderful discovery. What he meant by this is unclear. Perhaps in that moment he invented coordinate geometry,[6] that exquisitely nuanced language for describing the figure and motion of extended substances. Some believe his vision was that all true explanations of the world explained by means of a deductive system, though that was hardly a new idea, nor would he have thought it so. Or perhaps he was shown his own system, the descent into doubt where all of extended substance is stripped away, and one knows oneself only as thought thinking about itself, eventually given back the world but knowing from then on one's hidden core, made of a different substance than the stuff of this world. Whatever he saw, it came to him all at once, like a flash, he said. Like a vision, but this not indescribable, mystical, but a rational understanding.

The dualistic difficulty he would never solve: when the body becomes a machine, the mind becomes a ghost, a poltergeist, a bender of spoons. The body is more than a machine, it is mysterious. Consider the placebo effect. Or then again, consider moving your arm, quite as much a mystery in Descartes' scheme of things, as Elizabeth of Bohemia was quick to point out. As part of his attempt to answer her, he wrote *The Passions of the Soul*, endlessly compounding, say, laughter, out of three parts joy and two parts anger,[7] ingeniously describing by means of valves and the movements of vapors the hidden kinetic behind the kinesthetic effects we experience in our passions, but skipping very fast over the part about the pineal gland.

Elizabeth wrote him that she found it easier to conceive that the soul is something extended than to imagine a body's being moved by an immaterial substance. And indeed, the modern philosophical tradition in which I was raised may be said to have spelled out in some detail the way in which the mind is "something extended," identifying the cash value of "mental attributes" in bodies, their behavior, the kinesthetic sensations of their passions, their "dispositions to act," their "ways of life." Dualism is no more; mind and body are one. . . . Why do I find myself thinking of that old feminist joke about marriage: "The husband and wife became one, and that one was the husband"? . . . Mind and matter were one, and that one was located clearly in the public, the verifiable, the interpersonal.

Thank heaven for dreams. Though most people I knew took the conclusions of Norman Malcolm's book *Dreaming* seriously, it always seemed to me to be a sort of reductio ad absurdum of that publicly-oriented point of view, a way of thinking that led Malcolm to mischaracterize how we employ the concept of dreaming.[8] In the years since then dreaming has interested me more and more: the logic of dreams, their status as a way of knowing, and the questions they ask that cast their flicker over waking "daily life."

For Descartes, a dream is a parade of phantoms, the creases of the brain relaxing, releasing vapors and spirits, forming phantasms with no extension to their name. No reality. No meaning. So he thought when he theorized.[9]

There is, on the other hand, the series of dreams he had in his bed tucked over the stove, on the night of the day wherein his heated body/mind had come upon his "wonderful discovery." Far from thinking these dreams had no meaning, he considered them to be among the more significant sense data he had ever had in his life.

What Descartes wrote about the dreams is lost, but we have his biographer's version. In the first dream, among other things, a whirlwind revolved him violently upon his left heel; later a strong wind forced him to bend over to the left. In the second, a clap of thunder woke him. (A reverberation, perhaps, from the day's lightning strike of intuition?) When he opened his eyes, the room seemed filled with flying sparks. The third dream featured books appearing and disappearing on the table. Verses, full of significance, were found and quoted. "*Est et Non*," "Yes and No," "It Is and It Is Not." And "What road shall I choose in life?"

Descartes did not, of course, attribute *extensional* reality to the events and things perceived in these dreams; but still, they pointed beyond themselves. If they were phantasms, they were phantasms come to play with him, to bring him messages, to enact with him a story. If they deceived in one way, they spoke truths in another.

Perhaps in sleep the mind sleeps too, its watchful guardians of rationality and plausibility out cold, drunk beside the door; perhaps then angels come.

If Descartes' whole life were like a dream, a story with themes recurring and meanings on many levels, then I would be remiss not to tell you of another dream about finding verses in a volume, a dream that came to someone else near the end of Descartes' life, when he was in Sweden as the guest of Queen Christina.

Christina's library was next to her bedroom, the high walls lined with books all the way to the top. Halfway up, a suspended catwalk ran along the walls. This is the room where she met with Descartes at five o'clock, those freezing winter mornings before the fire, among a collection famed far and wide, though he was inclined to grumble at her passion for gathering "a lot of old books." But it was perhaps the fame of this collection that made it a fitting symbol for "the great library in the sky," the repository of all knowledge, in the following story found in one of Descartes' letters (as told in Jack Vrooman's biography *René Descartes*):

> It appears that at Dijon a learned man had struggled all day with a key passage from a Greek poet without being able to understand it. Tired and annoyed by the fruitlessness of his long effort, he went to bed. While deep in sleep, his spirit was transported to Stockholm, where he was introduced into the palace of the queen and led into her library. He looked at all the books, and his eyes fell upon a small volume which he opened. After having glanced through ten or twelve pages, he ran across ten lines of Greek verse that completely resolved the difficulty which had troubled him for so long. The joy he felt at this discovery woke him up. He repeated the verses contunually, and then wrote them down on a scrap of paper so that he would not forget them. The next morning, he thought about this nocturnal adventure, one of the most extraordinary of his life, and sent a letter to Descartes . . . to inquire if the queen's library, her palace, and the city were such as he had seen them in his dream. He asked him to look for the volume he had read to see if it did indeed exist, and if it contained the ten lines of Greek quoted at the end of the letter.
>
> Descartes was quick to answer . . . , telling him that even the most talented engineer could not have described the plan of the city more correctly, that the library was exactly as he had depicted it, and that he had found the book in question and had read the verses. Even though the book was extremely rare, one of his friends had promised to obtain a copy which he would send to Dijon as soon as possible as a token of his esteem. The story ends here, for there was no further correspondence between the two men. It was recounted in books published

during both the seventeenth and eighteenth centuries, and while it remains one of those curious sidelights that literary historians employ to entertain their students, no attempt at a rational explanation has ever been given (Vrooman 1970, 235-36).

It seems to me this event would have been very good news for Descartes, vindicating something about his conception of the mind; but what? Does it prove that the mind is extensionless? Far from it; it seems to say that the mind of the man from Dijon found itself in the Three Crowns castle, on the east corner, four floors up, in the library, near the shelf where the book that held the solution was filed.

If this occurrence does not show the mind to be nonextended, does it at any rate show that the mind is detachable? Detachable in fact, so therefore certainly differentiable in theory? Its own thing? A separate substance?

"His spirit was transported to Stockholm," Vrooman puts it. We need not take this too literally. We do not have to say the man's mind went to Stockholm, for motion is relative here; we could as well say that Stockholm came to the mind of the man in Dijon. Still, either way, it is an extraordinary occurrence, and one worth meditating on.

And if we do say he came to Christina's library, he did not come without his body. He was conducted to the palace, presumably by someone he could see and who could see him. (Though not necessarily. One may be shown around in a dream by an offstage announcer.)

But certainly he had a body! How else take the book from the shelf? If he'd found himself a disembodied spirit, and had had to levitate it out, he surely would have mentioned the fact. Probably he reached out, slid the book from the shelf, blew the dust off, like always, as something said, "This one!" "Take up and read!"

"But," we may ask, "if there had been someone there? Some servant, paid to stay awake all night, watching for any books moving, surely he would have seen nothing that night. In the morning, that volume's covering of dust, and ashes, would measure the same as its neighbors'.". . . Well, perhaps the dream would not have come in that case, like all magic, like Diana, would have hidden itself before the observer's heavy tread, vanishing behind a rose.

One has perceptions and passions in dreams, one walks and speaks and sees. Does one have a body? Indeed. It is the embarrassment of riches when it comes to bodies, as much as anything, that is odd here. There is the body seated before the fire in its dressing gown; there is the naked one lying in bed, eyes closed, snoring softly.

There are complex connections between the two. Think of the man who dreamed of being in the French Revolution, in the end being guillotined, waking to find that a part of the bedstead had fallen on his neck.[10] Think of the little boy who after long searching finally finds a bathroom. "Ah," he lets it go. Only to wake into being five years old at a boarding school off in a foreign country, shamefully wetting the bed once again. (Sometimes it matters mightily to be able to tell whether one is awake or dreaming.)

But if one can, in a way, have more than one body, and the two complexly related, does the fact that one is dreaming at least mean this: that one has *at least* one body? The extended, solid, weighted one with the rapid-eye-movements happening. Can we doubt the physical reality of our sleeping, extended, "real" body? Or does it underlie our ability to dream, both actually, as it lies there breathing, and conceptually, in its waking life? Do dream language and dream body rest upon our understanding of the real body?

. . . Or could they execute a flip? As dream body slides underneath now, supporting the dancing weight of real body on its own soft contours, folding it in its arms. So that suddenly dream body seems as real as any other, "real" body, as ephemeral. When one sees with a consciousness in the light of which both dream body and real body are parts of the passing show.

My friend Bethroot has a friend who may or may not be dying of a brain tumor. At one point when things were looking grim, Barbara, for that is her name, was having a long talk with her physician. At the end of it she asked him as a friend if he had any advice for her. "I don't know," he answered sympathetically, "maybe . . . practice solipsism?" They laughed until they cried. From some half-forgotten philosophy class each had salvaged that word, and with it, some sense of what it had meant for a moment to doubt the world away.

Possibly the point of wondering whether one is dreaming, wondering whether one has a body, is not to deliver ourselves from the valley of the shadow of doubt, but to find therein an awakening.

L. Aryeh Kosman: "The structure of the *Meditations* is the structure of one classical form of meditation. The meditator detaches himself from his world; experience is stripped of its content in order that there may be revealed . . . self and God" (Rorty 1986, 39).

Zen saying: "With a little doubt, there is a small awakening. With a great doubt, there is a great awakening. With no doubt, there is no awakening."

FOR SANDRA

As we drifted toward sleep,
our bodies still wound together,
I thought, for a while,
 that we slept
 in a spaceship,
 cylindrical, small,
 room only
 to stretch in.
 The round walls
 around us were
 lined all with books,
 row over row of
 women's writings
 saved from the
 destruction.
 Asleep, naked,
 we floated,
 fleeing down darkness
 and the stars.

THE FEMINIST EXISTENTIALIST STATE SONG

Amazing grace, how sweet the sound
That saved a causal mechanism like me.
I once was lost, now lost and found,
I close my eyes to see.

Amazing leap, how fine the point
Between the earth and sky
That moment free of gravity
Isadora shows us why.

In existential levity
Amazing *pas de chat*,
In cunning, punning brevity
In graceful *port de bras*. [11]

THE ANSWERS IN THE BACK
(Philosophy for Tap Dancing) [12]

1.

Oh, the outer is the inner
And the inner is the outer.
It's a crazy world!
You may try to do without Her
But the Inner is the Outer
As the film unfurls.
As the role goes rolling along,
As the singer's one with the song,
So the outer is the inner
And the inner is the outer.
It's a crazy, crazy world!

2.

Oh, is it out? Or is it in her?
Will the Outer be the winner
As the film unfurls?
Am I stout? Or am I thinner?
Wish my outer fit my inner!
It's a crazy world!
As the reel goes rolling along,
It's only Kali singing her song
Of the spider and the Spinner
Of the Outer and the Inner.
It's a crazy, crazy world!

3. (aberrant verse)

Well, now, the speed of light's a bummer
It's the same for every comer.
It's a crazy world!
And the rules that work for plumbers
Don't apply at higher numbers
As the fields unfurl.
Where the ruler's shorter or long,
It's just the Wu Li singing a song:
It's "The outer is the inner
And the energy is matter."
It's a crazy, crazy world!

4.

Oh, is it what I had for dinner?
Is it outer? Is it inner?
It's a crazy world!
You may doubt her; you may win her
If the Outer is the Inner
As the film unfurls.
Oh, it's the real world ringing along,
Only Alice singing a song
About the Outer in the Inner
And the Inner in the Outer.
It's a crazy, crazy world!
Thanks be!

NOTES

"Lesbian Slip," "*Est et Non*: The Dream Body," "The Feminist Existentialist State Song," and "The Answers in the Back" were presented at the Fall 1991 Conference of the Society for Women in Philosophy, Pacific Division. My thanks to the members of that audience. "2:00 AM, Valentine's Morning" was first published in Rooney (1991). The piece is excerpted from my unpublished book, *The Auto Biography of Deborah Carr*. For many helpful conversations and pointing out of sources that led to "*Est et Non*" I am grateful to Grace Iurilli. This paper was first read at the "Giving the Body Its Due" conference in Eugene, Oregon.

1. *Word Is Out* (Mariposa Films) is an excellent film of interviews with many kinds of lesbians and gay men.

2. In my ethics classes I send an orange around the circle, as a symbol of "who has the floor." For more about this, see Alexnder (1987).

3. Lyrics from "Singing for Our Lives," words and music by Holly Near, Hereford Music, 1979. All rights reserved.

4. ". . . with a shade of difference I could be there still." For this understanding I am indebted to Adrienne Rich's poem "The Roofwalker" (Rich 1967), which I read "not with indifference" back when I was a safe housewife.

5. The "path with a heart" is from another teacher of mine back then, the Yaqui sorcerer Don Juan, in Casteñeda (1968).

6. I confess this is a bit of poetic license; I know of no evidence to suggest he invented coordinate geometry at that moment—I wanted to remind readers that he had invented it. Though the more general possibility that the world could be described by mathematics may have been part of what Descartes glimpsed in his vision; Davis and Hersh suggest this. (Davis et al. 1986, 3-8).

7. While this reducing of "complex emotions" to mixtures of a few "simple" ones strikes me as the mathematical mind gone wildly awry, I remembered again why I like Descartes so much when I noticed that beginning the long list of passions he undertakes to describe, the first one that comes to his mind is "wonder" (Descartes 1931, 358).

8. For a great deal more on this subject, see Alexander (1975).

9. See, for example, *The Passions of the Soul* (Descartes 1931, 341).

10. This was Alfred Maury, a nineteenth century dream researcher. He theorized that though the whole dream had seemed a very long one, in fact it must have been caused by the headboard's falling on his neck, and so must have all taken place in the instant before he woke up. (There are alternative ways of looking at this.)

11. Ballet terms: *pas de chat*—a catlike, sideways leap; *port de bras*—a graceful movement of the arms.

12. My thanks to Hannah Blue Heron for the musical notation.

REFERENCES

Alexander, Tangren. 1975. Malcolm and dreaming and nonsense. Ph.D. diss., University of Oregon.

———. 1987. The womanly art of teaching ethics; or one fruitful way to encourage the love of wisdom about right and wrong. *Teaching Philosophy* 10(4): 319-28.

Casteñeda, Carlos. 1968. *The teachings of Don Juan: A Yaqui way of knowledge*. Berkeley: University of California Press.

Davis, Phillip J. and Reuben Hersch. 1986. *Descartes' dream: The world according to mathematics*. Boston: Houghton Mifflin.

Descartes, René. 1931. *The passions of the soul*. Trans. Elizabeth S. Haldane and G. R. T. Ross. In *The philosophical works of Descartes*, vol. 1. London: Cambridge University Press.

Gidlow, Elsa. 1982. *Sapphic songs, eighteen to eighty*. Mill Valley, CA: Druid Heights Books.

Katz, Jonathan. 1976. *Gay American history*, New York: Crowell.

Kosman, L. Aryeh. 1986. The naive narrator: Meditation in Descartes' *Meditations*. In *Essays on Descartes' meditations*.

Malcolm, Norman. 1962. *Dreaming*. New York: Humanities Press.

Rooney, Frances, ed. 1991. *Our lives: Lesbian personal writings*. Toronto: Second Story Press.

Rorty, Amèlie Oksenberg, ed. 1986. *Essays on Descartes' Meditations*. Berkeley: University of California Press.

Sue, Nelly, Dian, Carol, and Billie. 1976. *Country lesbians: The story of the WomanShare collective*. Grants Pass, OR: WomanShare Books.

Vrooman, Jack R. 1970. *René Descartes: A biography*. New York: G. P. Putnam's Sons.

On *Borderlands/La Frontera*:
An Interpretive Essay

MARÍA LUGONES

Borderlands/La Frontera *deals with the psychology of resistance to oppression.*
The possibility of resistance is revealed by perceiving the self in the process of being
oppressed as another face of the self in the process of resisting oppression. The new
mestiza consciousness is born from this interplay between oppression and resistance.
Resistance is understood as social, collective activity, by adding to Anzaldúa's theory
the distinction between the act and the process of resistance.

Borderlands has been a very important text for me. I have found company in
it. *Desde el primer momento pensé que éramos hermanas en pensamiento.* I have
carried Anzaldúa's insights and metaphors with me for several years in my daily
ruminations and in my daily exercise of triple vision. I could say that I have
lost perspective on this text in making it mine, or I could say that I have gained
perspective in finding borderdwelling friendship in it. I find her thinking
intertwined with my own. Thus this essay is highly interpretive. I will explain
what I learned from *Borderlands* and I will try to think my way around some of
the trouble that I have with some of the living that it suggests to me.

Work on oppressed subjectivity focuses on the subject at the "moment" of
oppression and as oppressed. Oppression theory may have as its intent to depict
the effects of oppression (alienation, ossification, arrogation, psychological
oppression, etc.), without an intention to rule out resistance. But within the
logical framework of the theory, resistance to oppression appears unintelligible
because it lacks a theoretical base. Anzaldúa's *Borderlands* is a work creating a
theoretical space for resistance.

Anzaldúa focuses on the oppressed subject at the "moment" of *being*
oppressed. Thus she can capture both an everyday history of oppression and
an everyday history of resistance. Her culture, though oppressive, also grounds
her resistance:

Hypatia vol. 7, no. 4 (Fall 1992) © by María Lugones

> At a very early age I had a strong sense of who I was and what
> I was about and what was fair. . . . Every bit of self-faith I'd
> painstakingly gathered took a beating daily. Nothing in my
> culture approved of me. (16)

But also,

> When I was seven, eight, nine, fifteen, sixteen years old, I would
> read in bed with a flashlight under the covers, hiding my
> self-imposed insomnia from my mother. . . . My sister, Hilda,
> who slept in the same bed with me, would threaten to tell my
> mother unless I told her a story. . . . Nudge a Mexican and she
> or he will break out with a story. So, huddling under the covers,
> I made up stories for my sister night after night. . . . It must have
> been then that I decided to put stories on paper. (65)

Anzaldúa describes two states of the self *being* oppressed: the state of intimate
terrorism and the *Coatlicue* state. These states are two sides of the experience
of *being* oppressed. In expressing this experience, Anzaldúa thinks of the self
as multiple. There is the self oppressed in and by the traditional Mexican world;
the self oppressed in and by the Anglo world; and the self-in-between—the
Self—herself in resistance to oppression, the self in germination in the borderlands. If the self is being oppressed, then she can feels its limits, its capacity for
response, pushed in, constrained, denied. But she can also push back. This is
not a fantastic or metaphysical leap out of the reality of oppressed. Rather
Anzaldúa knows the weight of oppressed worlds and the hard, risky work of
resistance.

In the state of intimate terror, the Self feels the oppression; she feels petrified:

> Alienated from her mother culture, "alien" in the dominant
> culture, the woman of color does not feel safe within the inner
> life of her Self. Petrified, she can't respond, her face caught
> between *los intersticios*, the space between the different worlds
> she inhabits. (20)

Anzaldúa sees the ability to respond as at the center of responsibility. She
connects the state of intimate terrorism with a lack of ability to respond, the
"very movement of life, swifter than lightning, frozen" (21). But as the Self is
being oppressed, she is at the crossroads of choice (21). Anzaldúa

> made the choice to be queer . . . It's an interesting path, one
> that continually slips in and out of the white, the Catholic, the
> Mexican, the indigenous, the instincts. In and out of my head.
> It makes for *loquería*, the crazies. It is a path of knowledge—one
> of knowing (and of learning) the history of oppression of our
> *raza*. It is a way of balancing, of mitigating duality. (19)

Anzaldúa thinks of homophobia as "the fear of going home." The fear of being caught in the *intersticios*, or the fear of being abandoned by *La Raza*. Abandoned "for being unacceptable, faulty, damaged" (20). The two fears so close, since abandonment is a powerful weight exercised on the in-between-self to give herself up, not to make full use of her faculties.

Anzaldúa tells us that *Coatlalopeuh* was an early Mesoamerican creator goddess that had two aspects: the underworld, dark aspect, *Coatlicue*; and *Tonantsi*, the light, the upper. *Coatlicue* was driven underground with other powerful female deities by the male dominated Azteca-Mexica culture, and *Tonantsi*, split from her dark aspect, became the good mother (27). The Spanish colonizers and the colonizing church continued the split when *Tonantsi*, desexed, became *Guadalupe*, the chaste protective mother (28).

> Today *la Virgen de Guadalupe* is the single most potent religious, political and cultural image of the Chicano/*mexicano*. Because *Guadalupe* took upon herself the psychological and physical devastation of the conquered and the oppressed *indio*, she is our spiritual, political and pyschological symbol. *Guadalupe* is the symbol of the ethnic identity and of the tolerance for ambiguity that Chicanos/*mexicanos* . . . , people who cross cultures, by necessity possess. (30)

Anzaldúa embraces a decolonized *Guadalupe* back into her dark and light ambiguity. She remembers the name *Coatlicue* and rejects the mind/body split imposed on *Tonantsi* by the Catholic church as well as her desexualization. *Coatlicue* is remembered in resistance to oppression, in creation.

> She, the symbol of the dark sexual drive, the chthonic (under-world), the feminine, the serpentine movement of sexuality, of creativity, the basis of all energy and life. (35)

The *Coatlicue* state is a state of creation. The self *being* oppressed, the self-in-between, *la terca*, *la hocicona*, the against-the-grain storyteller pushes against the limits of oppression. Caught in-between two harmful worlds of sense that deny her ability to respond, the self-in-between fashions herself in a quiet state. Anzaldúa recognizes here that the possibility of resistance depends on this creation of a new identity, a new world of sense, in the borders.

The *Coatlicue* state is one of stasis because it is a state of making new sense. It is a state of isolation, separation from harmful sense. This creation is a dangerous thing. The self risks her own familiarity and her being familiar to others. Though in intimate terror she is not safe but "a victim where someone else is in control," the in-between-self at the moment of germination may be unable to make new sense, and that is a terrifying possibility.

> She has this fear   that she has no names   that she has
> many names   that she doesn't know her names. . . . She has
> this fear   that if she takes off her clothes   shoves her brain
> aside   peels off her skin . . . strips the flesh from the bone . . .
> that when she does reach herself . . . she won't find anyone. . . .
> She has this fear that she won't find the way back (43)

So the self-in-between in the *Coatlicue* state, the resistant state, needs to enact both strategies of defense against worlds that mark her with the inability to respond and distractive strategies to keep at bay the fear of having no names. The strategies of defense against harmful sense are insulating strategies: she uses rage to drive others away and to insulate herself against exposure; she reciprocates with contempt for those who have roused shame in her; etc. (45).[1] Since she cannot respond in their terms, because in their terms she is not responsible, she must make a space apart for creation.

Anzaldúa sees repetitious activity and depression as distracting strategies:

> At first I feel exposed and opened to the depth of my dissatis-
> faction. Then I feel myself closing, hiding, holding myself
> together rather than allowing myself to fall apart.
>
> Sweating, with a headache, unwilling to communicate, fright-
> ened by sudden noises, *estoy asustada.* (48)

The new mestiza, an ambiguous being, is the borderdwelling self that emerges from the *Coatlicue* state:

> It is this learning to live with *la Coatlicue* that transforms living
> in the Borderlands from a nightmare into a numinous experi-
> ence. It is always a path/state to something else. (73)

This path leads to a consciousness that is born from "racial, ideological, cultural, and biological cross-pollinization" (77). The mestiza consciousness is characterized by the development of a tolerance for contradiction and ambiguity, by the transgression of rigid conceptual boundaries, and by the creative breaking of the new unitary aspect of new and old paradigms. The mestiza consciousness participates in the creation of a new value system through an "uprooting of dualistic thinking" (80).

La mestiza is captive of more than one collectivity, and her dilemma is which collectivity to listen to. She crosses from one collectivity to the other and decides to stake herself in the border between the two, where she can take a critical stance and take stock of her plural personality.

> *Pero es difícil* differentiating between *lo heredado, lo adquirido, lo
> impuesto.* (82)

She throws out what is worthless, the lies, the dulling of life, the runaways. She effects a rupture with all oppressive traditions at the same time that she makes herself vulnerable to foreign ways of thinking, relinquishing safety.

Anzaldúa makes it clear that remaining a being in two worlds without "cross-pollinization" is deadly for Chicanas and other women of color. It is to become a hyphenated being, a dual personality enacted from the outside, without the ability to fashion her own responses. She would agree with the Pachuco speaking in *Peregrinos de Aztlan* by Miguel Mendez-M. When the Pachuco asks the question "*que semos ese?*" (what are we?) and hears the response "*Bueno . . . pues mexico americanos*," he responds:

> *Chale, ese, es pura pinchi madera, la de mexicano domas pa' meterlo al surco, a las minas, nel, pos otra chinga pior. Lo de americanos, pos ya te daras cola, camarada, pa' darnos en la madre en sus pinchis guerras puercas.*

> [Roughly: Mexicanos to be put to work the land, or the mines, or something worse. Americans to kill us in their filthy wars.] (Mendez-M. 1979, 25)

Because I think it is important to distinguish this dual personality[2] from the plural personality and the operating in a pluralistic mode of new mestiza, I will venture my own sense of the distinction. I think this sense fits Anzaldúa's text well. The dual, hyphenated, personality is an Anglo creation. According to this concept, there is no hybrid cultural self. It is part of the Anglo imagination that we can keep our culture and assimilate, a position that would be contradictory if both cultures were understood as informing the "real" fabric of everyday life. But in thinking of a Mexican-American, the Anglo imagination construes "Mexican" as the name for a superexploitable being who is a practitioner of a superfluous, ornamental, culture. Being "American" is what supposedly gives us (dubious) membership in that "real" culture, the culture of the ideally culturally-unified-through-assimilation polis illegitimately called "America." Being American is what makes us functioning citizens.

The Mexican and the American in the dual-personality construct are both animated from the outside; that is why there is no cultural "cross-pollinization." But the plurality of the new mestiza is anchored in the borders, in that space where critique, rupture, and hybridization take place. Though she cannot choose not to be read, constructed, with a logic of hyphenation, demoralization, instrumentality, stereotyping, and devaluation, she can imbue that person with a sense of conflicted subjectivity and ambiguity.[3] So the dual, hyphenated, personality is externally animated and characterized by an absence of the ability to respond and create. The plural personality of the new mestiza is a self-critical, self-animated plurality.

A difficult question to answer in Anzaldúa's text is the question of the company that the Self-in-between, the border Self, keeps in resistant creation.

> A borderland is a vague and undetermined place created by the emotional residue of an unnatural boundary . . . a constant state of transition. *Los atravesados* live here . . . those who cross over, pass over, or go through the confines of the "normal.(3)

A social history of both *despojamiento* and resistance in the meetings between *gringos* and *mexicanos* crisscrosses Anzaldúa's understanding of the borderdweller's situation.

> *¿Quién está protegiendo los ranchos de mi gente? ¿Quién está tratando de cerrar la fisura entre la india y el blanco en nuestra sangre? El Chicano, si, el Chicano que anda como un ladrón en su propia casa.* (63)

Anzaldúa also tells us of the cultural backings for her own resistance in ancient Mesoamerican culture and in contemporary *mexicano, Tejano, Chicano* cultures. Her text draws from *corridos*, ancient myths, *dichos, cantares*, contemporary texts by Chicano/a and Latin American writers. She draws from Los Tigres del Norte as well as from Andres Gonzales Guerrero; from Gina Valdes and Alfonsina Storni; from El Puma and Miguel León-Portilla.

In depicting the borderlands, she tells us of a "place" or state populated by "the people who leap in the dark" (81), a people who are a new mixture of races, "*la primera raza síntesis del globo, una raza mestiza*" (77).

Yet Anzaldúa also depicts the crossing-over as a solitary act, an act of solitary rebellion. Maybe because the *Coatlicue* state and the state of intimate terrorism are described as states of the inner life of the self, because Anzaldúa is describing states in the *psychology* of oppression and liberation, she does not reveal the sociality of resistance. Yet, unless resistance is a social activity, the resister is doomed to failure in the creation of a new universe of meaning, a new identity, a *raza mestiza*. Meaning that is not in response to and looking for a response fails as meaning.

I see enough evidence in her text to develop an account of the sociality of resistance. If rebellion and creation are understood as processes rather than as acts, then each act of solitary rebellion and creation is anchored in and responsive to a collective, even if disorganized, process of resistance.

> *Los Chicanos*, how patient we seem, how very patient. . . . We know how to survive. When other races have given up their tongue, we've kept ours. . . . Stubborn, persevering, impenetrable as stone, yet possessing a malleability that renders us unbreakable, we, the mestizas and mestizos will remain. (63-64)

This society places borderdwellers in profound isolation. The barriers to creative collectivity and collective creation appear insurmountable. But that is only if we think of the act and not of the process of creation. As we author every act of resistance we can understand it as meaningful because it is inserted in a process of resistance that is collective, but we can also aspire to acts of collective resistance, breaking down our isolation against the odds prescribed by "the confines of the normal."

NOTES

1. I have analyzed these defense strategies in "Liberatory Strategies of the Chicana Lesbian: Active Subjectivity in the Absence of Agency," and in "Hard to Handle Anger," to appear in (Lugones, forthcoming).
2. For work on dual personality, see Rosaldo (1989), Madrid-Barela (1973), Chin (1991) and my "Colonization", unpublished manuscript.
3. I have developed these ideas further in Lugones (1987).

REFERENCES

Anzaldúa, Gloria. 1987. *Borderlands/la frontera*. San Francisco: Spinsters/Aunt Lute Book Company.
Chin, Frank. 1991. Come all ye Asian American writers. In *The big aiiieee! An anthology of Chinese American and Japanese American literature*, ed. Jeffrey Chan. New York: Meridian.
Lugones, María. 1987. Playfulness, "world"-travelling, and loving perception. *Hypatia* 2(2): 3-19.
———. Forthcoming. *Pilgrimages/peregrinajes: Essays in pluralist feminism*. Binghamton: SUNY Press.
Madrid-Barela, Arturo. 1973. In search of the authentic pachuco. *Aztlan* 4(1): 31-60.
Mendez-M., Miguel. 1979. *Peregrinos de Aztlan*. Berkeley: Editorial Justa Publications.
Rosaldo, Renato. 1989. *Culture and Truth*. Boston: Beacon Press.

Not Lesbian Philosophy

JOYCE TREBILCOT

Presenting reasoned rejections of the hierarchical implications of "philosopher" and the sexual implications of "lesbian," the author's method leads her to indicate that her resistance to these names is motivated partly by particular facts of her early life.

Am I alone in being alone? I respond to a call for papers on lesbian philosophy because I believe that this rubric will connect me with women with ideas like mine. I respond even though, most deeply, I feel myself a lesbian only by default and hardly a philosopher at all.

Oh, I have a job as a philosopher, and if someone were to ask "How many lesbians in the room?" I'd raise my hand. But "philosopher" and "lesbian" aren't names I choose for myself. Currently, the name I like best is "anti-hierarchist"—that's an idea I can cling to. Among anti-hierarchists, I imagine, lesbians are dykes and no one has the role of philosopher, the role of an authority who tells other people how things are and should be and who, because of being a philosopher, is entitled to be believed.

A concept of a philosopher—white, male, oldish, "wise"—was transmitted to me as part of the culture in which I was conditioned, and then I learned more about it when I got to college and began taking philosophy courses in which the "superiority" of philosophy was taught along with Plato and Russell and symbolic logic. I loved much of what went on in those courses: the working with words, the promise of being able to figure out what to believe and what to do with my life, the mystique of philosophy as difficult, profound, and of sublime importance. Philosophy was, after all, the "Queen of the Sciences"— what could be more suitable for a young woman who would sometimes answer questions about her life plans by saying that she intended to find out the "best" possible thing to do and then do it? The chairman of the philosophy department was of a different mind: he told me that philosophy was "not a good field for a girl"; but I insisted, and he relented. That philosophy admitted only a few women helped to maintain its status; that I was one of the few tended to elevate mine.

Hypatia vol. 7, no. 4 (Fall 1992) © by Joyce Trebilcot

In graduate school, elitism training got serious. The message was both that philosophy is "superior" to other disciplines (whose problems ultimately lead one to philosophy) and that academics in general are "better" than most other people (only academics have a chance at understanding what's really going on, than which there is nothing more important, because understanding is the means for controlling nature, systems, and people—and no questioning the value of controlling). I was learning well. For example, when the teacher of a large introductory course I was required to attend as a teaching assistant began the semester by saying that although this was a course on philosophy he did not call himself a philosopher because whether he was a philosopher or not was for others to decide, I sneered; how silly, I thought—a transparent attempt to enhance his own status. I had learned the importance of subtlety in inculcating the elitist message.

By the time I became an assistant professor, I was expected to be skilled in and thoroughly committed to the narrow path of analytic rigor, rejecting anything "soft," non-white, non-Anglo, non-supportive of the way my colleagues wanted to live. Further, if I wanted to "succeed," I would have to participate regularly in the dueling, the repartee, that they reveled in. But as the Second Wave of feminism broke, I had a framework for my resistance. I started to argue feminism with the other faculty members (all men) in my department. They were not persuaded, I came out, got tenure, and gradually reduced my relationship with all my male colleagues to a distant cordiality.

If the philosophers who, over the years, tried to make me conform were to defend their own "superiority," their arguments might be versions (probably fancier and more obscure) of this one: A philosopher's function is to uncover TRUTHS that benefit "the whole society" (by trickle-down); these truths are not just lying around to be noticed by anyone but require special intelligence, training, and resources—a *discipline*—to be uncovered; hence, philosophers are and should be taken to be authorities on the subjects they discuss.

One difficulty here, in my mind, is that the "truths" philosophers discuss are mainly *values* that presuppose other, unstated values (for example, the superiority of white male methods or the inevitability of hierarchy). Obviously I can't accept values that presuppose other values that I reject, and so the philosophers who propound them can't be "authoritative" for me. Perhaps it would help if thinkers would lay out all their presuppositions, but that's impossible because there is no end to presuppositions, no point at which the background of every idea has been completely explicated: each new explication requires explication itself and, also, life won't hold still long enough, new stuff keeps happening. So, instead of knowing all of a thinker's assumptions, one has instead to consider that person's life and situation and make a guess about whether the deep values are likely to be similar to one's own. In order to make that comparison, of course, one must know quite a bit about one's own values. But if I know my own values and also something about how to find out more about them, then I don't need an authority. Having developed a practice of discovering/creating my own values, I am my own "authority."

Another difficulty with the argument is in the claim that discovering "truths" requires a special discipline. In my experience, it is part of the ordinary life of many dykes who have not had advanced training in an academic discipline to think seriously and critically about values. I understand that developing a sustained presentation of ideas does require resources, particularly time and energy and concentration—but obviously it doesn't require training and licensing, as in academe.

So I think that professional philosophers have no claim to authority over other people's beliefs both because in order to accept an authority one needs to be in the process of developing one's own values, which means that one doesn't need an authority, and because the training of professional philosophers gives no special capacity for finding "truth." In particular, I think that dykes who are professional philosophers have no claim to authority among dykes. Indeed, the fact that parts of the intellectual lives of many academic lesbians are directly influenced by dominant white males on a nearly daily basis is reason to be *especially* cautious about their/our contributions to dyke thought.

A main function of academic philosophy (and other academic disciplines) in the larger context of the dominant culture is, in my opinion, to persuade people to accept hierarchies, for example by making power-over relationships appear natural, inevitable, or good or, more subtly, by promising power-over (sometimes by implying that if you can understand *this* obscure/complex/boring stuff, you're "better" than other people). By rationalizing hierarchy, philosophers strengthen the power of those hierarchically above them, secure their own places in the structure, and ensure that large numbers remain below. Maverick academics who don't want to play this game either do not survive— we get kicked out and down (many political dykes once in academe have left and many are part-time, peripheral); or we are tolerated as tokens; or we do a lot of pretending, hiding our true values, our true selves, from our colleagues; or we compromise, hiding our true values/selves from ourselves.

In any case, it seems clear to me—and, I expect, to most of the readers of this essay—that academic philosophy, "analytic" and otherwise, as it exists today in the U.S. and presumably elsewhere, is essentially oppressive, in part because most of its practitioners, following tradition, assume that they have a right to determine how other people should think and act. Why would a dyke want to be associated with such an enterprise?

Money, of course. I and others maintain a relationship with a philosophy department primarily so that we can buy what we need and/or so we can control our own money. Once, when I was just about to enter a Ph.D. program, a faculty member asked me why I had decided to come back to school and I told him that I needed the money (I thought then that I could speak honestly to faculty); I remember his disdain as he said that scholarly work should be done only by those who would do it for love even if no money were involved. But I knew that if I didn't need money, I would be moving around the world writing and reading and trying to figure out how my mind worked, as I had been doing before—not going to school. This fortyish, white, upper-middle-class male, who felt quite at home in the university, taught me something about academe and about himself by his remark. He learned nothing from me, though; he had no idea how being in school felt to me.

But philosophy for me is not just a matter of money. Sometimes I use my connection with philosophy as a source of status. I do so for good purpose when, for example, I use being a professor at the university to get access to resources for lesbian and feminist groups. But I also identify with the status sometimes when I have no such purpose because, like most people conditioned in hierarchical society (like all, I believe, who have not consciously changed), I have a hierarchical grid within me that puts people into slots according to what I imagine to be their value compared to me, usually either above or below. Although I work on dissolving this grid, it still operates within me much of the time.

Philosophy gives me a sounder sort of self-esteem too: I am proud that I was able to survive mid-century U.S. society by learning how to get paid by a university. Without being able to write and teach and have *some* control over my work, I would have had a much worse time.

But apart from my reasons for maintaining an association with institution-alized philosophy, I like some of the kinds of thinking and talking that go under the name "philosophy." These, of course, don't require academe. Indeed, it can be argued that "dyke philosophy" can barely be done—or at least can't thrive—in academe. In any case, for me, calling the anti-hierarchizing explo-ration of ideas "philosophy" brings hierarchy back in; for me, the terms "philosophy" and "philosopher" seem irredeemably contaminated with elit-ism.

But "dyke" has been redefined, why not "philosophy"? I don't mean here to suggest attempting to reform philosophy within academe. Many feminist projects in academe, including the development of women's studies, help make it a better place for women, but I think that the university will continue to be dedicated to hierarchizing people and that reform efforts need to be infused with that awareness. Outside of academe, however, "philosophy" is used to refer to a certain subject matter, a certain approach to thinking, that can and perhaps in some cultures does exist not only without reference to academe but perhaps also without assuming authority over knowledge. Perhaps "philosophy" can be and sometimes is used in such a way among dykes. Western academics do not own philosophy, although many think that they do.

Probably even now, in some dyke communities, dykes have a sense of "philosophy" whereby the term refers not to a professional role but to a kind of talk, or talk-action, that occurs alongside other forms such as telling about the past, making plans, explaining how to do something. It would be interesting to know whether, in such groups, philosophizing is a function supposed to be performed by only a few or is taken to be something nearly everyone does or can do. I am inclined to prefer the latter arrangement because I so much want each dyke's ideas and feelings to be valued, to be valued "equally." That many dykes are committed to processes whereby *every* womon is given serious attention and respect is, for me, part of the genius of dykes together, one of the great joys of being a dyke.

But the likelihood of the term "philosophy" being reconceived and becoming a regular part of dyke vocabulary is small, I think, at least where there is proximity to academe. It is one thing to wipe the dirt off "dyke," but quite another to wipe the power-over off "philosopher."

So although I have a job as a philosopher, "philosopher" is not a name I choose for myself. Nor do I now have—or need—a substitute.

"Philosopher" is not a name I choose, and neither is "lesbian." Regarding "lesbian" I will be brief. Although I like the company in this category a lot better than that in the category "philosopher," I reject its focus. In my experience, the meaning of "lesbian" is primarily sexual. Lesbian literature includes discussions intended to shift the meaning of lesbianism away from sex to other centers such as friendship or the rejection of patriarchy, but many, perhaps most, lesbians nevertheless define "lesbian" as centrally about sex, as do most heterosexuals.

But I am not primarily sexual and so do not like being named with a word that means "sex" to most people; defining women in terms of sex is a trick men play on women and I don't want to play it on myself. Sexuality is in me, in my life. It has had a VERY IMPORTANT role in my development, as is virtually inevitable in partriarchy. But I think of sexuality—sexuality/violence—as the main tool that men and boys use to control women and girls. Like some other lesbians, I certainly do not want it as a central part of my identity.

Instead of "lesbian," I prefer "dyke," with its message of resistance: "dyke" speaks more to—and of—my heart.

But why do I want to reject the name "lesbian philosopher"? I have just given reasons, but why are these reasons salient for me, why do I make them mine? Reasons are based on motives, in my opinion: one is moved by feelings rooted in one's situation, experiences, and temperament to find and adopt particular values along with reasons for them. So I want here to point to some of the parts of my background that are relevant to my dislike of "lesbian philosopher."

First, the process of detaching myself from academic philosophy occurs at this particular time in my life because, at fifty-nine, I begin to see the end of my economic reliance on the university. In a half-dozen years or less I will "retire" and, while some think of retirement as extended leave, continuing their academic identities, to me it is an opportunity for restructuring my work and, to some extent, myself. Having resigned from the university, I intend to be something less polite than a lesbian philosopher. At school the politeness is a protection from men in my immediate environment, but when I leave my job, there will be no men in my immediate environment. At that time I would like to be able to be simply a dyke, a dyke whose life includes writing and thinking about ideas—although I know that I will not shed my academic identity easily, quickly, or all at once.

My preparation for rejecting hierarchy, including both academe and heterosexuality, began in infancy. According to my mother, during my first few weeks of life I was often left alone in a room where I screamed from frustration and loneliness, wanting to be held, wanting company, feeling abandoned. The doctor had warned my mother that if she followed her feelings and picked me up whenever I cried between feedings, she would "spoil" me. So, trying to be a good mother, she left me alone. I screamed, enraged. I take this experience to be a first and deep lesson in the importance for me of being in control of my own situation.

My mother and I continued to have battles of will. I remember, for example, that when I was four or five she made me sit all afternoon over my lunch— strained spinach with bits of bacon in it, long gone cold—insisting that I eat; I refused. I was testing my power, learning the range of an idea that was to become part of the long-term music of my mind: "You can't make me." For many years, this refrain, "You can't make me," played over and over in my head along with another favorite, "My mother won't let me": songs of a dominated child. My mother's intention, which was supported by my father, was that every aspect of my life—behavior and appearance, thoughts and feelings—should be as she wanted (of course she read my locked diary: I remember putting a hair on a page to test her, and the next day it was gone). Being thus dominated prepared me to resist hierarchy both by making me super-aware of the frustration of not being in control of one's own life and by giving me practice in feeling alone, in being an outsider with respect to those who did not question hierarchy.

As I grew older, I struggled to reject my family of origin and also decided that I would not myself marry or give birth; later, I rejected the very concept of family, and now I want not to use the term at all, not even for dykes relating to dykes, because for me it inevitably resonates hierarchy—not only the hierarchy of my own particular experiences, but, more generally, the domination of females, of the young, and of the old that are part of the meaning of "family" in the mainstream culture I was trained in. In my teens and twenties I rejected also conventional ideas about work. I had no patience for any of the "careers" that I was supposed to choose from and devoted my energies instead to ideas, art, and adventure, partly for love of intense experience for its own sake and partly because I needed such experiences, I thought, in order to know how to live. I was called a nonconformist, a "bohemian," and, in my mother's word, a "drifter." (I remember being thrilled with the label "nonconformist"—a name for myself!—it was perhaps as welcome to me then as "lesbian" has been to some dykes-from-birth who grow up without any reflection of themselves.)

So, one might say, I rejected conventional values because of the combination of my temperament and my mother's domination of me and I was able to choose to be unconventional partly because I had learned to be by myself, growing up in a household where I was alone in confronting the monolithic power of my parents, and by myself also in the wider social context where my values were unacceptable to most of the people around me. With this background, I was overwhelmed when I finally learned, with the advent of feminism, that there are *good reasons* for my differences, that is, that my hatred of being controlled, my rejection of family, my refusal to conform to other people's standards, that all this resistance makes intellectual sense in the context of analyses of the oppression of women and children, of capitalism, of heterosexism, of hierarchy.

As I continue to discover/invent "theory" to attach to my deepest feelings and as I become more connected with other dykes, I realize also that I am *not* alone, not, at any rate, entirely alone. While no one else rejects the names "lesbian" and "philosopher" for just the same reasons I do (no one else has just the same stories), I am not alone in the rejecting. Anti-hierarchist dykes—disagreeing with one another on all manner of topics including what constitutes anti-hierarchism—abound.

NOTES

Ideas from Chris Cuomo and Sally Tatnall have been helpful for this writing (I heard both of them speak about philosophy at a meeting of the Society for Women in Philosophy in Edwardsville, Illinois, on March 7, 1992).

I appreciate also responses to an earlier version of the piece—but the rewriting has changed it so much that the earlier "version" is really a different piece—by Claudia Card, Marilyn Friedman, and two anonymous reviewers.

The Feminist Sexuality Debates and the Transformation of the Political[1]

BAT-AMI BAR ON

In this essay I examine the history of the sexuality debates among feminists. In both the nineteenth century and the recent sexuality debates the personal is taken to be foundational for a political stance, while simultaneously the debates transform feminist understandings of the extent to which the personal is political. I suggest that this transformation undermines the epistemological assumptions of the debates, resulting in a feminism that cannot be radical.

I.

Ann Ferguson has claimed in several articles that central to the most recent feminist sexuality debates is disagreement over the "correct" feminist theory of sexuality, social power, and sexual freedom (Ferguson 1983, 10-16; 1984, 106-12; 1986, 11-13). According to Ferguson:

a. While one party to the debates sees a fundamental connection between intimacy and sexuality, the other sees such a connection between pleasure and sexuality,

b. While the first party sees sexuality shaped by sexual objectification as a tool of male domination, the other sees sexuality as shaped by sexual repression that is the product of all institutions, interactions, and practices that distinguish the normal/legitimate/healthy from their opposites and privilege certain sexual expressions over others,

c. While the first party sees sexual freedom as presupposing equality and respect, as well as requiring the elimination of patriarchal institutions and sexual practices, the other sees

Hypatia vol. 7, no. 4 (Fall 1992) © by Bat-Ami Bar On

sexual freedom as requiring oppositional practices that transgress respectable categories.

Ferguson suggests that these are the central disagreements in the sexuality
debates because they are implied by the beliefs of each party about the "correct"
feminist position on sexuality. Moreover, she points out that

> d. While the first party believes that "feminists should repudiate
> any sexual practice that supports or 'normalizes' male violence"
> and "reclaim control over female sexuality by developing con-
> cern with our own sexual priorities which differ from men's,"
> the other believes that "feminists should repudiate any theoret-
> ical analyses, legal restrictions, or moral judgements that stig-
> matize sexual minorities and thus restrict the freedom of all"
> and "reclaim control over female sexuality by demanding the
> right to practice whatever gives us pleasure and satisfaction."
> (Ferguson 1984, 108-09; 1986, 12).

According to Ellen Carol DuBois and Linda Gordon, the most recent feminist
sexuality debates are similar to debates among first wave, that is, nineteenth
and early twentieth century, feminists (Dubois and Gordon 1984, 31-49).
DuBois and Gordon, like Ferguson, point out the major foci of disagreements
between the parties to the first wave feminist sexuality debates. It seems that
first wave feminists also disagreed about sexuality itself, one party believing
that male and female sexual desire differ fundamentally, the other believing
that both are healthily lusty. Consequently, the first party saw male sexuality
as dangerous to women, while the second saw a double standard that represses
women as bad and, as a result, while the first party looked for means to impose
boundaries on male sexuality, the second looked for means to liberate female
sexuality.

In light of the similarity between past and present sexuality debates among
feminists, it is tempting to believe that the terms of the sexuality debates have
been steady. But, this is not so. In what follows, I will argue that even the terms
of the sexuality debates among second wave feminists have not been steady.

The most recent sexuality debates are not the first for second wave feminists.
Those that preceded them expressed an underlying tension in the feminist
movement and resulted in an open heterosexual—lesbian split. I will examine
a history of the earlier and later sexuality debates among second wave feminists.
I will use the history to point out that in both the nineteenth century and the
recent sexuality debates the personal—especially the experiential connection
of marginality, difference, sexuality and consciousness—is taken by the parties
to the debates as foundational for a political stance, while simultaneously the
debates bring with them a transformation of feminist understandings of the
extent to which the personal is political. I will end by examining the conse-

quences of this transformation and suggest that it undermines the epistemological assumptions of the debates. I will show that the result is a feminism that cannot be radical.

II.

I stated above that the current sexuality debates are not the movement's first and that the previous ones expressed the tension and brought out into the open a heterosexual-lesbian split. In retrospect, neither the tension nor its eventual expression is surprising in a movement that adopted as a slogan and took seriously the claim that the personal is political and, therefore, did not shy away from examining sexuality and practices and institutions that legitimize specific sexual relations, such as love, marriage, the family and sexual violence. Second wave feminists made strong claims about sexuality and its setting from the start. Thus, for example, the 1970 manifesto of the New York Radical Feminists states:

> Radical feminism recognizes the oppression of women as a
> fundamental political oppression. . . . The oppression of women
> is manifested in particular institutions, such as marriage, moth-
> erhood, love, and sexual intercourse. . . . Through those insti-
> tutions the woman is taught to confuse her biological sexual
> differences with her total human potential. . . . Biology is des-
> tiny, she is told . . . She is told that sexual intercourse, too, is
> her function, rather than a voluntary act which she may engage
> in as an expression of her humanity. (Connell and Wilson 1974,
> 253-54)

That same year Kate Millet declared in "Sexual Politics: A Manifesto for Revolution" that a sexual revolution would bring about "the end of sexuality in the forms in which it has existed historically—brutality, violence, capitalism, exploitation, and warfare—that it may cease to be hatred and become love" (Millett 1973, 365-67).

These strong claims forming the kernel of early second wave feminist critique of sexuality and the practices and institutions that legitimize specific sexual relations also form implicitly the kernel of a critique of male-dominated heterosexuality and heterosexism. They were quickly followed by an open critique of male-dominated heterosexuality and heterosexism that was intimately tied with the examination of lesbian practice. The feminist connection of experiential marginality, difference, sexuality, and consciousness as foundational for a political stance is first made in this context.

Two documents are very instructive in this respect Radicalesbians' "Woman-Identified Woman" (1973, 240-45) and Charlotte Bunch's "Lesbians in Revolt" (Bunch 1975, 29-37). Both analyze the symbolic value of lesbian practice in a heterosexist world. The first document opens with the question "What is a lesbian?" and answers as follows:

> A lesbian is the rage of all women condensed to the point of explosion. She is the woman who, often beginning at an extremely early age, acts in accordance with her inner compulsion to be a more complete and freer human being than her society—perhaps then but certainly later—cares to allow her. . . . She may not be fully conscious of the political implications of what for her began as personal necessity, but on some level she has not been able to accept the limitations and oppression laid on her by the most basic role of her society—the female role. (Radicalesbians 1973, 240)

Charlotte Bunch further develops this answer.

> In our society which defines all people and institutions for the benefit of the rich, white male, the Lesbian is in revolt. In revolt because she defines herself in terms of women and rejects the male definitions of how she should feel, act, look, and live. . . . The Lesbian rejects male sexual/political domination; she defies his world, his social organization, his ideology, and his definition of her as inferior. (Bunch 1975, 29)

Though she points out clearly that a lesbian does not choose women to escape oppression but because she loves women, Bunch emphasizes the political nature of lesbian practice. She states:

> Woman-identified Lesbianism is . . . more than sexual preference; it is a political choice. It is political because relations between men and women are essentially political; they involve power and dominance. Since the Lesbian actively rejects that relationship and chooses women, she defies the established political system. (Bunch 1975, 30)

Even after pointing out that not all lesbians are politically conscious and therefore are not necessarily aware of their choices as political choices, Bunch adds:

> The lesbian's independence and refusal to support one man undermines the personal power that men exercise over women. Our rejection of heterosexual sex challenges male domination in its most individual and common form. We offer all women something better than submission to personal oppression. We offer the beginning of the end of collective and individual male supremacy. (Bunch 1975, 33)

Thus far, lesbian practice has been presented as a challenge to male domination. Bunch goes on to call attention to the relative marginality of lesbians in a heterosexist society and proclaims distrust in heterosexually committed women. She writes:

> Heterosexuality separates women from each other; it makes women define themselves through men; it forces women to compete against each other for men and the privilege which comes through men and their social standing. . . . The lesbian receives none of these heterosexual privileges or compensations since she does not accept the male demands on her. She has little vested interest in maintaining the present political system since all of its institutions . . . work to keep her down. (Bunch 1975, 34)

And she ends by saying:

> As long as straight women see lesbianism as a bedroom issue, they hold back the development of politics and strategies that would put an end to male supremacy and they give men an excuse for not dealing with their sexism. . . . Lesbianism is the key to liberation and only women who cut their ties to male privilege can be trusted to remain serious in the struggle against male dominance. Those who remain tied to men, individually or in political theory, cannot always put women first. (Bunch 1975, 36)

I have quoted from Bunch's essay at length because her formulation of the connection between the personal and the political and her claims about experiential marginality, difference, sexuality, and consciousness as foundational for a political stance are striking, and also because in the two decades that have passed since the publication of "Lesbians in Revolt," they have been forgotten. I believe that the forgetfulness is not due to this formulation's lack of theoretical sophistication nor to "dyke baiting," a common movement experience in the early and mid seventies. The forgetfulness is the result of the *normalization* of both lesbian practice and lesbian-feminism. This normalization naturalized lesbian practice and robbed it of its symbolic value, thereby robbing it of its earlier political significance. It clipped the political wings of lesbian-feminism by validating lesbianism as one among a plurality of feminist perspectives.

The normalization of lesbian practice and the normalization of lesbian-feminism are interrelated and mutually reinforcing. The poorer the symbolic value believed to be embodied in lesbian practice, and the less the practice is perceived as deeply political because of its fundamental opposition to male-dominated heterosexual society, the less compelling is the claim that lesbian-feminism, as a conscious articulation of the politics of lesbian practice, provides a vanguard understanding of women's experience in male-dominated heterosexual society and the strategies needed to radically transform that society. Similarly, the less a radical feminist political promise is seen as special to lesbian-feminism, the less compelling is the claim that lesbian practice should be perceived as deeply political and rich in symbolic value.

III.

Among the products of the normalization of lesbian practice and lesbian-feminism was a containment of the critical force that lesbians in the second wave feminist movement claimed for themselves. By 1979 both the feminist critique of the practices and institutions that legitimize specific sexual relations and the feminist experimentation with alterative practices and institutions were in decline, and the New Right was on the rise. Responding to this threatening combination, some socialist-feminists that were not identified as lesbians, like Barbara Haber, called for the reinitiation and development of a feminist critique of personal life, especially of the family as a setting in which personal life takes place (Haber 1979, 417-30).

At first it may seem that what Haber was calling for in her essay "Is Personal Life Still A Political Issue?" was simply the continuation of an examination of practices and institutions that legitimize specific sexual relations. But I believe that Haber's essay is an example of the ways in which the normalization, hence the containment of the critical force of lesbian-feminism worked.

Haber saw the critique of personal life as the most relevant contribution that the feminist movement could make to the lives of women in the late seventies. Because she was aware that by 1979 the movement had been trying to bridge the heterosexual-lesbian split, and because she also saw dangers in the bridging, she stated that "a feminist movement that attempts to maintain its gay-straight unity at the price of ignoring the crisis that faces the majority of women makes itself irrelevant" (Haber 1979, 422).

Though she may have hoped otherwise, Haber seems willing to risk resplitting the movement. Moreover, her call for the initiation and development of a critique of personal life was a call to heterosexual feminist women. She appealed to them because, like the women the critique was to speak to, they belonged to what she calls the "American sexual mainstream." She believed that while (a) lesbians "have maintained to a far greater degree than heterosexual feminists a cohesive, critical view of the family and heterosexuality," and (b) lesbians have a vantage point that is invaluable in future development of a critical theory of personal life," nonetheless, (c) "the feminist movement must take advantage of the experience of both gay and straight women" (Haber 1979, 421).

Thus Haber puts the lesbian-feminist and heterosexual-feminist perspective on the same plane. Moreover, she goes beyond normalization to identifying indirectly lesbian-feminism as the cause of the heterosexual-lesbian split in the movement. She describes the split as the product of the early seventies lesbian moralism and the dismissal of heterosexuality. She writes:

> Having discovered that smashing monogamy and heterosexuality were inadequate programs for their lives, women who were committed to their sexual preference for men and unwilling to write off family life became defensive and eventually (more or less) silent on sexual and family issues. (Haber 1979, 422)

The most subtle of Haber's containment moves is her call for a critique of personal life that is focused on the family as the setting of personal life. A critique of the family can demystify it without necessarily being critical of the family or of personal life. Thus in *Capitalism, The Family and Personal Life* Eli Zaretsky argues that under capitalism, personal life—the life of people as individuals capable of and seeking intimacy and happiness—while still falling short of what it can be, which is autonomous life activity, is served by the family, the only existing, even if not wholly satisfactory, institutionalized refuge from the brutality of capitalism (Zaretsky 1976). And in *The Reproduction of Mothering* Nancy Chodorow exposes the complex relations between gender and generation as structures underlying the family, but it is only the family as engendering, the family insofar as it reproduces women as mothers and men as fathers, that is the subject of Chodorow's criticism (Chodorow 1978). According to her, it is the function of the family as an engendering agency that is the core problem of the family, but this function can be disposed of and the family can be restructured and preserved.

Neither Zaretsky's nor Chodorow's work includes an examination of the family as a social institution that legitimizes specific sexual relations, or explores its connections to other practices and institutions that do this such as romantic love, marriage and sexual violence. Both Zaretsky and Chodorow concede that the family is male dominated, yet they believe that the family is redeemable and affirm its value. Indeed, Zaretsky's work can be used to assign the family and personal life the same kind of symbolic political value that Bunch assigned to lesbian practice because the family and personal life, as he sees them, stand opposed to capitalism and the alienation and dehumanization it produces.

Zaretsky's and Chodorow's treatment and affirmation of the family tends to make the family immune against a lesbian-feminist critique. Thus, they have contributed to the more than decade-long reprivatizing and depoliticizing personal life, processes to which Haber also contributes. These processes stand in tension with and even undo the deprivatizing and politicizing of personal life begun by the New Left and carried on by feminism. Chodorow's contribution to the re-privatization and depoliticization of personal life has two dimensions. Her work has been used to naturalize and, therefore, normalize lesbian practice. She showed that in the engendering family girls became psychologically women and mothers without separating themselves from women and mothers in the radical way that boys separate themselves from women and mothers in order to become men and fathers. This has been used by some, such as Adrienne Rich, to suggest that lesbian attraction rather than heterosexual desire is natural (Rich, 1980).

IV.

While large segments of personal life became and stayed taboo subjects, sexual practices and choices became the focus of a feminist critique as a by-product of the attempt to organize a feminist response to pornography in the late seventies. There was already a beginning of a feminist critique of pornography and the pornographic imagination in the late sixties.[2] But during most of the seventies feminist energies were focused on sexual violence—on rape, battering, sexual harassment, and child abuse—and not on pornography. Feminist energies that had been focused on sexual violence were slowly drained as they were submerged in victim service organizations that were dependent on state, federal, or other funding agencies whose interest was not in the feminist critique of the sexual victimization of women nor in the development of strategies of social transformation. At the same time, a feminist critique of pornography and a related critique of sadomasochistic practices gathered momentum.

A feminist critique of sexual violence, because it is a critique of systemic victimization and it is not victim-blaming, is not a critique of women's personal lives and life choices. At first, it may seem that a feminist critique of pornography and sadomasochism is merely an extension of the feminist critique of sexual violence and that it, too, is not critical of women's personal lives and life choices.[3] But this is not so since some women, including women with unquestionable feminist credentials, find pleasure in partaking in the pornographic imagination and in sadomasochistic practices. For these women a critique of pornography and sadomasochism is a critique of their sexual practices and choices.

The critical feminist response to the feminist critique of pornography and sadomasochism together with that critique and the ensuing debate between feminists on both sides of the issues form the most recent feminist sexuality debates. They have followed and developed the pattern set for the containment of the critical role that lesbians claimed for themselves in the feminist movement in the early seventies. This is especially clear in Gayle Rubin's "Thinking Sex: Notes for a Radical Theory of the Politics of Sexuality" (Rubin 1984, 267-319).

In this essay Rubin relies on Foucault's work to develop a description of the common discourses about sexuality. According to her, these discourses share several assumptions: they take sex as a natural, thus a pre-social force; they consider this force to be dangerous, destructive, and negative; they assign it special significance in human life; they provide a single standard to which all sexuality has to conform; they appraise sex acts or practices according to a hierarchical system of values about sex and their distance from the standard; and they take there to be some line in sexual conduct that if crossed, only peril can follow.

Rubin claims that feminism, specifically what she calls "anti-sex" feminism, shares a variant of these assumptions. She makes this point most explicitly in relation to her extensive description of the hierarchical system of values about sex:

> According to this system, sexuality that is "good," "normal," and "natural" should ideally be heterosexual, marital, monogamous, reproductive, and non-commercial. It should be coupled, relational within the same generation, and occur at home. It should not involve pornography, fetish objects, sex toys of any sort, or roles other than male and female. Any sex that violates these rules is "bad," "abnormal," or "unnatural." (Rubin 1984, 280-81)

Later she describes the "anti-sex" variant of feminism:

> Proponents of this viewpoint have condemned virtually every variant of sexual expression as anti-feminist. Within this framework monogamous lesbianism that occurs within long-term intimate relationships, and which does not involve playing with polarized roles, has replaced married procreative heterosexuality at the top of the value hierarchy. Heterosexuality has been demoted to somewhere in the middle. Apart from this change, everything looks more or less familiar. The lower depths are occupied by the usual groups and behaviors: prostitution transexuality, sadomasochism, and cross-generational activities. (Rubin 1984, 301)

Rubin's comparison of the common discourses about sexuality with "anti-sex" feminist discourse of sexuality points out both the latter's achievements and its limitations. A comparison of these achievements and limitations in the context of the previous comparison establishes one thing very clearly—the absence of radicalism in "anti-sex" feminism and, by implication, in certain lesbian practices.

According to Rubin, there are radical lesbian practices and they are radical because they are transgressional. Their practitioners are a true vanguard in the current struggles about sexuality. They are, however, not alone:

> The women's movement may have produced the most retrogressive sexual thinking this side of the Vatican. But, it has also produced an exciting, innovative, and articulate defense of sexual pleasure and erotic justice. This "pro-sex" feminism has been spearheaded by lesbians whose sexuality does not conform to movement standards of purity (primarily lesbian sadomasochists and butch/femme dykes), by unapologetic heterosexuals, and by women who adhere to classic radical feminism rather than to the revisionist celebrations of femininity which have become so common. (Rubin 1984, 302-03)

By identifying certain sexual practices, whether lesbian, homosexual, or heterosexual as long as they are transgressional, as providing a vantage point from which one can understand and transform sexuality in a better way than "anti-sex" feminism understands and transforms it, Rubin in the early eighties, like Bunch in the early seventies, treats experiential marginality, difference, sexuality, and consciousness as foundations for a political stance. Bunch's connections led her to claim the feminist vanguard for lesbians. However, Rubin's connections lead her away from feminism. After acknowledging that feminism has provided guidance to progressive thinkers interested in thinking about sex, she states:

> I want to challenge the assumption that feminism is or should be the privileged site of a theory of sexuality. Feminism is the theory of gender oppression. To automatically assume that this makes it a theory of sexual oppression is to fail to distinguish between gender on the one hand and erotic desire on the other. (Rubin 1984, 307)

Denying that feminism, any feminism, is capable of a theory of sexuality that explains sexual oppression and sexual liberation, Rubin denies the value of the current sexuality debates. In addition, she removes from the domain of feminist discourse another segment of personal life. In doing so she contributes to the construction of a feminism for which the personal is not political.

V.

Rubin's strategy of containment was successful. By now, but for a few letters to the editor in feminist newspapers, the current sexuality debates have turned into a lukewarm debate over various legal strategies against the pornography industry. Still, Rubin's ability to distance herself from feminism is dependent on her belief that experiential marginality, difference, sexuality, and consciousness are foundations for a political stance, especially for one that is superior to those it competes with. Because of Rubin's flight from feminism, and similarly because of Haber's call for a feminist critique of personal life, albeit one led by heterosexual feminists, it is not obvious that there is something problematic about believing that the personal is foundational to one's political stance while at the same time actually constraining the political critique of the personal. But something is definitely problematic here.

In the context of a feminism that takes seriously the claim that the personal is political, it makes sense to believe that the personal is foundational for one's political stance. This is so because in the context of that kind of feminism, one's political stance articulates the political structures and discourses, the relations of power, domination, and submission in which one is enmeshed. One's political stance is then, among other things, immediately and directly about and for oneself.

A feminism that takes seriously the claim that the personal is political because it takes the personal as foundational for the political is a standpoint feminism. It is a feminism that not merely denies the possibility of separating the personal and the political but one that could be described, following Nancy Hartsock, as a feminism according to which:

> 1. Material life . . . not only structures but sets limits on the understanding of social relations.

> 2. If material life is structured in fundamentally opposing ways for two different groups, one can expect both that the vision of each will represent an inversion of the other and that the vision of the ruling class will be partial and perverse.

> 3. The vision of the ruling class structures the material relations in which all parties are forced to participate and, therefore, cannot be dismissed as simply false.

> 4. In consequence, the vision available to the oppressed group must be [politically] struggled for and represents an achievement. . . .

> 5. Because the understanding of the oppressed is an engaged vision, the adoption of a standpoint exposes the real relations among human beings as inhuman, points beyond the present, and carries a historical and liberatory role. (Hartsock 1983, 118-232)

According to Sandra Harding in "The Instability of the Analytical Categories of Feminist Theory," standpoint feminism is a descendant of the Marxist reformulation of the Enlightenment's belief that men, and only men, possessed the innate abilities for objective and, therefore, emanicipatory understanding of reality (Harding 1986, 645-64). According to Harding, Marxism reformulated the "Enlightenment vision so that the proletariat, guided by Marxist theory and class struggle, became the ideal knower, the group capable of using observations and reason to grasp the true form of social relations, including our relation to nature" (Harding 1986, 654). Under standpoint feminism, women became the ideal knowers.

However, a standpoint feminism that is silent about personal life, that does not critically examine sexuality and the practices and institutions that legitimize certain sexual relations, that is not critical of love, marriage, the family, heterosexism, and sexual violence is a standpoint feminism that cannot be used fruitfully by a woman for a critical awareness of her self in her socio-cultural context. It is a standpoint feminism that does not, because it cannot, have a dynamic dialectical relation of the personal and the political and, therefore, it is a standpoint feminism whose growth is necessarily stunted.

This is the kind of feminism that Haber and Rubin and the many who have contributed to the re-privatization and de-politization of personal life—including the naturalization of lesbian practice and normalization of lesbian-feminism—offer by contributing to the constraints on a feminist discourse of personal life. This is also the kind of feminism that all premature closures of past and present sexuality debates partake in creating. No matter how heated, a discussion, a debate, a struggle for power and control of the terms of the discourse, keeps the issues alive and makes growth possible. And at this point, if it is not too late, growth in the feminist critique of personal life, which means repoliticization, is essential to a reradicalization of feminism.

NOTES

A version of this paper was first presented at the National Women's Studies Association conference, June 1988.

1. Throughout the paper I use "feminist" and "feminism" in the singular, though there are many kinds of feminists and many forms of feminism. Most of those that fall under my singular "feminist" and "feminism" when I discuss specific positions are mainstream radical socialist, lesbian, and lesbian SM feminisms and feminists. At times, however, my use of the singular "feminist" and "feminism" is abstract and idealized, which is, I believe, rather problematic because of the departure from the historically situated movements. I suspect that my abstract and idealized uses of "feminist" and "feminism" are a kind of what Iris Young calls "a utopian moment." I do struggle with it but I was unable to eliminate it from this paper.

2. The 1968 demonstration against the Miss America Pageant was motivated by criticisms of the use of women as sex objects. In 1969, Bay Area Women's Liberation

protested a local underground paper's decision to publish pornography. For writing from this time see, for example, Dunbar (1969).

3. This is very clear from the approach to the issues. See, for example, the analyses by Barry, Griffin, Morgan, and Russell in Lederer (1980) and Linden et al. (1982) in comparison with Brownmiller (1975) and Russell (1975), the classic feminist analyses of rape.

REFERENCES

Brownmiller, Susan. 1975. *Against our will: Women, men and rape.* New York: Simon and Schuster.

Bunch, Charlotte. 1975. Lesbians in revolt. In *Lesbianism and the women's movement,* ed. Nancy Myron and Charlotte Bunch. Baltimore, MD: Diana. First published in *The Furies* 1(1), January 1972.

Chodorow, Nancy . 1978. *The reproduction of mothering: Psychoanalysis and the sociology of gender.* Berkeley: University of California Press.

Connell, Noreen and Cassandra Wilson, eds. 1974. *Rape: The first sourcebook for women.* New York: Plume Books.

DuBois, Ellen Carol and Linda Gordon. 1984. Seeking ecstasy on battlefield: Danger and pleasure in nineteenth century feminist sexual thought. In *Pleasure and danger: Exploring female sexuality.* Boston: Routledge & Kegan Paul.

Dunbar, Roxanne. 1969. Sexual liberation: More of the same thing. *No More Fun and Games* 3 (November).

Ferguson Ann. 1983. The sex debate within the women's movement: A socialist-feminist view. *Against the Current* September/October: 10-16.

———. 1984. Sex war: The debate between radical and libertarian feminists. *Signs: Journal of Women in Culture and Society* 10(1): 106-12.

———. 1986. Pleasure, power and the porn wars. *The Women's Review of Books* 3: 11.

Haber, Barbara. 1979. Is personal life still a political issue? *Feminist Studies* 5: 417-30.

Harding, Sandra. 1986. The instability of the analytic categories of feminist theory. *Signs: Journal of Women in Culture and Society* 11(4): 645-64.

Hartsock, Nancy C. M. 1983. *Money, sex and power.* Boston: Northeastern University Press.

Lederer, Laura (ed). 1980. *Take back the night: Women on pornography.* New York: William Morrow.

Linden, Robin Ruth, Darlene R. Pagano, Diana E. H. Russell, and Susan Star Leigh, eds. 1982. *Against sadomasochism: Radical feminist analysis.* San Francisco: Frog in the Well.

Millett, Kate. 1973 [1970]. Sexual politics: A manifesto for Revolution. In *Radical feminism,* ed. Anne Koedt, Ellen Levine, and Anita Rapone. New York: Quadrangle. First published in Notes from the second year.

Radicalesbians. 1973 [1971]. Woman-identified woman. In *Radical feminism,* ed. Anne Koedt, Ellen Levine, and Anita Rapone. New York: Quadrangle. First published in *Notes from the third year.*

Rich, Adrienne. 1980. Compulsory Heterosexuality and Lesbian Existence *Signs: Journal of Women in Culture and Society* 5(4): 631-60.

Rubin, Gayle. 1984. Thinking sex: Notes for a radical theory of sexual politics. In *Pleasure and danger: Exploring female sexuality,* ed. Carole S. Vance. Boston: Routledge & Kegan Paul.

Russell, Diana E. H. 1975. *The politics of rape: The victims' perspective*. New York: Stein and Day.

Zaretsky, Eli. 1976. *Capitalism, the family and personal life*. New York: Harper and Row.

Sadomasochism and Exclusion

LORENA LEIGH SAXE

Should Lesbian and women's events have policies banning sadomasochists or sadomasochistic acts? This question is being heatedly debated in the Lesbian community. In this paper, I examine the moral and political problems with sadomasochism from a Lesbian-feminist perspective, concluding that sadomasochism is antifeminist and antiliberatory for many reasons. Then, given this conclusion, I explore how events such as women's music festivals should determine their policies about sadomasochism.

Recently, in the Lesbian communities, there has been a great deal of debate over the moral and political appropriateness of the presence of sadomasochists and open sadomasochistic practice at women's and Lesbian events. This debate has occurred in the women's and Lesbian press, as well as at events such as conferences and the annual women's music festivals in the United States. Here I take up, from a Lesbian-feminist perspective, the question of whether sadomasochism (s/m) should be prohibited from such events. Is sadomasochism profeminist, antifeminist, or neither? I address this question first. I use the book *Coming to Power* (Samois 1981) as my primary source on sadomasochist ideology, as this is one of the few long s/m works that claims to be profeminist.[1] I then address what the answer to this question about whether sadomasochism is feminist implies about the presence of sadomasochists at events such as women's music festivals.

SADOMASOCHISM: PROFEMINIST, ANTIFEMINIST, OR NEITHER?

In the debates about the morality and political soundness of sadomasochism, all sides—sadomasochists, those tolerant of sadomasochism, and those opposed to it—have focused on the *consent* of the masochist. Sadomasochists, and those tolerant of them, claim that this consent is what distinguishes the sadomasochistic relationship from one of battering. Or, they state that one should be able to do whatever one wants, or consents to, as long as no one else

Hypatia vol. 7, no. 4 (Fall 1992) © by Lorena Leigh Saxe

is wronged, and that it is a patronizing restriction of freedom to insist otherwise. Feminists opposed to sadomasochism have offered lucid arguments on the limits of this consent, basically noting that our desires are formed largely by social ideologies and institutions and thus it makes little sense to speak of fully and freely consenting to the masochistic role that men already prescribe for women (e.g., Wagner 1982; Rian 1982). Additionally, it has been noted that sadomasochism has an engulfing and addictive quality to it—partly in virtue of being (at least superficially) an outlaw culture, which makes it difficult for practitioners to move between sadomasochistic and nonsadomasochistic cultures, and partly because sadism creates physical tolerance in the masochist, so that both sadists and masochists demand more and more forceful actions to get aroused. Thus, what the masochist is initially "consenting" to may not be at all what she ultimately ends up participating in (and it may be very difficult for her to leave).

While these disputes about freedom and consent are intellectually stimulating, I think they are misfocused. Sadomasochism, in these discussions, is treated as a seamless whole—even the name seems to refer to a single thing. But sadism and masochism are different behaviors, and they can be evaluated separately. Too much attention has been paid to masochists, as if settling this question of consent will settle the entire issue. All too little attention has been paid to sadists. How are we, as feminists, to evaluate sadism?

Some ways of interacting with another Lesbian are not acceptable, regardless of whether she has consented to that treatment, regardless of whether we think her consenting is acceptable. Sexual sadism is one of those unacceptable ways of treating a Lesbian. In many other situations, this moral belief seems to be understood, or at least understandable. So, for instance, one may think it is all right for a woman to choose to smoke cigarettes since it is her own health she is risking (putting aside the issues of secondary smoke and increased health insurance rates for others). Even so, cigarette companies deserve condemnation for manufacturing and making a profit from a product that kills thousands of women. Tobacco companies profit from behavior that shows disrespect, even contempt, for the lives and health of women. To show a basic disrespect for a woman is unacceptable, to profit from such contempt unjust, even if she is not harmed or even if she enjoys it.[2] This is a basic critique of ethical hedonism. Ethically—because of the sort of beings that women are—and politically—as a necessary part of female liberation—women should be treated with basic respect.[3] This respect should be directed toward female strength and health and integrity, not only toward pleasure. Sadism, while it "respects" the pleasure of the sadist and of the desiring masochist, is nevertheless based on contempt for women, as the essence of sexual sadism is the degradation and humiliation of the masochist.[4]

Thus, I am suggesting that we stop evaluating the actions of the masochist by considering her consent and instead move to evaluating the actions of the sadist, using a standard of respect.

The question of consent also assumes and exacerbates a misleading distinction between private and public spheres of behavior. Consent is conceived as the private exchange of permissions between isolated individuals. Yet little about the permitted behaviors is private, nor are the effects of sadomasochism, as individuals are rarely isolated with respect to sexual cultures. It is on this point that the argument is convincing that our desires are socially constructed and thus our "consent" to sexual activity is not really free: it is not free in the sense of being the autonomous choice of an atomic individual. But then, no choice is wholly free in that sense; even the choice to rebel against oppression draws on the meanings found in both oppressive and rebellious cultural politics. The social and cultural nature of choice, per se, is not problematic, nor is it specific to sadomasochism, for we are social creatures. What is crucial is to acknowledge that "private consent" is nonexistent and go on from there.

The consent to be masochistic is not private (nor "free"); neither is the behavior of either sadism or masochism, nor its consequences, private. Those practicing sadomasochism often make the claim that the violence, humiliation, and domination involved are limited to the bedroom and do not spill over into other areas of life. As a justification for sadomasochism, this is suspect in at least two ways. First, for the past two decades, the bedroom has been a major focus of feminist political and ethical analysis: the so-called private sphere of the bedroom is the site of much of women's worst misogynist oppression. Even if sadism and masochism were confined to the bedroom, I would still be very concerned about the disrespect—the humiliation, degradation, and physical destructiveness—in the actions of sadists. Second, it is highly doubtful that sadomasochism stays completely within the bedroom, not affecting other Lesbians. Sadomasochism is a highly *visible* practice: practitioners often wear uniforms or leather (and identify themselves—as "leather dykes"—by this public dress), symbols such as swastikas and handcuffs, codes such as keys and colored handkerchiefs. The results of sadism—whip marks, cuts, bruises and scars—are also visible to others. It is also a very *group-oriented* activity: orgies are popular and common, with invitations sent out generally to the local sadomasochistic or the Lesbian community, and they sometimes occur in public places, such as bathhouses or festivals. That this public behavior does indeed reach the Lesbian public was made clear to me from a story I heard from a Lesbian who attended a recent women's music festival on the West Coast. She worked in the kitchen during her work shift, and, unknown to her, this was the work shift that many sadomasochists liked to work together. During the entire work shift, the other workers engaged in a sadomasochistic scene while chopping their vegetables, and she was compelled (unconsenting) to participate by being placed in the s/m role of voyeur. No sexual behavior is entirely private—as Lesbians, we know that what we talk about *or* stay silent about says much to others about our sexual lives. But sadomasochism is one of the least private sexual practices. Its public nature is generally without the consent of other Lesbians and, more importantly, has significant effects on Lesbian sexuality and community.

For Lesbians in community, the nonprivate nature of sadomasochism calls into question our *identity* as sexual and political beings. Far from being limited to "the bedroom," sadomasochism seems to be not only a public behavior but a *total identity*. Thus, for instance, one writer in *Coming to Power* states that "[with] S/M everything gets charged, so that even subtle movements of the hands and body have an S/M connotation to me now" (Samois 1981, 38). Sadomasochism is part of, and also creates, a world view in which the world is imbued with domination and violence. As a Lesbian feminist, I know already how difficult it is to resist that world view, which forms the core of heteropatriarchal culture (e.g., Hoagland 1988). Sadomasochism appears to refine, crystallize, and sexualize this world view so that it becomes even more absolute and comprehensive than it is otherwise.[5] Two world views—one nourished by and nourishing sadomasochism, the other, Lesbian feminism—are irreconcilably at odds. One view sees domination and humiliation in every female movement, and the other can envision a Lesbian free from these things, with strength and integrity. One's vision of the world and of Lesbians is the foundation from which she builds the world, and one cannot create liberation without being able to imagine liberation consistently.

Politically, sadomasochism also presents a problem both for Lesbian identity and for creating a community that would foster liberatory values. Pat Califia, for example, urges that sadomasochists of all sorts work to "have a common identity as *sadomasochists* (instead of gay men who are into leather, lesbian feminists who are into S/M, businessmen who are clients of professionals, etc.)" (Califia 1981, 271; italics in original). This common identity, she claims, arises from their common problems, such as "attacks in the media, and bad attitudes in City Hall" (ibid.). Community is sought not with Lesbians who are battling our common problems imposed on us by a misogynist culture, but rather with men who go to prostitutes and thereby participate in the subordination of women! One vision of community and identity seeks the liberation of women and Lesbians; the other, the release from the "bad attitudes" of sexual "repression." This last is not liberatory for women or girls, who are, in a sexist society, the prey of the unrepressed.

Is sadomasochism antifeminist or merely outside the realm of feminism? Sadomasochism actively works against feminism in two critical ways. Lesbian feminism is a jewel with many facets, some more crucial than others. One of the most important aspects of feminism is its goal of liberating women from oppression—male oppression and other forms. Many have argued that sado-masochism is consistent with, and even strengthens, such oppressions as anti-Semitism, racism, and sexism by both sexualizing and publicly displaying the symbolisms of Nazism, slavery, prostitution, and incest. Such symbols are not removed and transformed from the oppressiveness out of which they arise as it is precisely oppression and domination that *make* Nazism, slavery, and incest a turn-on for sadomasochists. Despite their claims to the contrary, sadomasochists are not playing with power and control in the abstract. For the purpose of fun the drama in their scenes uses (publicly, thus endorsing) the real-life horrors of oppression that real women and Lesbians have endured. Such reversal of the meaning of oppression and such public sanction of this reversal are antagonistic to women's liberation.

A common theme in the stories of *Coming to Power* is the use of sadism to escape from the *feelings* of female powerlessness. This can be contrasted with the goal of actually liberating women and Lesbians from oppression. This escape from the feeling of powerlessness is obvious for the sadists, or tops, who temporarily can forget their social role as oppressed females by dominating another.

Equally common is the *masochists'* use of others' sadism to escape feeling powerless. This type of escapism (which is not a genuine escape from oppression) takes several forms, each using either the sadist's violence or the fantasy created in the s/m "scene" as the vehicle of escape. In all cases, of course, the masochist is part of a "scene" in which she is being whipped or hit or violently penetrated, and generally this is accompanied by some shared fantasy and role playing derived from an oppressive situation, such as a gang rape, adult-child sex, enforced femininity (being forced to wear feminine clothing that the masochist hates), slavery, or "puppy training". Masochists in these stories use the *violence* directed at them to escape their feelings of powerlessness in the world by allowing themselves to be pushed so far by pain that they become disoriented, unable to think and unable to feel. This temporary inability to think is often mentioned in the stories as the goal of sexual activity and is considered in many stories to be a positive way of escaping from the dreariness and pain of one's everyday life.

Masochists in these stories use the *fantasies* in the scenes to "escape" from their oppression by acting as if their original, real oppression were being relived during a scene. This reenactment of one's real oppression allows for three ways of seeming to escape powerlessness, or rectifying it in fantasy. One way to "rectify" such oppression is to treat it as if it were chosen (the masochists are, after all, choosing to participate in it now) and thereby controllable. And, of course, another way to "correct" the brutalities of one's oppression is to make them sexually arousing. A third method of using fantasy to escape or undo real oppression is evident in a common part of a scene where the masochist is treated in a very domineering fashion and punished for "transgressions" until some point is reached, such as orgasm or the disorientation mentioned above, when the masochist is then greatly pampered by the sadist. The meaning of this entire scene seems to be that your oppressor really loves you and will reward you with great affection and kindness if you only stick with the pain and domination long enough. The masochist/oppressed is a truly *good* and deserving girl (slave, dog, woman); the sadist/oppressor is kindly. Affection and pampering naturally and necessarily are "earned" through submission (and *only* through submission; at least, affection and pampering without submission, such as that found in so-called vanilla sex, is devalued by masochists). In each of these escapist fantasies, the reality of oppression is reworked and reversed entirely, to be falsely escaped and ultimately propagated.

This approach to domination and submission is presented by sadomasochists as a way of learning how to "deal with" power and thus as an important learning tool for liberation in the "real" world. Sadistic power is, however, never satisfactorily "dealt with." Sadists learn to perfect techniques of power over other Lesbians. Masochists erase the real meaning of such power and replace it with the fantasy that such power over them is chosen, deserved, and rewarded. Both eroticize this power. None of this provides a useful tool for escaping or dismantling the real power oppressors have over us, nor does it inform us how to act with integrity, using personal and community power without oppressing others. There is no vision here of power, as strength, with freedom.

Another facet of Lesbian feminism is the valuing of the female. This valuing is connected to the goal of liberating women: what is valued is the female as she would be if free from male domination or as she is in resistance to oppression. Thus, much of Lesbian-feminist cultural work has been centered on recovering or creating images of female skill and power when women are free of male domination. This is seen to be an important contrast to heteropatriarchal culture, which devalues, erases, co-opts, or warps female strength. The importance of this work lies in the power of cultural images to shape our sense of personal and communal *possibility* for strength and freedom. Sadomasochism is contradictory to Lesbian-feminist culture and valuing of the female. As noted above, its sexual attraction is rooted in its disrespect for women, which is acted out in the form of humiliation and physical mutilation. For masochists, it glorifies female weakness: subservience, self-effacement, femininity. For sadists, female strength is twisted away from the power to resist oppression oneself or to create good for other women. For both the sadist and the masochist, the valuing of the female is wholly in accord with patriarchal values.

Finally, sadomasochists are openly and actively antifeminist. In *Coming to Power* this joke is presented:

> Riddle: How many S/M dykes does it take to change a light bulb?

Answer: Two—one bottom to do it and one top to tell her what to do.

Riddle: How many anti-S/M feminists does it take to screw in a light bulb?

Answer: At least four. One to handle the bulb, one to critique the word "screw," one to lend professional credentials to the operation, and one to find common ground with the utility company. (Samois 1981, 146)

The message in this joke is a frequent theme in the stories in Coming to Power: feminism is too complicated and difficult and time-consuming to be worthwhile. This is consistent with the ethical-hedonist stance of sadomasochists: a project is worthwhile only to the extent that it is fun and easy. And it is true that feminism is not always fun and easy. In fact, feminism is considered by sadomasochists to be so complicated and tiring that feminism itself is one of the things that masochists used pain and humiliation to escape. One story, for example, involves a woman who is just returning from a National Women's Studies Association conference, where she had to act responsibly and thoughtfully, and who now needs the numbing pain of sadistic abuse against her to release her from feminism's constraints. Other stories that show a masochist using pain to become disoriented and stop thinking make the point that she wants to stop thinking about the difficult responsibilities of feminism and of liberation. Feminism is too arduous to be worth the bother of giving it the intellectual attention it demands and should be "escaped" just like the feelings of powerlessness are "escaped" by masochists.

SADOMASOCHISM AT "PUBLIC" WOMEN'S AND LESBIAN EVENTS

I have argued above that sadomasochism is antifeminist in a variety of ways. Simply put, it is contemptuous of women, antagonistic in its world view to female and Lesbian liberation, and openly hostile to the intellectual and rebellious rigors of feminism. If this is true, what policy should women's or Lesbian events take on sadomasochism?

Many women's and Lesbian events occur each year, including music festivals, spirituality retreats, and conferences. For convenience I will restrict my comments to music festivals, but my analysis can apply to any women's or Lesbian event. Music festivals are large annual events: attendance varies from several hundred to several thousand depending on the festival. Some festivals have been running for more than 15 years and are a very important part of Lesbian culture. They occur all over the United States. In the rest of this paper, I will refer to a midwestern women's music festival, which I will abbreviate as MWMF.[6] MWMF is the largest and one of the oldest women's festivals and has been the site of much overt controversy about sadomasochism in the last few years. What sort of policy about s/m should MWMF adopt?

The policy toward antifeminist practices taken by an event may depend on whether it is a feminist or merely a "women's" event. After all, many women's groups are clearly not feminist, such as the DAR. Is MWMF feminist? Nowhere in the written literature of this festival does it claim to be a feminist festival. However, one must look at more than the stated policy of an event to determine whether it is really feminist. Several points in MWMF's policy and its history lead me to believe that it really is a feminist festival, and the organizers should just own up to this fact and state it outright. For example, the 1990 festival booklet states that the festival is the place to "leave learned prejudices out beyond the country roads" and thus it is "an *expectation* [that] acts or attitudes of racism, sexism, anti-semitism, classism, ableism, homophobia or violence against womyn in any form are not acceptable in this community, on this land" (italics in original). This is about as close as MWMF could come to calling itself a feminist festival without explicitly saying so. The festival is considered a community, one that is seen to be resistant to the prejudices learned outside, and also one that has an expectation of its members that behaviors oppressive to women are not to be practiced. MWMF is not merely a big female party, with no liberatory values. While women are there to have fun, it is also a place to "celebrate the beauty, strength, competence, wisdom . . . of women", a viewpoint in keeping with the profemale cultural goals of feminism. Historically, MWMF originated for feminist reasons: to encourage female talent and skills (musical, production, building, organizational); to "[celebrate] lesbian heritage" and provide "one of the few places where lesbian identity is the dominant culture"; to provide female-only space. These are all feminist goals. They provide opportunities for female development in roles from which women have been excluded, celebrate a frequently erased resistant female culture, and challenge the prescription of heterosexuality with female-only space.

As a feminist festival, MWMF has several options for a policy on sadomasochism.[7] It would be consistent with its general ban on racism, sexism, violence against women, and other oppressive acts against women to simply ban sadomasochism. This ban could take either of two forms: excluding sadomasochists or allowing those who practice s/m into the festival while banning the behavior and dress. The latter is actually more consistent with MWMF's policy on racism, sexism, and so forth: the acts, not the persons, are excluded. A third possibility would be to allow sadomasochistic practice but to make a firm statement that it is antifeminist and thus inconsistent with the goals of the festival community.

This last option seems contradictory and an unfair mixed message to give to sadomasochistic attendees. To determine what MWMF should do, however, one must look specifically at what feminist goals might be served by any of these options as well as exactly what sort of feminist function the festival serves in the Lesbian communities.

Some perceive MWMF to be a "piece of our Lesbian-feminist future": a week-long experiment in Lesbian-feminist community in which we practice our ideal values. Here we interact, as much as possible, as if we were no longer subjected to patriarchy and develop our vision of our future by living it. This understanding of the political function of MWMF would rule out sadomasochistic acts and dress, and possibly even the presence of sadomasochists, for these have no place in a Lesbian-feminist future.

I once viewed MWMF as a piece of our future, but no longer do. The producers of the festival were originally more overtly feminist in their goals for the festival, as were most of the attendees and performers. That has changed. Now the producers often do not make decisions according to feminist or liberatory values. Many performers are nonfeminist or even antifeminist and most attendees are not feminists and do not see the festival as a brief political community. Given this, MWMF, as a "feminist festival," must serve different goals than those achieved by conferences and festivals that more closely and deliberately resemble a piece of our future. (Some newer music festivals, such as one occurring on the East Coast, seem to be more of a political Lesbian community and, I think, should determine their sadomasochism policy on this basis.)

While MWMF is most properly seen as a feminist festival because of its stated policies, it is far from being a consciously political community. In contrast to some other conferences that are deliberately political, one cannot presume that most women in attendance at MWMF are feminists. Many are barely acquainted with feminism, and many others have distorted impressions of it. One very important goal for MWMF, then, is to be a place where Lesbian feminists can present feminist ideas to others, to be a place where liberatory teaching, discussion, and cultural activity occur. The inclusion of sadomasochists at the festival could serve two feminist educational goals. One would be to directly reach sadomasochists about feminism. Some may reevaluate their actions. Some masochists do seek escape from sadomasochistic relationships, and a feminist community could provide personal and ideological foundations for such escape.[8] Another goal would be to expose the uncertain or the s/m-tolerant to the realities of sadomasochism; all the feminist talk in the world doesn't convince someone of the degrading and antiliberatory aspect of sadomasochism as rapidly as witnessing a woman being tied to a tree and whipped. Such actions have been witnessed by women at music festivals. If it were made clear by feminists, and by the festival literature, that this was unacceptable and why, then an important teaching function could be served (much as it is crucial to actually *show* women the misogyny in pornography).

On the other hand, festivals are, as Pat Califia (1981) points out, places where sadomasochists network and also educate each other about their values.

To not exclude them could seem analogous to allowing a racist group or the *Playboy* photographers in to organize among women there. If sadomasochism is a serious threat to female liberation, then it would be an important goal for festivals such as MWMF to hinder such networking.

So, what is at issue here is a conflict in feminist goals for festivals such as MWMF—large festivals that are feminist in essence, but where many who attend are not feminist. Such festivals are attractive, because of their size, as educational, organizing, and recruiting places for both feminist and antifeminist groups.

My own sense about this conflict of goals is to favor the educational goals of feminism while trying to minimize the worst effects of sadomasochistic behaviors on the profeminist culture of MWMF as a whole. Thus, at this point I would favor allowing sadomasochists into festivals like MWMF, while banning sadomasochistic actions and dress.[9] For feminists, the educational and organizing opportunities presented by festivals the size of MWMF are rare, and introducing women (including sadomasochists and those tolerant who might not come if there was a no-sadomasochists policy) to the values of feminism is crucial for feminist longevity.

As a former conference organizer myself, I have learned that no policy decision is carved in stone and no single year's conference will achieve all the desired goals. Festivals and conferences are ongoing community projects, and any decision should be seen as an experiment, to be evaluated against the political goals of the project. If MWMF were to make the decision I recommend—to ban sadomasochistic dress and behavior but to allow sadomasochists to attend—they would need to evaluate this decision over time. Is this decision in fact allowing some women who might otherwise be involved in or tolerant to s/m to be exposed to a feminist analysis of s/m? Is it giving some masochists enough safety and support to leave the practice? Crucially, is the feminist organizing success outweighing (however one ended up determining this) the sadomasochist organizing success? Are the feminist goals of the festival shifting (e.g., is it becoming more consciously political) such that the decision should shift as well? Too often, attendees forget that both goals and policy decisions can change and should be viewed as political experiments. Of course, such experiments require clarity in the understanding and formulation of goals and policies, which many festivals have lacked with the s/m issue. I hope that the analysis in this paper serves to spark festival organizers and attendees toward such clarity.

NOTES

I heartily thank the following women for helpful comments at various stages of this paper: Claudia Card; Chris Cuomo; Noretta Koertge; the women at the March, 1992

Midwest Society for Women in Philosophy (SWIP) meeting; the two anonymous *Hypatia* reviewers; and especially Anna Lee. These women raised thoughtful questions and/or suggested ways to make this essay clearer; they do not necessarily agree with all (or any) of the points raised.

1. For feminist writings about sadomasochism see: Linden, Pagano, Russell, and Star (1982); Barry (1982); Jeffreys (1986); Penelope (1987).

2. This same analysis applies to Dow Corning's selling of silicone breast implants, given that the company knew of evidence of their dangers. In the fall of 1991, Dow Corning hired spokeswomen (mastectomy survivors) to proclaim publicly how much they valued the implants, and many journalists were pointing out that many women may choose the implants even with their dangers, and that now that the dangers were known, the implants should not be made illegal. These arguments about choice and consent missed the point that Dow Corning was being contemptuous of women by selling such dangerous devices (especially given the device's purpose).

These corporate examples show that one may be disrespectful out of motives other than a desire to see someone suffer. One may have a primary desire to make a profit. Similarly, one may even act disrespectfully as a sadist without having primarily sadistic motives. In a discussion about this paper, both Chris Cuomo and Claudia Card noted that some women are reluctant sadists. They may, for example, get talked, or even forced, into performing sadistic acts by a masochistic lover. Thus, they may not have a positive desire to see another suffer and may not enjoy this suffering. The desire to see another suffer or degraded (what we think of as sadistic motivation) certainly seems to add to the disrespect one is showing another, but it is not the only part of disrespect. How one actually treats another is primary. Even reluctant sadists are treating another with disrespect (and they are generally not evincing a positive motivation to see the other flourish; see note 3).

3. Traditionally philosophers use the term "respect" to mean a belief that the other person (animal, etc.) has inherent value and therefore should not be treated merely as a tool for one's own, another's, or the greater good. I mean this, but also more than this by "respect." Respecting another woman or Lesbian includes, minimally, believing she has inherent value and not using her merely as a tool, but it also implies certain *feelings* toward her. My respecting another includes feelings of wishing her well and positively wanting her to flourish, even if I do not like her or otherwise have bad feelings about her. Thus, for example, I might respect the writing of another even if I do not like it or do not agree with it; then, I would wish the writer well at her work and hope she develops it the best she can. This would stand in contrast to thinking that someone's work (such as, for example, that of pornographers) does not deserve respect, whereupon I would feel indifference (from a lack of respect) or glee (from contempt) at its failure. To show a woman or a Lesbian respect, then, includes being glad that she is flourishing.

What does it mean for a woman or a Lesbian to flourish? I think that flourishing for women and Lesbians means at least resisting oppression and also moving toward becoming what we might be if we were not oppressed. Patriarchy and other forms of oppression diminish us, do not allow us to flourish. Thus, I do not think that a woman can flourish being treated sadistically because the humiliation and degradation involved, as well as the reenactment of scenes of oppression involved in sadism, diminish her flourishing as a woman resisting patriarchy and as a proud woman (part of how I think we would be if not oppressed). This is true even if she is a masochist; that is, I don't think a masochist can flourish *as a Lesbian*, even though she may be getting what she wants from a sadist. A sadist is showing disrespect by acting in ways that prevent—and by possibly not *wanting*—someone's flourishing in resistance to patriarchy and by (perhaps) being *glad* that another woman is suffering or is degraded.

4. The violence that sadists do to masochists is part of the disrespect but not really the most crucial aspect. Most sadomasochistic scenes center on various forms of deep humiliation of masochists, such as derogatory name-calling, verbal (as well as physical) punishment for alleged "transgressions" (e.g., not following the sadist's orders), and having the masochists take on subservient roles. This humiliation seems to me to be the most disrespectful part of sexual sadism—the most undermining of personal agency, of pride, and of developing resistance to oppression (of flourishing).

Biz Huiras pointed out (at the SWIP meeting where I read this paper) that in addition to the humiliation that is heaped on masochists by sadists, the very act of masochists *consenting* to humiliating and sadistic treatment also serves to confer disrespect to the masochist. (Who, the sadist and the masochist might ask, would consent to such treatment unless she were worthless, or deserving of it, etc.?) That is, the "consent" of the masochist, far from morally excusing sadistic treatment, serves to *amplify* the moral problem posed by sadism.

5. This world view also includes some peculiar reversals about the meaning of violence in Lesbian's and women's lives. A sadomasochist (a sadist, I believe) at a 1990 women's music festival stated that "sadomasochism isn't violence against women; it is violence for women." Thus, not only does this view imbue the world with violence, but it also inverts the meaning of such violence. Other such reversals are part of this world view; I explore these later in the paper.

6. I decided to abbreviate names of festivals and conferences, or to use only general descriptions of them, in order to protect the organizers and attendees from those who, on learning of the presence of sadomasochists or of lesbians there, may want to cause trouble.

7. Some of the dykes who read drafts of this paper asked me how I thought such decisions about policy should be made and by whom. My beliefs and feelings about this arise from my own experience in organizing a Lesbian conference for four years. I think that the *organizers* of the event should make the policy decisions. In those four years, some have complained that this gives organizers too much power, or that it is undemocratic or otherwise unrepresentative, or that it might lead to bad decisions because there are always things that organizers are less knowledgeable about than others. I think that these complaints raise valid concerns but that organizers should still make the final policy decisions. It is very important that they make the decisions taking into account as much information as possible. To counteract the possible problems noted above, they should solicit ideas from actual and potential attendees; carefully research areas of concern, such as accessibility; read as much as they can about the issues; think very carefully about the political implications of all their decisions; and make the decisions that they believe will have the best political outcomes.

The problems with some more purely democratic form of decision-making are numerous. It is difficult to determine who should be included in this democracy (or open decision-making). Should this year's attendees make the policy decisions for next year's? That doesn't seem very representative, especially if there is some political problem in the event that excludes dykes for bad reasons (e.g., it is not accessible to disabled dykes). Then those dykes won't be there to make decisions for following years. But if not attendees, then who could make this decision democratically?

Should the decision be made by consensus? My experience is that that is impossible with more than about five people. Trying to attain consensus on decisions actually leads to decisions being made by those who are most charismatic, or who have the most energy to win in a conflict (favoring the able-bodied and healthy), or who are most manipulative or dramatic, or who are the most skilled at arguing (often favoring the educated)—or in some other politically useless way. This often does not lead to the *best political decision*, which is what I consider the goal. The best decisions are made, generally, by those who have given them the most detailed thought, which is usually the organizers, in consult with others whom they know may have been thinking through the issues, because the organizers are working on these decisions all year (as compared to many attendees who may have only started thinking about the issue the minute it is brought up for a decision).

Based on my experience, it is also crucial to have continuity in decision-making from year to year so that experiments can be tried and evaluated, and generally this continuity is best achieved by organizers. And finally, it is important to have someone who will be held responsible for decisions made, and who will articulate the reasoning behind a decision (so that dykes can make sense of the decision, suggest changes, understand exceptions or seeming contradictions, etc.), for which one needs a small and clearly defined decision-making body.

One thing to keep in mind here is that events such as music festivals have become crucial in helping to create and maintain our community, but they are *not* themselves, for most of us, our community. That is, most of us consider our day-to-day community to be distinct from the festivals. What may be ideal in terms of decision-making (that it be more representative and, perhaps, closer to consensus, while still achieving political goals over time) may be more possible in our day-to-day communities, where there is continuity as well as more time to meet about decisions.

A second question raised by those reading and hearing this paper was one of enforcement of decisions. To what extent should questions of policy enforcement determine what the policy should be, and what would this mean for the policy on sadomasochism? I do not have the space here for a comprehensive analysis of this question, but I would like to suggest some points to think about. Part of the enforcement issue is a practical concern. One might consider what decision to make to best achieve a political goal, assuming that there would be no complications arising from enforcement. Then, one would modify the decision if there were problems with enforcement that undermined one's goals or created other political problems. For example, in the conference I co-organized for four years, we thought that it was ideal to ban current batterers from the conference, but we quickly discovered that this was so difficult to enforce (because there is so little agreement about what constitutes battering) that we could not institute this policy without acting too capriciously. With the s/m issue, enforcement of a no-sadomasochists policy would be problematic for very large festivals because if the attendees were not self-identifying as sadomasochists and were not dressing as such, identification of them would be largely by hearsay and rumor, which would be very difficult to confirm and to enforce fairly. (We were able to have a no-sadomasochists policy for our small conference—about 100 participants.) For this reason, a no-sadomasochistic-dress-or-actions policy may be preferable.

One woman at SWIP noted that enforcement considerations are more than practical because how enforcement of decisions is practiced says something very important about feminist leadership in the community. This is an excellent point, and an important reason for avoiding decisions that can only be enforced capriciously, randomly, merely via rumor, or otherwise unfairly.

On the other hand, as Kathleen Barry (1979) points out, the policy or law one makes gives the community an important message about one's moral and political values, and one should ban or outlaw misogynist practices such as prostitution even if enforcement is impossible or politically costly. To do otherwise is ultimately to appear to endorse the practice. This would be one strong argument for large festivals having a full no-sadomasochists policy, even if this proved unenforceable.

8. In terms of personal support, the festival could provide a place where masochists can physically separate themselves from sadists and the s/m community and receive physical safety, a space to explore what sadism and masochism mean in their lives, and practical support for leaving s/m. At the SWIP meeting where I read this paper, the question arose about how explicitly this space should be advertised as safe for those wanting to leave s/m. One woman, whose name I did not get, suggested that it was important to be explicit so that masochists would know that the safe space was there for them, especially since there are places in the community that are hostile to sadomasochism. Sarah Hoagland responded to this by noting that many masochists may be too turned off to an explicitly sadist-free (which may be perceived as anti-s/m) space to chance visiting it. Perhaps this is one of those decisions that should be tried as an experiment to determine which sort of description of the space best attracted those who want it. (To this end, it would be useful if various festivals coordinated their decision-making just enough that different experiments were occurring at different festivals and notes were compared.)

9. Victoria Davion suggested that another reason for banning s/m behavior and dress at festivals is that s/m dress includes weapons that pose a threat to both the safety and the sense of safety of attendees. Indeed, rapes and other attacks do occur at large music festivals, and the presence of weapons facilitates those attacks and also adds to a climate of fear that many women go to festivals to escape.

REFERENCES

Barry, Kathleen. 1979. *Female sexual slavery*. Englewood Cliffs, NJ: Prentice-Hall.
———. 1982. "Sadomasochism": The new backlash to feminism. *Trivia* 1: 77-92.
Califia, Pat. 1981. A personal view of the history of the lesbian s/m community and movement in San Francisco. In *Coming to power*, ed. Samois. Berkeley, CA: Samois.
Hoagland, Sarah Lucia. 1988. *Lesbian ethics*. Palo Alto, CA: Institute of Lesbian Studies.
Jeffreys, Sheila. 1986. Sado-masochism: The erotic cult of fascism. *Lesbian Ethics* 2(1): 65-82.
Linden, Robin, Darlene Pagano, Diana E. H. Russell, and Susan Leigh Star. 1982. *Against sadomasochism*. East Palo Alto, CA: Frog in the Well.
Penelope, Julia. 1987. The illusion of control: Sadomasochism and the sexual metaphors of childhood. *Lesbian Ethics* 2(3): 84-94.
Rian, Karen. 1982. Sadomasochism and the social construction of desire. In *Against sadomasochism*, ed. Robin Linden, Darlene Pagano, Diana E. H. Russell, and Susan Leigh Star. East Palo Alto, CA: Frog in the Well.
Samois, ed. 1981. *Coming to power*. Berkeley, CA: Samois.
Wagner, Sally Roesch. 1982. Pornography and the sexual revolution: The backlash of sadomasochism. In *Against sadomasochism*, ed. Robin Linden, Darlene Pagano, Diana E. H. Russell, and Susan Leigh Star. East Palo Alto, CA: Frog in the Well.

Audre Lorde's (Nonessentialist) Lesbian Eros

RUTH GINZBERG

Audre Lorde reopened the question of the position of the erotic with respect to both knowledge and power in her 1983 essay "Uses of the Erotic: The Erotic as Power." This is not a new question in the philosophical literature; it is a very old one. What is different about Audre Lorde's examination of Eros is that she starts with a decidedly lesbian conception of Eros, in marked contrast to other Western philosophers' work.

> Reclaiming the erotic in our own terms, redefining power(s)
> in our own terms, are inseparable acts for women.
> —Robin Morgan (1990, 323)

THE EROTIC

Audre Lorde identifies the erotic as "a considered source of power and information within our lives" that "rises from our deepest and non-rational knowledge." The erotic, she claims, provides "the power which comes from sharing deeply any pursuit with another person," as well as "the open and fearless underlining of [one's] capacity for joy." This is important because

> the sharing of joy, whether physical, emotional, psychic, or intellectual, forms a bridge between the sharers which can be the basis for understanding much of what is not shared between them, and lessens the threat of their difference. (Lorde 1984, 56)

This is a political claim, not a claim about hedonism or rights to pleasure. When Lorde asks the philosophical question, "Why is the erotic a good thing?" she answers it quite differently from those who would claim its main value to be some sort of an end, or teleological pleasure. She sees the erotic as a virtue: a social, political, and epistemic capacity that tempers the individualistic sense

Hypatia vol. 7, no. 4 (Fall 1992) © by Ruth Ginzberg

of self. For her it is a source of power and information that encourages resistance to atomism and unchecked individualism, opening up an entire realm of human understanding otherwise unavailable.[1] Thus, the suppression or mis-representation of the erotic constitutes a primary social, political, and episte-mic harm. She further claims that the suppression of this gynocentric, or lesbian, eros is one of the major social arrangements that has perpetuated the oppression of women. As such, it deserves further philosophical attention.

I take Lorde's notion of the erotic to be a metaphysical yearning to integrate, or to connect, that which subjectively seems separate. She applies this not only to the creation of connections between and among individuals but also to the creation of connections between apparently different aspects of one's own life and work. She is not interested only in lust or genital activity; indeed, such characterizations of the erotic are exactly the misrepresentations against which she argues. "The erotic," she warns, "has often been misnamed by men and used against women."

> It has been made into the confused, the trivial, the psychotic, the plasticized sensation. For this reason, we have often turned away from the exploration and consideration of the erotic as a source of power and information, confusing it with its opposite, the pornographic. But pornography is a direct denial of the erotic, for it represents the suppression of true feeling. Pornog-raphy emphasizes sensation without feeling.(Lorde 1984, 54)

The word "erotic," Lorde reminds her reader, "comes from the Greek word *eros*, the personification of love in all its aspects—born of Chaos, and person-ifying creative power and harmony." Yet, turning to the *Oxford English Dictio-nary*, we find an etymology that encourages the very misunderstanding against which she argues; the *OED* defines the Greek Ερος only as "sexual love,"[2] while "erotic" is defined as

> of or pertaining to the passion of love; concerned with or treating of love; amatory.

Following the lead to "amatory," we get,

> of or pertaining to a lover, to lovemaking, or to sexual love generally.

There is no definition of "sexual love" despite four pages devoted to "love," though perhaps the closest is the fourth definition:

> that feeling of attachment which is based on difference of sex; the affection which subsists between lover and sweetheart and is the normal basis for marriage.

As a lesbian feminist of African descent who explicitly attributes her own understanding of the erotic to her rejection of "an exclusively european-american male . . . mode of living and sensation," Lorde is clearly not thinking of the erotic as a source of power and information that is "based on difference of sex" or that is the "normal basis for marriage." She is speaking of a specifically lesbian *eros*, or at least an *eros* that is not part of a phallocratic conceptual scheme. It is, as she says,

> . . . a particular feeling, knowledge, and understanding for those sisters with whom I have danced hard, played, or even fought . . . (Lorde 1984, 59)

But we shouldn't be surprised that the OED excludes this sense of the erotic. In *The Politics of Reality*, Marilyn Frye argues that lesbians are systematically excluded entirely from the phallocratic conceptual scheme. This, she claims, is accomplished through terms that point into semantic abysses, rather than referring to other terms that have meaning within that conceptual scheme. Tracing the etymology of the term "lesbian," Frye argues that lesbians are defined in such a way as to be logically, naturally, and semantically impossible. Etymologically, lesbians turn out to be "women who 'have sex' with other women," where "having sex" turns out to be something that can only happen when a penis is present. Since women do not have penises, she notes, speaking of lesbians as "women who have sex with other women is like speaking of ducks who engage in arm wrestling" (Frye 1983). Analytically, indeed tautologically, "lesbian" is self-referentially meaningless.

There is a semantic hole here into which the word "lesbian" disappears. A semantic hole is analogous to an astronomical black hole, from which even light cannot escape. It is an analytic position to which terms may refer within a conceptual scheme but from which meaning, like light waves entering a black hole, can never re-emerge. In this sense Lorde and Frye seem to agree that patriarchal forms of life exclude any lesbian notion of the erotic. Frye attributes this to the exclusion of "lesbian" from the patriarchal conceptual scheme; Lorde attributes it to a patriarchal distortion of the erotic. But they both maintain that there is some (other) form of life in which both lesbians and a lesbian eros do exist.

It is not coincidental that knowledge of such an eros has emerged primarily from the work of women who identify as lesbians. The ability to find or to construct meaning within the interior of this particular semantic hole can emerge only from that lived experience which is unmediated by phallocratic language. That, by definition, is lesbian experience.

The point here is that Frye has identified how it is that lesbian forms of life are excluded from phallocratic language games. Lorde has identified a meaning of the erotic that has been excluded from phallocratic language as part of this process. Using the analogy of the semantic hole, we can see what links Lorde's notion of the erotic to lesbian forms of life. Semantic holes don't just happen; they are formed as part of the process of language creation, metadistortions in the conceptual scheme across which ordinary meaning cannot travel in any ordinary ways.

In *Eros and Power*, Haunani-Kay Trask identifies other lesbians in addition to Lorde who have been major contributors to the articulation of this non-patriarchal understanding of the erotic, including Adrienne Rich, Mary Daly, Jill Johnston, and Cherríe Moraga. Yet Trask claims that "love cannot spring from theory, no matter how persuasive," and that "lesbian theory will not persuade the majority of women, even feminists, of the desirability of lesbian love" (Trask, 1986, 115). While undoubtedly it is true that lesbian theory will not persuade the majority of women to engage in exclusive or separatist lesbian sexual practices, that is not necessarily evidence against the persuasiveness of lesbian theory or against the ability of women to choose their sexual identities or practices, or indeed their conceptual schemes, for political reasons. It may be only evidence regarding the stronghold of patriarchy or the incontinence of the human will. Before exploring further this lesbian erotic, I want first to review briefly lesbian feminism, without, I hope, falling into any of the treacherous quicksand along the way.

LESBIAN FEMINISM

Lesbian feminism is not unproblematic. I will not discuss here one sense in which some may consider lesbian feminism to be "problematic": the sense in which generalized cultural homophobia makes some people fear being associated with anything lesbian, which causes them to fear or disdain feminism on the basis that it is, or is perceived as being, "too lesbian." Rather my intent is to discuss the ways in which lesbian feminism is problematic internally.

Among those who claim that "feminism is the theory, lesbianism is the practice,"[3] there is a tendency to regard nonlesbian feminists as, at best, naive or unreflective victims of false consciousness and, at worst, hypocritical, unreliable, untrustworthy, and potentially harmful. Among nonlesbian feminists there is a tendency to regard lesbian feminists as demanding an almost dictatorial degree of conformity or "political correctness." Among nonfeminist lesbians, nearly the same charge is made. These differences continue to be the source of not a small amount of divisiveness within lesbian and feminist communities, partly because of continuing struggles over what is meant by the term "lesbian" and by the term "feminist." The ongoing tensions surrounding differing claims about the meanings of these terms have become a central political issue around which alliances continue to be formed and broken, sometimes tragically.

Since the late ninteenth century, sexual orientation and identity have been construed against a background of essentialism. That is, a woman is these days thought to "be" a lesbian or a nonlesbian in some essential way. I will argue momentarily that it is this essentialism that underlies a large number of the problems internal to both lesbian and feminist theories. But first let's review three competing essentialist claims about the sense in which one "is" or "is not" a lesbian.

I can't help it. The first of these is the claim that lesbian identity is either something with which one is born or something that develops at a preconscious level of development. This notion is often expressed by those who claim that they have always been lesbians or who report that they knew they were lesbians, or at least very different from heterosexual women, from a very early age. This is also the underlying belief behind the idea that a formerly heterosexually active or heterosexually interested woman can discover that she "really is" a lesbian, although she had not recognized it previously. It also underlies the psychotherapeutic notion that someone who "is" gay or lesbian cannot be "changed" into someone who "is" straight (although they might be threatened, coerced, intimidated, or argued into changing "their behavior").

There are two reasons for taking this idea seriously. One is simply the fact that there are a large number of lesbians who report this sort of self-knowledge. To ignore or reject these reports of self-knowledge would be to import into lesbian theory some of the worst of patriarchal theorizing; that is, it would be to assert that the theorizer knew better than the "subjects" of the theory what was true about them. A second reason for taking this idea seriously is that there are political implications of such an idea that some lesbians believe to be valuable. There is a long tradition in moral and liberal political theory of not judging a person for that which she cannot help. Gay rights organizations have had some degree of success in the United States since the late 1960s arguing that a person either "is" or "is not" gay or lesbian but that, whichever he or she is, it is not something over which he or she has control. This civil rights approach to gay political activism is also a strategy that has convinced a fair number of liberal nonlesbian feminists to take lesbian concerns seriously within the women's liberation movement. It is, not coincidentally, quite parallel to the civil rights approach to women's liberation itself, which has argued that one cannot help whether one is female or male, and thus that whether one is female or male should have no bearing on one's civil and political rights. Depending on a lesbian's interest in allying herself with the gay civil rights movement, the drawing of this parallel will have more or less appeal.

The most compelling reason to consider rejecting the idea is because, as Frye points out, it leaves intact the assumption that if one could help it, one surely would. That is, it ignores or invalidates the responsibility some lesbians want to claim for choosing to be lesbian.

Another reason for lesbians to be wary of it is because although this sense of homosexual identity overwhelmingly is claimed by most gay men, it is claimed by a considerably smaller percentage of lesbians. Lesbians need to remain wary about the extent to which lesbian identity is assimilated as a "female version" of gay male identity. At least to whatever extent gender identity and its formation are not analogous for women and for men, lesbian and gay sexual identity formation are equally unlikely to be analogous.

I chose it. Another common essentialist claim, articulated in both Mary Daly's and Marilyn Frye's work, for example, is that lesbian sexuality is primarily an "orientation of attention" on the part of women who do choose to see women, and—importantly—not to see men, in particular ways. One often finds the notion of "woman-identified women" associated with this conception of lesbian identity. The idea here is that "being a lesbian" is not only, or even primarily, a matter of who rubs genitals with whom, but rather that it constitutes an entirely different way of seeing the world. From this perspective, women are no longer in the background, helping hands in the drama of patriarchy. Instead, women are the primary focus of all sorts of attention, including erotic attention. Lesbians who identify themselves in this way perceive lesbianism as a consciously chosen path, one that they could have rejected but did not. Many regard it as at least partly a political decision, to choose to focus their attention on women rather than on men.

Again, a major reason for taking seriously this notion is the large number of lesbians who report that this is true of themselves. The lesbian literature is full of works by lesbians who report having chosen lesbian lives as a political act, often as an explicitly feminist political act. To claim that so many smart, politically aware lesbians might actually be mistaken about themselves seems dauntingly arrogant. Another reason for taking it seriously is that, as theory, it resonates well with feminist standpoint epistemologies.

One reason to be wary of this framework is that it raises questions about whether a lesbian who claims that she has not made this choice, but rather that she can't help who it is to whom she is attracted, "is" "really" a lesbian. The thing that would distinguish someone as "really" a lesbian, on this account, is exactly the making of the choice, which the lesbian who claims she can't help it didn't do. A second reason for wariness is that this framework creates problems about how to regard women who claim to have shifted their attention in the requisite way(s) but who do not, themselves, claim lesbian identities.

I'm no different; all women are lesbians. A third way of conceiving lesbian identity, which some see as continuous with the second, is reflected in Adrienne Rich's "lesbian continuum." Rich argues that women interact with each other in a wide variety of intimate ways, from best friend to nurse to lover. One of the examples she cites is that of women who, in their capacities as nurses, caretakers, or daughters-in-law, care for women elders, creating woman-centered spiritual, emotional, and physical intimacies within the context of those relationships. Another example is that of the nursing woman suckling a girl-child, who vicariously recalls the pleasures of suckling at her own mother's breast. All of these, Rich claims, lie on a lesbian continuum; there is at least a bit of lesbian eroticism in many relationships between women, probably experienced to some extent by all women, whether acknowledged or not. What she says all women need is to rid ourselves of the homophobia that prevents us from acknowledging our own lesbian interests when and where they do occur (Rich 1980).

An important reason to take seriously the idea of a lesbian continuum is that it addresses two vexing problems at once. First, it provides a framework for recognizing, accounting for, and perhaps even stirring the lesbian imaginations of women who have not previously encountered lesbian capacities within themselves. Second, it serves to reorient lesbian theory away from the issue of the lesbian/nonlesbian dichotomy.

Clearly, neither for Rich nor for Frye is "having sex" with other women a necessary condition of lesbian identity. Indeed, a reason to be wary of both accounts is that they both seem to desexualize lesbians; that is, lesbian identity is in danger of becoming reduced to some kind of mystical spiritualism. More than a few lesbians have noted that if heterosexual women who breast-feed girl babies get to co-opt the term "lesbian," then they want another, different, word to describe themselves as women who are sexually active with other lesbians.

There is another difficulty common to all three of the views described above, raised primarily by lesbians for whom lesbian identity constitutes a chosen worldview. Basically the difficulty is this: any functional definition of "lesbian"—that is, any description defining "lesbian" in terms of acts rather than in terms of agents—would allow that some women who have not escaped from the phallocratic conceptual scheme might "be" lesbians, by virtue of what they "do." That is, it would definitionally accommodate the existence of androcentric, or at least nonfeminist, lesbians. Crisis points provoked by this problem show up infamously—for example, as the bitter divisions within lesbian communities about how to regard the sadomasochistic practices engaged in by some lesbians. The question here is whether any behavior engaged in between lesbians qua lesbians is, by definition, necessarily "lesbian" behavior. Some feminist lesbians want to claim that sadomasochistic behavior is patriarchal behavior, not lesbian behavior, even if it occurs between two lesbians.

At the same time, any functional definition of "lesbian" would not allow that there could be any women who have managed to escape from patriarchy's worldview who do not engage in lesbian activities. That is, it would definitionally preclude the existence of nonlesbian feminists. Some lesbians endorse this result, claiming that nonlesbian feminism is not possible, that the willingness to engage in heterosexual activities is itself evidence that the woman so willing is still enmeshed in patriarchy. They view heterosexual women who make such

claims as, at best, self-deceived. However, many women who consider themselves to be both woman-centered and heterosexual, and some lesbian feminists, deny this, pointing out that worldviews cannot be defined behaviorally.
That is, worldviews can only be defined mentalistically in terms of characteristics of the agent, not in terms of how she acts. Crisis points provoking this
problem show up as divisions between lesbians and heterosexual women, and
sometimes even as challenges from profeminist men, about what it means to
"be" a feminist, or even about what it means to "be" a lesbian. Such claims
often suggest that there are, or might be, ways for men or heterosexual women
to act that are "newly created" or "outside of patriarchy," because attitude and
not behavior is thought to be "what really counts."

ESSENTIALISM

Part of the problem here is that the underlying ontological essentialism
remains unquestioned. It is only since the latter half of the nineteenth century
that psychological theory has supported the idea that whole persons can "be"
essentially heterosexual or homosexual, or even bisexual.[4] It is difficult for me
to grasp the notion of a whole person "being" lesbian or not, especially when
"lesbian" is construed in Lorde's terms rather than in terms of some other,
phallocratic, conceptual scheme.

Taking seriously Lorde's distinction between the erotic and the pornographic, it begins to appear as though much of the debate about whether
mental states or behaviors define who is and who is not a lesbian is exactly an
instance of conflating the pornographic with the erotic. She argues that "the
dichotomy between the spiritual [psychic and emotional] and the political
is . . . false" and that this is part of the pornographing of the sexual.[5] This, she
says, results from an "incomplete attention to our erotic knowledge."

> For the bridge which connects them is formed by the erotic—
> the sensual—those physical, emotional, and psychic expres-
> sions of what is deepest and strongest and richest within each
> of us, being shared: the passions of love, in its deepest meanings.
> (Lorde 1984, 56)

Thus, the entire debate about whether "real" lesbianism consists of genital
activities or acts of attention or political acts rests on this dichotomy that Lorde
wishes to deny. Sarah Hoagland also resists this dichotomy when, in explaining
why she refuses to define the word "lesbian" in her book *Lesbian Ethics: Toward
New Value*, she states that "to define 'lesbian' is . . . to succumb to a context
of heterosexualism" (Hoagland 1988). Furthermore, the idea that whole
persons can be defined by their erotic or sexual connections seems to import
into lesbian theory some things that feminists very much want to reject.

Some of the earlier and least controversial feminist arguments were against constructing the identities of whole women in terms of their relationships to men: daughter of, wife of, employee of. Surely a woman is more than just Joe's daughter, John's wife, Harvey's secretary, no matter how much influence these men have over her. Defining whole persons in terms of their erotic attachments or sexual arrangements is both underdescriptive and overdescriptive.

Indeed, it is probably true that persons are shaped and perceptions influenced by the erotic attachments and sexual arrangements that they engage in. But persons are underdetermined by *only* the erotic attachments and sexual arrangements they engage in. They are also shaped by the work that they do, the food that they eat, the neighborhoods they live in, the chemicals they are exposed to, the ethnic backgrounds with which they identify, and the genes they were born with. Imagining the personal identities of two lesbians—one of whom is middle-aged, a lesbian activist, owns a small business, lives in Seattle, eats in fast-food restaurants, and uses a wheelchair, and the other of whom is not yet out of her teens, lives in Tehran, has servants who grow and prepare her food organically, has sexual intercourse with her husband from an arranged marriage, is a devout Muslim, and has no independent economic means—it is a fairly good guess that these two lesbians are influenced at least as much by other things about their lives as they are by their lesbianism. It may be true that they both "see" the world through "lesbian eyes," but one also sees the world through "Muslim eyes" and the other presumably doesn't; one also sees the world through "American capitalist" eyes and the other presumably doesn't. It is in this sense that lesbian essentialist theories of personal identity are underdescriptive.

But they are also overdescriptive. Lesbians of color, notably Barbara Smith, Audre Lorde, and María Lugones, have talked about the personal and cultural dissonance created when they (or others) try to identify themselves as somehow primarily lesbian in their identities. There is an irresolvable dissonance in trying to say, "Most essentially I am a lesbian; in addition, I am also Black, Chicana, a woman, a philosopher, or whatever."[6] The idea here is that it is one of the privileges of relatively white, relatively middle-class, relatively young, relatively healthy American women, who do not experience many other forms of oppression, to be able to identify lesbianism as a primary feature of themselves; this occurs because they have the privilege of considering themselves to be otherwise "ordinary" or unremarkable in the ways in which they do not deviate from the demographics of the dominant group. Few white Americans think of themselves as essentially white or think that their whiteness constitutes an essential part of their racial identities. They think of themselves as raceless. A great many more African Americans think of themselves as essentially Black or think that their Blackness constitutes an essential part of their identities. This is some indication of the strength of dominant-group privilege and its impact on identity.[7]

The problem lies in the essentialism. But there is more to be said here than that. One of the objections of feminist philosophers, lesbian and nonlesbian, is that things such as gender have always been taken by androcentric philosophers to be contingent characteristics of persons. This is one of the views that allows many mainstream philosophers to question whether feminist philosophy really is philosophy at all. An alternative solution to that of characterizing lesbianism as either a contingent or an essential characteristic of persons is needed.

Without addressing here the more general problems with essentialism (a topic widely discussed elsewhere), I would like to suggest that part of the problem lies in characterizing *persons*, rather than *acts, moments, relationships, encounters, attractions, perspectives, insights, outlooks, connections,* and *feelings,* as lesbian. If one takes "lesbian" to have Lorde's, Frye's, and Hoagland's sense of externalness to the phallocratic conceptual scheme, it is easier to imagine that there are events, interactions, and feelings that occur in that context than it is to imagine that there are whole persons whose very existence permanently "is" or "is not" in that context. One can see, implicit in their descriptions of a "lesbian context," or that which is outside of the "phallocratic conceptual scheme," or the "lens through which we scrutinize all aspects of our existence," glimpses of one of the "worlds" to which María Lugones invites us to travel when she recommends that "we learn to love each other by learning to travel to each other's 'worlds' " (Lugones 1987, 4).[8]

Lugones claims that "world"-travellers become different people in different worlds. Of course, she is not saying that Pat Robertson becomes Jesse Jackson by visiting Watts, or anything equally ontologically ridiculous. Nor is she speaking of potentialities or different possible worlds; she is speaking of actual "worlds" between which individuals move, becoming different in context-switch. It is "the shift from being one person to being a different person" that she calls travel. She writes:

> Those of us who are "world"-travellers have the distinct experience of being different in different "worlds" and of having the capacity to remember other "worlds" and ourselves in them.... So, the experience is of being a different person in different "worlds" and yet of having memory of oneself as different without quite having the sense of there being an underlying "I." (Lugones 1987, 11)

This is not quite so mystical as it might first sound; I believe it is a common, ordinary experience. Most people have the experience of "being" different persons in different contexts. For example, the mature academic who teaches, conducts research, runs a household, and makes economic and personal decisions generally quite competently may find herself "being" a different person when she visits her parents' home for two weeks. She "shifts" who she actually is in different contexts. As Lugones says:

> The shift may not be willful or even conscious, and one may be completely unaware of being different than one is in a different "world," and may not recognize that one is in a different "world." Even though the shift can be done willfully, it is not a matter of acting. One does not pose as someone else, one does not pretend to be, for example, someone of a different personality or character or someone who uses space of language differently from the other person. Rather one is someone who has that personality or character or uses space or language in that particular way. The "one" here does not refer to some underlying "I." One does not experience any underlying "I." (Lugones 1987, 11-12)

Lugones is arguing here against identity-essentialism. Her claim is that there is no essence of self that is unchanging outside of context. It is not, of course, that she "is" a philosopher but "is not" Hispanic in Minnesota and "is not" a philosopher but "is" Hispanic in New Mexico, or vice versa. Her claim is that the experience of such an essence of self is not available to " 'world' travellers"; it would only be available, if at all, to those who live very homogeneous lives. But she recommends against living such a homogeneous life, even if one is able. "World"-travelling is a practice that she recommends as "a skillful, creative, rich, enriching, and, given certain circumstances, as a loving way of being and living." So Lugones has suggested a method for engaging in non-ordinary travel across Frye's nontransversable semantic warps; it is this she calls "world"-travel.

I suggest that Lorde's conception of lesbianism is one that is ontologically a matter of positioning oneself in a lesbian "world" and allowing oneself freely to become who one is constructed as in that "world." This includes all of the physical, emotional, psychic, intellectual, and probably other dimensions of lesbian existence. But who one "freely becomes" in that context will probably vary in intensity and kind from individual to individual. Undoubtedly, there are some for whom the physical or sexual aspects of lesbian existence will seem most prominent. There are some who experience lesbian existence primarily in its intellectual or emotional aspects. There are also undoubtedly some who will choose to spend more time in this "world" than others, and some who will choose to spend less, regardless of which dimensions of it are most prominent or intense for them.

The danger of this suggestion is that I imagine it raises horror in some lesbians, who envision themselves being asked to act as perpetual tour guides to "world"-travelling ontological tourists who schedule brief stops in Lesbian-Land for the sake of being able to say they've been there. This fear is not unfounded. There is something horrible about the idea of millions of lesbians opening up their beds, their bars, their hearts, their souls, their homes, their music festivals, and their conferences to heterosexual "tourists" who are passing on through, taking mental snapshots and sending philosophical post-cards on home to their menfriends, saying "Having a wonderful time; wish you were here." This is not my suggestion at all, nor is it Lugones's recommenda-tion.

Such ontological tourism is perception through what Frye calls the "arrogant eye," which is in contrast to the "loving eye" through which Lugones invites "world"-travellers to see. For both Frye and Lugones, the loving eye is "the eye of one who knows that to know the seen, one must consult something other than one's own will and interests and fears and imaginations."[9] Lugones concludes that

> there are 'worlds' that we can travel to lovingly and travelling to them is part of loving at least some of their inhabitants. (Lugones 1987, 3)

This is not ontological tourism. The reason for doing this is because

> travelling to someone's 'world' is a way of identifying with them . . . because by travelling to their 'world' we can under-stand what it is to be them and what it is to be ourselves in their eyes. (Lugones 1987, 17)

This is the same political claim as the one made by Lorde: that is, the development of particular, erotic connections is a social, political, and episte-mic activity that tempers the individualistic sense of self maintained by phallocratic conceptual schemes, opening up an entire realm of human under-standing otherwise unavailable. It also explains in what sense Lorde's *eros* is specifically lesbian.

EROS AS LESBIAN

It would be intellectually dishonest not to describe what some people have called the "feminist eros" as lesbian. The uncovering and explication of this conception of the erotic, the work of describing it, overwhelmingly has been the work of women who claim lesbian identities. Indeed, if Frye is right about semantic holes, and I think that she is, then production of this sort of knowledge is possible only as a result of of insights and memories that emerge from specifically lesbian experience. This is not to say that no nonlesbians have contributed to these developments. Trask (1986, 117) finds traces of this theme in the works of Robin Morgan, Nancy Chodorow, and Dorothy Dinnerstein, all of whom do not identify themselves as lesbians. Belenky, Clinchy, Gold-berger, and Tarule (1986, 141-44) find it in the work of Sara Ruddick and

Virginia Woolf. One possible move here, often actually made with respect to Virginia Woolf, would be to claim that these women "really are" lesbians, though they may not realize it or identify themselves as such. But I reject such essentialism.

I would not, however, reject the notion that they were exploring a lesbian "world," in Lugones's sense of a "world," in their more lesbian work. And it is not incidental that lesbian "world(s)" are maintained primarily by and for those who choose to spend most of their time in those worlds—those who most readily adopt lesbian identities.

There is a long tradition of failure to notice, or failure to remember, or failure to attribute, or failure to mention that important insight, theory, or practice is discovered or created by members of oppressed groups. To fail to attribute the notion of the so-called feminist eros to lesbian theory would be to perpetuate this erasure. Notice that even already that erasure has begun in the developing practice of referring to the feminist eros rather than to the lesbian eros. There are pressures on both lesbian and feminist intellectual communities to engage in this erasure.

One pressure is that of making it more "respectable" or less threatening by not calling it lesbian. Many academics reencounter our own fears and homophobia each time our offices and desks are full of books and journals with the word "**lesbian**" printed in large typeface on the cover or when we regularly walk around carrying such books and journals.

The problem is illuminated even more when one thinks of the times and places that colleagues and students have declined to borrow such books and journals because the word "**lesbian**" is on the cover, for lack of a suitably concealing backpack or briefcase or a plain brown wrapper. "It's not that I'm prejudiced," they mumble apologetically, "It's just that I'm afraid that other people might think . . ." and their voices trail off, unable to articulate what, exactly, are the thoughts of "other people" that they fear. Such generalized cultural hatred and fear of that which is lesbian, fear that would make it seem, or actually be, dangerous to be in possession of a book or journal with the term "**lesbian**" in the title, is reminiscent of the very worst of McCarthyism. Intellectual honesty requires that scholars resist this intimidation; human cowardice makes it hard to resist, but does not excuse a failure to do so.[10]

Another pressure comes from nonlesbian feminists, and sometimes even from nonfeminists or nonwomen, who wish to claim for themselves the exciting epistemic possibilities discovered by lesbian feminists. They have a stake in denying that there is something distinctively lesbian about the lesbian conception of the erotic; if the lesbian component of the experience and theory is denied, then nonlesbians can partake of this compelling source of information and power without dealing with their own self-knowledge and their own identities in what may be frightening ways.

Consider, for example, the "me too" phenomenon experienced by many teachers and students of women's studies. When lesbian existence and lesbian theory are explored in a positive light, there are invariably some number of students, including occasionally male students, who want to jump on the "Me Too" bandwagon, claiming all kinds of ways to have discovered their own lesbianism. Some women, presumably those most convinced that lesbianism is a mental state, do this without actually changing their behavior in any discernible way; i.e., they continue to sleep with boyfriends or husbands in overtly sexist and heterosexist relationships while making these claims. Other women dissolve relationships with boyfriends and husbands and eagerly seek sexual relationships with other lesbians, many of whom are quite wary of these neo-dykes. While some of these women undoubtedly do continue to maintain lesbian identities following the end of the semester, my impression is that a large number of them discover that daily lesbian existence is a great deal more mundane, a great deal less exciting, and a great deal more risky than they had first imagined it to be. Some of them discover that they "are not actually" lesbians and may even feel that they were somehow misled by the intellectual encounter that caused the "mistake." Occasionally, and sometimes danger-ously, they may claim to have been "brainwashed" or coerced in some way by the teacher. One might want to ask what is happening here, a question not unrelated to essentialism, "world"-travel, and the position of lesbianism with respect to lesbian theory.

It helps to see these students as having engaged in "world"-travelling, in Lugones's sense of the term. They have travelled to a lesbian "world" in the context of the class and have "loved at least some of [its] inhabitants" in the process of doing so: often classmates, authors of the assigned readings, or the teacher. In other words, they have formed the beginnings of erotic connections in the context of a lesbian "world." My sense is that for many of these women it is the confusion brought on by essentialism that causes them to believe that this means that they, therefore, "are" lesbians. Having noticed that they are able to form erotic connections in a lesbian context leads them to belive that they must then "really be" lesbians.[11]

But having formed the beginnings of erotic connections in the context of a lesbian "world" is not all there is to "being" a lesbian. "Being" a lesbian means choosing to spend a certain amount of one's time in this "world"; it also means feeling "at ease" in this "world." Lugones cites four ways that one might be at ease in a "world." One way is by being fluent—one knows the language and the "moves" of discourse of that "world." Another is to be normatively happy, to agree with the norms of the "world." The third is by being "humanly bonded"—that is, by being with those one loves, who love one in return. The final way she suggests is by sharing a history. It is in these ways that one adopts a "world" as one's own. She notes:

> One may say of a "world" that it is "my world" because one is
> at ease in it, i.e.[,] being at ease in a "world" may be the basis
> for the evaluation. (Lugones 1987, 12-13)

It is my sense that the usual way in which one might say "I am, or I am not, a lesbian" corresponds with Lugones's ability to say that a "world" is "my world." Translated into her language, the essentialist notion of "being" a lesbian becomes the nonessentialist notion of being able to call the lesbian "world" one's own. The student who decides that she "is" a lesbian after encountering the lesbian "world" and beginning to form connections within it is confused by the essentialist notion of lesbianism. It may be that after travelling in that "world" for some amount of time, she will come to be at ease in it. But making that decision upon first encountering the "world" may be, in many cases, premature.

Viewing lesbianism in this nonessentialist way also gives us a clue, however, about what to make of those who do not identify themselves as lesbians but who nonetheless travel within lesbian "worlds" at some times, on some occasions. It is my belief that it is possible for a woman to travel in a lesbian "world" regularly, over long periods of time; to work in that context, to form friendships in that context, and to create theory in that context, without ever feeling that that world is wholly "her own." Without feeling that a "world" is wholly her own, without feeling wholly at ease in that "world," she might never say that she "is" who she is in that world; she might never feel that she "is" a lesbian.[12]

And in some nontrivial sense, she is correct. A woman who travels frequently within a lesbian "world," who lives and works and plays in that "world" but does not consider it to be her own, is not a lesbian in the same sense that Marilyn Frye or Audre Lorde or Sarah Hoagland "is" a lesbian. This is more than a simple "coming out" distinction. Some might characterize such a woman as a lesbian who is not yet "out," even to herself; she remains, in a sense, deluded in her own self-knowledge. I reject this view.

But I also reject the essentialist view that she "is not" a lesbian. To the extent to which she travels frequently within the lesbian "world," forms erotic connections within that "world," lives, works and plays in that "world," she is experiencing some aspects of lesbian existence deeply, and as her own experience. To the extent to which she does this, she is not one of those so enmeshed in the phallocratic conceptual scheme that, for her, lesbians don't exist. It is precisely to the extent to which she travels in the lesbian "world" that lesbians *do* exist.

This illustrates the brilliance of Lorde's lesbian notion of the erotic. It is an epistemic and ontological capacity, not a mystical or a hedonistic commitment, nor a set of genital activities. Most importantly, it is a nonessentialist conception of the erotic.

It is my sense that such a nonessentialist lesbian conception of the erotic could go a long way toward healing some of the most bitter divisions between and among gynocentric women, including the rifts created by the so-called sex wars of the 1980s and including the continuing distrust between lesbians and heterosexual feminists. Lorde has articulated such a conception. Frye has given a language-based explanation of how it could be that this lesbian eros is necessarily lesbian. Lugones has suggested how such a warp in the conceptual scheme could be traversed by those who desire to travel beyond language warps in extraordinary ways. My claim is that this combined conception of a lesbian erotic and its ontology is far more important than may have been previously recognized. It has deep epistemic, political, and moral implications to which we must now turn.

NOTES

Special thanks to Claudia Card and to the anonymous reviewers for *Hypatia* who helped me considerably in thinking through these issues. Thanks also to Susan Bernick, Marilyn Frye, Jenifer Langdon, R. Ruth Linden, Naomi Scheman, Elise Springer, and Terry Winant for helpful comments or discussions at various stages of this work and to Maggie Collins for wordprocessing and other practical assistance.

1. This sort of understanding seems to be what Belenky, Clinchy, Goldberger, and Tarule refer to as "connected knowing." They found that connected knowers seek to understand people's ideas in the other people's terms rather than in their own terms" and that these connected knowers "were attached to the objects they sought to understand: they *cared* about them" (Belenky et al. 1986, 124).

2. One wonders if Plato would agree—but thats another discussion entirely. For more on this see, for example, Keller (1985) or Schott (1988, esp. #3-18). Gregory Vlastos also had been writing about Plato's *eros* shortly before his death.

3. Sarah Hoagland gives the following history of this oft-repeated phrase: in 1970 Ti-Grace Atkinson wrote, "Feminism is a theory, but lesbianism is a practice," in distinguishing between feminists and lesbians; five years later, Jill Johnston said, "Feminism is the complaint and lesbianism is the solution" (Hoagland 1988, #306).

4. See Card (1987). For further reading, see also Boswell (1980) and Weeks (1977). Thanks to Claudia Card and the anonymous reviewer(s) for pointing out the relevance of these works.

5. Thanks to Susan Bernick for introducing me to the possibilities and understandings illuminated by the use of the verb-form of "pornography": to pornograph, meaning "to make pornographic." Catherine MacKinnon used the word "pornographed" at least as far back as 1982 when, speaking about Linda Marchiano on a panel at Stanford University (April 2, 1982), she said, "The film *Deep Throat*, in which Linda was pornographed, became a chic success.

6. See Lorde (1983), especially the essays "Sexism: An American Disease in Blackface," "Age, Race, Class, and Sex: Women Redefining Difference," and "Eye to Eye: Black Women, Hatred, and Anger." See also Hull and Smith (1982) and Lugones (1990).

7. For a somewhat compelling account of how this could be so, see Harding (1991), especially chapter 8 (. . . and Race? Toward the Science Question in Global Feminism).

8. It is only fair to Lugones to note that she was addressing "women of color in the U.S." in making this recommendation, and since I, and possibly you, may not fit that discription, my suggestion that she invites "us" to do this may be a misrepresentation of her work. But elsewhere in the paper she does offer this to white/Anglo women in the U.S. as a solution to our "failure to love women across ration and cultural boundaries."

9. Lugones quotes Frye (1983, 75) approvingly, so long, she says, as Frye does not mean "that I should not consult my own interests nor that I should exclude the possibility that my self and the self of the one that I love might be important ties to each other in many complicated ways."

10. In all honesty, doing the work for this article required making some snap, but nonetheless difficult, decisions not to rearrange books or shuffle papers around to conceal titles or notes when certain students, colleagues, or administrators walked into my office. This in addition to those not-transient-enough worries about having the word "Lesbian" appear on my yet-untenured c.v.

11. Incidentally, I don't think that this dynamic occurs only in women's studies classrooms. I believe that there are many students who have decided to be biologists or musicians or journalists or philosophers in much the same way. The difference here is that deciding to "be" a biologist is a career choice that allows a great deal of one's personal identity to remain unchanged, in ways that deciding to "be" a lesbian does not.

12. This observation rekindles my interest in the artificial language "e-prime" created by linguists. It is different from ordinary English only in that it contains no forms of the verb "to be." I.e., rather than saying "She is a lesbian," one would have to convey the information without using the form of the verb "to be": "She identifies herself as a lesbian," "She has important lesbian relationships," "She told me of some important lesbian experiences in her background," "She lives and sleeps with a woman lover."

REFERENCES

Belenky, Mary Field, Blythe McVicker Clinchy, Nancy Rule Goldberger and Jill Mattuck Tarule. 1986. *Women's ways of knowing: The development of self, voice, and mind.* New York: Basic Books.

Boswell, John. 1980. *Christianity, social tolerance, and homosexuality.* Chicago: University of Chicago Press.

Card, Claudia. 1987. *Intimacy and responsibility: what lesbians do.* Madison: Institute for Legal Studies, University of Wisconsin-Madison Law School.

Frye, Marilyn. 1983. *The politics of reality: Essays in feminist theory.* Trumansburg, NY: Crossing Press.

Harding, Sandra. 1991. *Whose science? Whose knowledge?* Ithaca, NY: Cornell University Press.

Hoagland, Sarah. 1988. *Lesbian ethics: Toward new value.* Palo Alto, CA: Institute of Lesbian Studies.

Hull, Gloria and Barbara Smith. 1982. The politics of black women's studies. In *All the women are white, all the blacks are men, but some of us are brave,* ed. Gloria T. Hull, Patricia Bell Scott, and Barbara Smith. Old Westbury, NY: The Feminist Press.

Keller, Evelyn Fox. 1985. Love and sex in Plato's epistemology. In *Reflections on gender and science*. New Haven: Yale University Press.

Lorde, Audre. 1984. Uses of the erotic: The erotic as power. In *Sister outsider: Essays and speeches by Audre Lorde*. Trumansburg, NY: Crossing Press.

Lugones, María. 1987. Playfulness, "World"-travelling, and loving perception. *Hypatia* 2(2): 3-19.

———. 1990. Hispaneando y lesbiando: On Sarah Hoagland's Lesbian ethics. *Hypatia* 5(3): 138-46.

Morgan, Robin. 1990. *The demon lover: On the sexuality of terrorism*. New York: Norton.

Rich, Adrienne. 1980. Compulsory heterosexuality and lesbian existence. In *Signs: Journal of women in culture and society* 5(4): 631-60.

Schott, Robin May. 1988. *Cognition and eros: A critique of the Kantian paradigm*. Boston: Beacon Press.

Trask, Haunani-Kay. 1986. *Eros and power: The promise of feminist theory*. Philadelphia: University of Pennsylvania Press.

Weeks, Jeffrey. 1977. *Coming out*. London and New York: Quartet Books.

Queer Ethics; or, The Challenge of Bisexuality to Lesbian Ethics

ELISABETH D. DÄUMER

Due to its problematic political and social position between two opposed sexual cultures, bisexuality has often been ignored by feminist and lesbian theorists both as a concept and a realm of experiences. The essay argues that bisexuality, precisely because it transgresses bipolar notions of fixed gendered and sexed identities, is usefully explored by lesbian and feminist theorists, enhancing our effort to devise an ethics of difference and to develop nonoppressive ways of responding to alterity.

In her recent book *Lesbian Ethics: Toward New Value*, Sarah Hoagland affirms that lesbian existence, because it "challenges the social construction of reality," holds a promise for a transformation of consciousness: "the conceptual, material possibility of female agency not defined in terms of an other" (Hoagland 1988, 6). Concerned with nourishing this promise, Hoagland offers a wealth of strategies for creating values that would enhance lesbian capacity to separate from heterosexualism—"a way of living," in Hoagland's words, "that normalizes the dominance of one person and the subordination of another" (7)—and to respond to differences among lesbians in ways that do not replicate forms of domination but enable moral agency and authentic choice. That the experiences and views of bisexual women are absent from a book on lesbian ethics might surprise only a few of its readers. In this essay, however, I shall propose that an exploration of bisexuality—as an experience as much as a moral, social, and epistemological point of view—contributes significantly to feminist and lesbian theorizing, and especially to the endeavor, so admirably advanced in Hoagland's work, of devising alternative, non-oppressive ways of responding to alterity.

Beginning with a poetic rendition of the experiences and fitful reflections of a fictitious woman named Cloe, I will, in the second part of the essay, explore the theoretical implications and transformative promise of Cloe's ostensibly missing or indeterminate sexual identity for a feminist antihomophobic under-

Hypatia vol. 7, no. 4 (Fall 1992) © by Elisabeth D. Däumer

standing of sexuality and gender.[1] Finally, I will show how a serious examination of bisexuality draws out the implications of recent work on lesbian ethics, most fully developed in Hoagland's book, for a "queer ethics": an ethics dedicated to creating values that would nourish the queer in all of us and help us—whether we are male or female, gay- or lesbian-identified, bisexual, heterosexual, or undecided—separate from straightness or, as Hoagland terms it, heterosexualism. I do not anticipate a grand conclusion to the medley of voices and perspectives that I am here assembling. But I do hope to contribute to the burgeoning dialogue on what is still a strangely repressed and uncomfortable subject—the instability and fracturedness of our gendered, sexed, social and political selves—by showing its centrality to our attempt at developing an ethics of difference.[2]

I.

We are increasingly aware that sexuality is about flux and change, that what we call "sexual" is as much a product of language and culture as of nature. But we earnestly strive to fix it, stabilize it, say who we are by telling of our sex—and the lead in this conscious articulation of sense of self has been taken by those radically disqualified for it by the sexual tradition. (Weeks 1985, 186)

In an age of constructed sexualities a new type of constructed being is claiming our attention. She identifies as female. Let us call her, like earlier heroines of feminist history, Cloe. Neither straight nor gay, Cloe is also not bisexual, at least not in the traditional, still current, sense of the word—pregenderized, polymorphously perverse, or simply sexually undecided, uncommitted, and hence untrustworthy. Cloe can make up her mind; but she would be so much better at explaining how indeed she is making up her mind, if others—her lesbian friends worried about her relapse into an inevitably heterosexist heterosexuality, her straight friends enchanted or disquieted by her exoticism—if many of these well-meaning friends wouldn't try to make up her mind for her.

To be historically exact, Cloe owes much of her existence to the valiant struggles of lesbian feminists who established oases of political and sexual sisterhood, which despite certain censorious tendencies allowed women like Cloe to move away from straightness, to explore their sexuality, their emotional, sexual attraction to other women in a welcoming environment—an environment quite different from that which older lesbians had faced and many other lesbians are still struggling with. Thus Cloe is deeply grateful to these women who weathered homophobic ostracism and enabled their younger—i.e., newer—sisters to explore their "deviancy" joyfully, often playfully, safe from the twin specters of internalized guilt and external ostracism.

Of course, these differences in experience invariably produced tension and at times division. While Cloe no longer feels straight (i.e., heterosexual), indeed is passionately nonstraight, she also does not, if the truth be told, feel that she ever came out of the closet. There had been for her no closet to begin with. Rather, her experience of being closeted coincided with her coming out as a lesbian or, to be more accurate, with her first female lover, whose hand she dared not hold in public, whose presence she needed to explain—not once, but again and again—to friends, family, colleagues, who, until then, had had no reason to assume she was not heterosexual, like them.

Like other women coming to feminism in the 1970s and 1980s, Cloe fell in love with women not out of a deep-seated sense of sexual orientation but in the course of political bonding and passionate intellectual conversations. Nor was it sexual or social aversion to men that drove her to women, but something positive—enchantment and delight with the company of people who excited her intellectually, emotionally, then sexually, who did not expect, like men she had known, nonreciprocal access to her at all times. Over the months and years, Cloe simply preferred being with women; and it seemed to her a small, and natural, step from intellectual passion to sexual intimacy.

Nevertheless, when she took that step she was deeply startled by the difference it made. Nothing had prepared her for the sweetness of a woman's mouth, the mystery of a woman's breast. Nor could she have described how she changed. Falling from her old sense of self, she was reborn into a new way of experiencing her body, her sexuality, her femininity. She could not even say that her new way of being in the world was *truer*. On the contrary, she walked about like a stranger, newly alive to what had appeared to her a familiar world, a familiar body, a familiar self. But most of all, she felt enlarged, filled with wonder at her ability to give abundantly and to receive joyfully. And to her mother, who could not help observing the flowering of confidence and well-being in her daughter, Cloe said that now, for the first time in her life, she felt she had a choice—a choice about whom to love, a choice in creating and re-creating her sexuality.

Cloe soon found out, however, that choosing to love a particular woman was not, for her, the same as affirming a specific sexual identity. Not that she didn't try to become a lesbian. She did. But after a brief and enthusiastic effort at making herself into a real sister, when Cloe lovingly invested herself with all the paraphernalia of lesbian feminism and fell in and out of love with a small-boned dark-haired woman, after what should perhaps be described as a second adolescence, Cloe began to wonder: Could it be possible to relate to men and women, or the creatures answering to these names, not as men and women, as straight or gay, but—and here she would whisper to herself embarrassedly—as *humans*? Of course, she was wise and self-resisting enough not to voice such deluded, liberal gibberish.

Nevertheless, she could not help dreaming. She would see herself at a table with a beloved—was she male, he female, she a celibate androgyne, he a lesbian mother?—with whom, over glasses of deep red wine, she could engage in beautiful, deliciously double- or triple-voiced conversations. She was dreaming not of a genderless, sexless creature, nor of an androgynous one (although this was closer to her vision), but of somebody with whom she was not primarily a woman, a lesbian, or a misrecognized heterosexual. Navigating questions of identity in a postmodern age, Cloe dreamed not of instability or indecidability so much as of an intimacy not regulated through positionings in ostensibly stable sexual identities. Cloe longed for people with whom she could create herself anew, again and again, and for whom she could do the same.

What delusions, we might say. Poor Cloe! After a brief relapse with a man, closely monitored by her lesbian sisters, the question of her sexual identity became pressingly imminent. She refused, passionately, to return to straightness, but neither could she in good conscience call herself a dyke. So why not say she was bisexual, as some sympathetic friends had tentatively suggested? Yet somehow Cloe wasn't happy with that label, even if in terms of her sexual and emotional experience it seemed closest to the truth. After all, she had loved men in her life and she had loved women, and she could not imagine ceasing to love either. But to assume the label of bisexuality? That gave her pause. A host of little comments, brief remarks, as well as her own assumptions made this a less than savory, and hardly political, identity: it seemed one was bisexual by default, for lack of commitment and the ability to make up one's mind. True, a male friend—now homosexual, formerly married, and in both apparently happy—had remarked that bisexuals have the best of both worlds. A lesbian friend disagreed. To her it seemed a bisexual had the worst of both worlds: who, she asked, would your friends be?

And Cloe agreed with her. For even if her heterosexual or hetero-identified friends tended to view bisexuality with tolerant, sometimes condescending, curiosity, the lesbian community—as community—expressed above all suspicion, even contempt, for women "who went back to men," women who were "ac-dc," on the fence. The threat of AIDS has only exacerbated such suspicion, leading many lesbians to view bisexual women as potential AIDS-carriers. Inherently contaminated, they endanger lesbian purity. Moreover, because such women might refuse to assume either a clearly lesbian or heterosexual identity, they carry the taint of promiscuity, as if they were floundering, promiscuously and opportunistically, back and forth between people of either gender—exploiting heterosexual privilege on the one hand, while savoring, unrightfully, the honey of lesbian sisterhood on the other. And while Cloe was careful not to minimize the social ostracism endured by gays, she could not help but feel that those who dared to call themselves bisexual were also subjected to a sort of ostracism, not only by the larger society but by lesbians as well.

II.

> It is a rather amazing fact that, of the very many dimensions along which the genital activity of one person can be differentiated from that of another (dimensions that include preference for certain acts, certain zones or sensations, certain physical types, a certain frequency, certain symbolic investments, certain relations of age or power, a certain species, a certain number of participants, etc. etc. etc.), precisely one, the gender of object choice, emerged from the turn of the century, and has remained, as *the* dimension denoted by the now ubiquitous category of "sexual orientation." (Sedgwick 1990, 8)

Prompted by my reading of Sedgwick's *Epistemology of the Closet*, from which the above quotation is taken, I recently argued during a dinner with friends that we ought to problematize more stringently the relations between sexual acts, sexual identity, politics, and gender. Inspired by Sedgwick's dazzling description of the infinite multitude of ways in which sexuality could be defined were we not as exclusively fixated on riveting it to the gender of whom we are attracted to or sexual with, I impersonated Cloe and wondered if it was possible for a woman and a man to engage in a lesbian relationship. After all, if, as some lesbian theorists like Monique Wittig have suggested, a lesbian is "outside the categories of sex (woman and man), because the designated subject (lesbian) is *not* a woman, either economically, or politically, or ideologically" (Wittig 1981, 53), why, then, could it not be possible for a man to resist his designated gender (including the relations of domination embodied within it) and assume a lesbian identity?[3] On a theoretical level, at least, Sedgwick's observations add a twist to Wittig's construction of lesbian that gives rise to exciting—or disturbing—questions and possibilities: How would we define the relationship between a female lesbian and a gay man, who, like a character in Caryl Churchill's *Cloud Nine* wants to be a lesbian? Would their relationship be heterosexual, even though neither partner views her/himself as straight? Could such a union not be called "lesbian" in the utopian feminist sense of the term? Both partners, after all, insist on being *not* a woman and *not* a man; and for both, gender identification is secondary to, or entirely determined by, their commitment to establishing a relationship that resists the domination of heterosexually gendered positions.

One of my friends immediately pinpointed what was to her most problematic about this proposition. It would, she said, efface her own identity as a lesbian, and, by stretching the term beyond any intelligible, useful boundaries, perpetuate lesbian invisibility in new and dangerous ways. She also asked, disbelievingly, who—i.e., what woman, what man—would want to define their relationship in this manner, and how would the concept of heterosexual privilege fit into this scheme? Since these are serious charges, I'd like to respond to them in some detail.

Let us start with the second. In light of Cloe's desultory attempt to fashion for herself a sexual identity from the startling dearth of currently available options (hetero, homo, or bi), we ought not be surprised that she would think up something as improbable as a lesbian relationship between a woman and a man. Since she herself feels no longer straight, she wonders, of course, how to name her current relationship to a man. Is it heterosexual just because it implies certain sexual practices—namely, penetration—that can or cannot be performed? Is it heterosexual because clearly she is a woman, at least anatomically, and he a man? Is it heterosexual because it conforms to the dominant idea of a "normal" relationship—and thus also reaps the benefits of heterosexual privilege—despite the fact that the individual members in this relationship might view themselves as "queer"?

Cloe is not oblivious to the sociopolitical connotations of engaging in what to most would look like a heterosexual relationship. Nor is she unaware of the privileges conferred upon this relationship: social endorsement and a certain visibility; legal and financial benefits; relative safety from homophobia (she is also affected by homophobia, if differently from a woman who is lesbian-identified and lives in a relationship with another woman).[4] Cloe would not, moreover, seriously insist on describing either herself or her relationship as lesbian. Yet her half-mischievous proposal to do so reflects her increasingly dizzying awareness of the many possible sexual and gendered selves, the many passions and attractions, fantasies and relationships—whether sexual, erotic, affectional or intellectual—that remain frustratingly silenced, unspoken in the discourses of sexuality currently available to us. Her own sense of the fissures and contradictions (between sexual and political identities, political and personal, emotional commitments, etc.) that attend her way of being in the world has produced in her a hunger for language differentiated enough to capture the wealth of contradictions that pervades the efforts of individual men and women to subvert or modify dominant constructions of gender and sexuality.

I have so far resisted calling Cloe "bisexual" because it seems to me that the term "bisexuality," rather than broadening the spectrum of available sexual identifications, holds in place a binary framework of two basic and diametrically opposed sexual orientations. Contributors to a recent anthology on this subject, Bi Any Other Name, affirm that bisexuality, when made visible, disrupts a "monosexual framework" by challenging "assumptions about the immutability of people's sexual orientations and society's supposed divisions into discrete groups" (Hutchins and Kaahumanu 1991, 3).[5] Yet the various efforts chroni-

cled in this anthology to construct a bisexual identity—distinct from heterosexual and homosexual identities while comprising aspects of both—do not
always bear out the radical potential of its affirmation.[6]

Some of the contributors, for instance, view themselves as divided between
homosexual and heterosexual orientations; thus Loraine Hutchins, one of the
editors, describes her struggle to "[accept] myself as the 70-percent straight
person I probably really am," while "constantly [fighting] to have the 30-per-
cent lesbian side not be ridiculed or misunderstood" (xv). Others think of
themselves as integrating both orientations and thus, as one of the editors,
quoting Robin Morgan, maintains, "[sacrificing] nothing except false categories and burned-out strategies" (xxiv). Yet such tropes of bisexuality as either
neatly divided between or integrating heterosexuality and homosexuality
threaten to simplify bisexuality: on the one hand, they retain a notion of
sexuality—and sexual identity—based exclusively on the gender of object
choice, thus implying that a bisexual woman, for instance, would be heterosexually involved with a man, homosexually involved with a woman. (Cloe,
for one, finds it impossible to say, with the absolute certainty that such
definitions of bisexuality imply, that she loves men and women differently; and
although she finds it equally impossible to say that she loves them the same,
she is reluctant to ascribe the difference in these encounters—whether imaginary or real—to gender alone. Is it really always that easy, she wonders, to
keep straight whom one was loving and how? What if, by mistake, one forgot
that the person holding one's hand was a man—or a woman—and if one,
equally by mistake, were to slip into a heterosexual relationship with a woman,
a lesbian relationship with a man?)

On the other hand, in their tendency to reduce bisexuality to a third sexual
orientation (or a mixture of orientations), these tropes of bisexuality simplify
its sociopolitical implications. Bisexuality is not merely a problem of an
unrecognized or vilified sexual preference that can be solved, or alleviated,
through visibility and legitimation as a third sexual option. The problems of
bisexuals are social and political ones, resulting, as Lisa Orlando, one of the
contributors to the anthology, points out, "from [our] ambiguous position . . .
between what currently appear as two mutually exclusive sexual cultures, one
with the power to exercise violent repression against the other" (224-225).

To be sure, the affirmation of an integrated, unified bisexual identity,
fostered within supportive bisexual communities, might boost the psychological well-being of many bisexual people. It remains to be seen, however, if and
how such increased visibility would contribute to our struggle against homophobia, sexism, and heterosexism—the forces that have made the formation
of an oppositional sexual culture necessary in the first place. Put differently, as
long as there are two mutually exclusive sexual cultures, and as long as it is
politically essential to maintain oppositional cultures—based on sexuality as
much as on gender—the effort to disambiguate bisexuality and elevate it into

a sign of integration might counteract the subversive potential of bisexuality as a moral and epistemological force, as well as obscure its contribution to current discussions among feminist and lesbian theorists on the limitations of identity politics and the urgent need to respect differences among women.

I propose, therefore, that we assume bisexuality, not as an identity that integrates heterosexual and homosexual orientations, but as an epistemological as well as ethical vantage point from which we can examine and deconstruct the bipolar framework of gender and sexuality in which, as feminists and lesbian feminists, we are still too deeply rooted, both because of and despite our struggle against homophobia and sexism.

What are the advantages of assuming bisexuality as a perspective? I can think of many:

1. Because bisexuality occupies an ambiguous position *between* identities, it is able to shed light on the gaps and contradictions of all identity, on what we might call the difference *within* identity. This ambiguous position, while it creates painful contradictions, incoherences, and impracticalities in the lives of those who adopt it, can also lead to a deep appreciation of the differences among people—whether cultural, sexual, gendered—since any attempt to construct a coherent identity in opposition to another would flounder on the multiplicity of at times conflicting identifications generated by the bisexual point of view.

2. Because of its nonidenticalness, bisexuality exposes the distinctive feature of all politicized sexual identities: the at times radical discontinuities between an individual's sexual acts and affectional choices, on the one hand, and her or his affirmed political identity, on the other. By doing so, bisexuality reactivates the gender and sexuality destabilizing moment of all politicized sexual identities, at the same time that it can help us view contradiction, not as a personal flaw or a danger to our communities, but as a source of insight and strength, as a basis for more inclusive "we's" that enable rather than repress the articulation of difference.

3. Because of its ambiguous position between mutually exclusive sexual cultures, bisexuality also urges us to problematize heterosexuality in ways that distinguish more clearly between the institution of compulsory heterosexuality and the efforts of individual men and women to resist heterosexualism within and without so-called heterosexual relationships. Thus as feminist and lesbian theorists we need to inquire more intently into the possibility of antiheterosex-ist heterosexual relationships and describe such relationships in ways that neither obscure how they are impacted by heterosexualism nor collapse them univocally with heteropatriarchy. Marilyn Frye took an important step in this direction in a speech delivered at the 1990 National Women's Studies Asso-ciation conference, "Do You Have to Be a Lesbian to Be a Feminist?" In this

speech, which was published later that year in *off our backs*, Frye firmly asserted that we do not but that we need to be "virgins" in the radically feminist lesbian sense—i.e., women "in creative defiance of patriarchal definitions of the real, the meaningful" (Frye 1990, 23). A series of letters to *off our backs* in response to Frye's speech revealed, however, that many non-lesbian-identified or heterosexual women understood her to affirm the opposite—that you need to be a lesbian to be a feminist. This misreading on the part of the respondents reflects, perhaps, their sense that many lesbian feminists, because they tend to equate the difficulty of being a feminist in relation to a man with its impossibility, are unable to be curious about, or respectful of, the antipatriarchal, antiheterosexist struggle waged by many non-lesbian-identified women and mothers. Of course, heterosexually identified feminists need, on their part, to embrace more emphatically feminism as a sign of sexual ambiguity and refuse to disavow the destabilizing "queer" force of feminism by, for instance, publicly dissociating themselves from lesbianism.

4. Because the bisexual perspective enacts within itself the battle of contradictory sexual and political identifications, it can also serve as a bridge between identifications and communities, and thus strengthen our ability temporarily to "forget" entrenched and seemingly inevitable differences—especially those of race, gender, and sexuality—in order to focus on what we might have in common.

III.

It is the queer in me that empowers—that lets me see those lines and burn to cross them; that lets me question the lies we all were told about who women are, who men are, how we may properly interact . . . what nice girls do and don't do. The queer in all of us clamors for pleasure and change, will not be tamed or regulated, wants a say in the creation of a new reality. (Queen 1991, 20-21)

Cloe, as I mentioned previously, fell from straightness—from an assumption of heterosexuality as natural and, at least for herself, unavoidable—within her group of lesbian-feminist friends. In this close-knit circle of friends, Cloe began to conceive of loving another woman erotically and sexually. But neither her dreams and fantasies nor her actual experience of falling in love with a woman could entirely convince her that now a truer, more authentic self had surfaced within her. Instead she experienced the exhilaration of being offered a choice that she had not known—or felt—to exist: the choice to explore her sexuality and the complex depth of her bonds to women, the choice to act in resistance to institutionalized compulsions, to her own socialization, to her fear of familial rejection and social ostracism.

Making that choice did not, for Cloe, automatically eliminate other options—e.g., the option to love a man. Rather, Cloe entered a new perceptual framework—what I would like to call a "queer universe"—in which the fluctuations and mutabilities of sexuality, the multitude of different, changing, and at times conflicting ways in which we experience our sexual, affectional, and erotic proclivities, fantasies, and practices can be articulated and acknowledged. In the queer universe, to be queer implies that not everybody is queer in the same way. It implies a willingness to enable others to articulate their own particular queerness.

Yet if, in Cloe's experience, the lesbian-feminist community had opened up this vision of queerness by enabling her to explore her difference, she often felt that the same community and culture had also restricted her own and other women's self-exploration for the sake of communal cohesion and self-protection. Thus, although many lesbian theorists insist on attributing lesbianism to a political choice against heterosexualism and urge heterosexual feminists to realize that they, too, do not simply follow a natural calling but choose to be, or at least to remain, heterosexual, few of these theorists have displayed any curiosity about the whole range of choices that might be opened by such initial resistance against heterosexualism. A recent example of such lack of curiosity is Bette S. Tallen's "How Inclusive Is Feminist Political Theory? Questions for Lesbians," in which she asserts that "non-lesbian feminists, to the degree that they refuse to separate from men and masculine values and identify with lesbian existence, participate in the maintenance of patriarchal order" (Tallen 1990, 250). Not only does such affirmation uncritically collapse heterosexuality with the maintenance of heteropatriarchy, on the one hand, and lesbianism with resistance to patriarchy, on the other, but Tallen's article also displays no interest in other possible ways of resisting patriarchy and straightness. It demands that nonlesbian women identify with the "L-word," while demonstrating no reciprocal concern for the struggles of bisexual or other nonstraight women against heteropatriarchy.

Although there is no evidence to suggest that Hoagland would not agree with analyses such as Tallen's, *Lesbian Ethics* proffers a needed and exciting antidote to the tendency of some lesbian thinkers to place the needs of lesbian identity and unity over the articulation of differences, a tendency that ultimately works to contradict the centrality of choice and individual moral agency in feminist and lesbian ethics. Believing that "if we are to form an enduring community, it will not be on the basis of outside threats . . . of a rich tradition nor of what we find here . . . but on the basis of the values we believe we can enact here" (Hoagland 1988, 154), Hoagland maintains that we can only foster moral agency in others and ourselves if we are willing to acknowledge differences between ourselves and others. Indeed, her whole book is dedicated to the creation of a new ethic that would nourish lesbian connection but not at the expense of suppressing differences. In pursuit of this aim, she proposes alternative ways of thinking about alterity, designed to enhance our capacity, as a group and as individuals, to respond affirmatively to forces that have often been experienced as threatening to lesbian identity and community—the tensions, ambiguities, and contradictions arising from differences of race, class, age, able-bodiedness, as much as from differences of sexual, affectional, and intellectual choices.

The strength of Hoagland's ethical model lies in its conceptualization of moral agency according to which we choose to act with a full awareness of what constrains our ability to choose. "Choice," Hoagland affirms, "is at the very core of the concept of 'moral agency.' *It is not because we are free and moral agents that we are able to make moral choices. Rather, it is because we make choices, choose from among alternatives, act in the face of limits, that we declare ourselves moral beings*" (231). From the vantage point of this revisionary concept of moral agency, Hoagland takes a close and critical look at the way in which lesbian notions of choice are still, and often destructively, rooted in traditional ethics, which assume "that to be ethical we must be able to control external forces or, at the very least, that a proper moral choice would be one in which there were no constraints on us, no limits" (198). As a result, she explains, the focus of traditional ethics is exclusively "on whether we can blame or praise others for what they have done and whether we can be blamed or praised for what we have done" (198). Pointing to the implications of such ethical notions—for instance, the belief that it is always easy to distinguish between good and bad choices, since good choices have only good consequences and will not harm anyone—Hoagland proposes instead that we direct our energies to making our choices "intelligible" and to understanding the "complexity" emerging from them (220-28).

Although this conceptualization of agency raises compelling questions about bisexuality as a moral choice, the experiences and views of bisexual women and lesbians are, as I mentioned previously, absent from Hoagland's work. Since her study draws on the narratives of U.S. lesbians from a variety of communities, we might, of course, conclude that there were no bisexual women in these communities. Equally likely is the possibility that, if there were such women, they did not speak up about their experiences, silenced both by their own sense of disloyalty and by fear of not being understood, of not being able to make themselves, or to be viewed as, "intelligible." Certainly, Hoagland's own references to women whose experiences imply a certain measure of bisexuality do not reflect an interest in the complexity of their existence. Once, for instance, a married heterosexual woman is mentioned who "keeps trying to get closer to [her lesbian friend] and start something even though she just got pregnant and so is situating herself in a way that will make it much harder to leave her husband" (218). My quarrel is not with the fact that Hoagland's attention is in this case centered on the lesbian friend and her difficult choices, but with her manner of describing the other woman as "heterosexual," a designation that reduces the complexity of her being and even seems to imply that her desire for another woman is somehow less legitimate than that of a self-identified lesbian.

From a bisexual vantage point, however, what is promising in *Lesbian Ethics* is that Hoagland's apparent indifference to choices that challenge notions of fixed sexual identities (whether lesbian or heterosexual) coexists with her insistence *not* to define "lesbian." To do so, she explains, is to "succumb to a context of heterosexualism. No one ever feels compelled to explain or define what they perceive as the norm. If we define 'lesbianism,' we invoke a context in which it is not the norm" (8). In addition, her refusal to define lesbianism indicates a reluctance to make identity simply and unproblematically the cornerstone of lesbian ethics. In a compellingly "universalizing" or "queer" gesture, Hoagland equates lesbianism with support of female agency not defined in relation to man, on the one hand, and separation from heterosexualism on the other.[7] Thus, while retaining a notion of lesbian that is necessarily rooted in dominant categories of gender, even as it resists those (only a woman can refuse to belong to the category "woman"), Hoagland drives a wedge between the automatic linking of sexuality and gender, thereby opening her inquiry to an awareness of both the actual permeability of sexual identity and the plurality of ways in which people of all genders and sexualities resist straightness. In its universalizing force, then, lesbianism is not only separation from men (i.e., defined in terms of the gender of object choice) but also "a challenge to heterosexualism." Heterosexualism, in turn, by designating "a way of living that normalizes the dominance of one person and the subordination of another," is not confined to the relations between men and women but includes as well other, not specifically gender-based, relations: "the 'protective' relationship between imperialists and colonized, the 'peace-keeping' relationship between democracy (u.s. capitalism) and threats to democracy" (8).

Consonant with what I have called Hoagland's universalizing gesture is her acknowledgment, however cursory and enigmatic, that heterosexual women and men might also fit into her ethical scheme: "Heterosexual women can fit in this schema, for example. However, they fit in exactly the way lesbians fit in with heterosexual society. We fit there, but not as lesbians. Heterosexual women can fit here, though not as heterosexual women—that is, not as members of the category 'woman.'" When Hoagland speculates, in a whimsical remark relegated to a footnote and parentheses, whether "men could change in such a way as to be able to function in the framework of lesbianism," her answer is less reassuring: "I think it is possible. For example, if men changed themselves to become like dolphins—playful, intelligent, non-intrusive creatures—they could well fit" (95).

Hoagland's universalizing impulse ought not to be confused with an endeavor to be more inclusive, for while the latter sustains a conceptual framework of identifiable essences constituted in reference to an outside that serves as a foil to the community's internal boundaries, a universalizing gesture undercuts this framework by challenging the belief in immutable categories of gender and sexuality itself. Thus Hoagland is aware that our capacity to respond affirmatively to differences within a community is enhanced not necessarily through a call for more inclusivity but rather through a rethinking of the ways in which a community defines itself. Letting go of the "urge to define" the borders of lesbian community, and thus of "the metaphor of a fortress which requires defending from invasion," Hoagland begins to reenvision community in terms of a shared focus of attention, a "ground of lesbian be-ing, a ground of possibility" (9). Moreover, given this universalizing or queer impulse of her work, there is no intrinsic reason for Hoagland's exclusion of the moral choices of bisexuals from lesbian ethics. On the contrary, since bisexuals transgress boundaries of sexually identified communities and thus are always both inside and outside a diversity of conflicting communities, a serious consideration of their experiences and moral choices would help us develop the insight that I find so promisingly implied in Hoagland's *Lesbian Ethics*— that our ability to respond to diversity *within* lesbian community is linked to our capacity to articulate and reimagine the complex relations and interactions, as well as the shifting boundaries and allegiances, *between* communities.

Hence, as a sign of transgression, ambiguity, and mutability, bisexuality also provides a necessary theoretical link between lesbian theory and the rapidly expanding field of queer theory, on the one hand, and lesbian ethics and queer ethics, on the other. In its current usage, "queer," as Teresa de Lauretis explains, is intended "to mark a certain critical distance" from the designations "lesbian" and "gay," and a desire to "transgress and transcend them—or at the very least problematize them" (de Lauretis 1991, v). Among other things, queer theory is dedicated to opening up differences that, in de Lauretis's words, "are, paradoxically, elided, because taken for granted, in 'lesbian and gay' " (vi). A queer ethics, as I have briefly and provisionally proposed at the beginning of this essay, would support and nurture the queer in all of us—both by questioning all notions of fixed, immutable identities and by articulating a plurality of differences among us in the hope of forging new bonds and allegiances. In doing so, queer ethics poses a creative challenge to lesbian ethics, which need neither supercede nor undercut such ethics but can further its aim of enabling female agency and authentic choice through separation from heterosexualism. In addition, however, a queer ethics would stress the interrelatedness of different, and at times conflicting, communities and thus emphasize the need to combine forces in our various antihomophobic and antisexist endeavors.

NOTES

1. The first part of this essay served as an introduction to my presentation "Feminist Biphobia; or, What Does Sexuality Have to Do with Gender?" delivered at the 1991 North Central Women's Studies Association conference in Athens, Ohio. I would like to thank Sandra Runzo and Kate Mehuron for their helpful and challenging responses to the present, extended version of this presentation.

2. For recent work problematizing sexuality and gender, see especially Butler (1990), Sedgwick (1990), Fuss (1989 and 1991), de Lauretis (1991).

3. Diana Fuss asks a similar question when she points to Monique Wittig's and Adrienne Rich's problematic attitude to male homosexuality: "given the way in which gay men, in their social and sexual practices, radically challenge the current notions of masculinity and the 'naturalness' of heterosexual desire, one would think that they, too, disrupt and disable the logic of the straight mind (or what Rich prefers to call the 'institution of compulsory heterosexuality')" (Fuss 1989, 47).

4. In the welcome and useful anthology Bi Any Other Name: Bisexual people speak out, which I will discuss in more detail below, the painful difficulties of bisexual passing are compared, by a number of contributors, to the problems of multiracial people. Indeed, in her review of the anthology, Aurora Levins Morales points out that "bisexuality and mixed racial heritage feel so similar because they pose the same kind of challenge to society. Both represent a claim to a complex humanity that undermines deeply held ideas of category: the societal belief in immutable, biologically based groupings of human beings" (Morales 1992, 24).

5. According to the editors of Bi Any Other Name, "Monosexual is a term coined by the bisexual movement to mean anyone (gay or heterosexual) who is attracted to just one sex, their own or the opposite one" (Hutchins and Kaahumanu 1991, 10).

6. By saying this I wish in no way to question the tremendous usefulness and timeliness of this anthology. Apart from reassuring me that my own thoughts and experiences were shared by many other people, the anthology has also provided an important starting point for the present study of bisexuality and lesbian ethics.

7. I take the term "universalizing" from Sedgwick's useful distinction between "minoritizing" and "universalizing" understandings of homo/heterosexual definition. According to the first view, homo/heterosexual definition is "an issue of active importance primarily for a small, distinct, relatively fixed homosexual minority"; from the latter perspective, it is an "issue of continuing, determinative importance in the lives of people across the spectrum of sexualities" (Sedgwick 1990, 1). My linkage between "universalizing" and "queer" is one that emerges clearly within recent work in queer theory. Thus, to Michael Warner, the preference for the term "queer" over "lesbian" and "gay" "represents, among other things, an aggressive impulse of generalization; it rejects a minoritizing logic of toleration or simple political interest-representation in favor of a more thorough resistance to regimes of the normal. The universalizing utopianism of queer theory does not entirely replace more minority-based versions of lesbian and gay theory—nor could it, since normal sexuality and the machinery of enforcing it do not bear down equally on everyone" (Warner 1991, 16).

REFERENCES

Butler, Judith. 1990. *Gender trouble*. New York: Routledge.

Churchill, Caryl. 1985. *Plays*. London: Methuen.

Däumer, Elisabeth. 1991. Feminist biphobia; or, what does sexuality have to do with gender? Paper presented at North Central Women's Studies Association conference, 19 October, Athens, Ohio.

de Lauretis, Teresa, ed. 1991. Special issue of *Differences: A Journal of Feminist Cultural Studies* 3(2).

Frye, Marilyn. 1990. Do you have to be a lesbian to be a feminist? *off our backs* August/September.

Fuss, Diana. 1989. *Essentially speaking*. New York: Routledge.

———. ed. 1991. *inside/out: Lesbian theories, gay theories*. New York: Routledge.

Hoagland, Sarah Lucia. 1988. *Lesbian ethics: Toward new value*. Palo Alto: Institute of Lesbian Studies.

Hutchins, Loraine, and Lani Kaahumanu, eds. 1991. *Bi any other name: Bisexual people speak out*. Boston: Allyson Publications.

Morales, Aurora Levins. 1992. First but not least. Review of *Bi any other name: Bisexual people speak out*, ed. Loraine Hutchins and Lani Kaahumanu. *Women's Review of Books* 9(6): 23-24.

Orlando, Lisa. 1991. Loving whom we choose. In *Bi any other name*. See Hutchins and Kaahumanu.

Queen, Carol A. 1991. The queer in me. In *Bi any other name*. See Hutchins and Kaahumanu.

Sedgwick, Eve Kosofsky. 1990. *Epistemology of the closet*. Berkeley: University of California Press.

Tallen, Bette S. 1990. How inclusive is feminist political theory? Questions for lesbians. In *Lesbian philosophies and cultures*, ed. Jeffner Allen. Albany: State University of New York Press.

Warner, Michael. 1991. Introduction: Fear of a queer planet. *Social Text* 29: 3-17.

Weeks, Jeffrey. 1985. *Sexuality and its discontents*. London: Routledge and Kegan Paul.

Wittig, Monique. 1981. One is not born a woman. *Feminist Issues* 1(2): 47-54.

Male Lesbians and the Postmodernist Body

JACQUELYN N. ZITA

This essay explores the criteria for lesbian identity attribution through the case study of "male lesbians": biological males who claim to be lesbians. I analyze such sex/gender identity attribution through the lens of postmodernism, which provides a workable theoretical framework for "male lesbian" identities. My conclusions explore the historicity and cultural constructedness of the body's sex/gender identities, revealing the limitations of both "the postmodernized body" and "the essentialized modernist body."

The owner's manual, interior, and T-shirt all say Porsche. But it still runs like a Volkswagen. And no matter how much you scream at it, beat it, love it, or hate it, it is still, deep down a Volkswagen. . . . I felt somewhat awkward about a car analogy, but I love cars and my Volkswagen is very much a part of my life and my identity. No, it does not have a Porsche engine in it, but I have often felt that I'm a lesbian trapped inside a man's body.
(Commentary written by an undergraduate male student)

My Future Memories: Being the recently discovered ideas of a twentieth-century penis-wielding adrogynite; or, The possible accounting of a lesbian trapped in a man's body.
(Essay title written by an undergraduate male student)

You're not welcome in this bar/ You're not welcome at this party/ You're not welcome in my home. And I say I don't know why separatists won't let me in—I'm probably the only lesbian to have successfully castrated a man and gone on to laugh about it on stage, in print and on national television.
(Transsexual Kate Bornstein, 1991)

Hypatia vol. 7, no. 4 (Fall 1992) © by Jacquelyn N. Zita

The "male lesbian" seems to be an oxymoron. Yet I have met more than a few. Other lesbians report similar encounters. Is there a problem here? Our commonsense definition of "lesbian" as a woman who has emotional and sexual relationships with or erotic desires for other women renders the "male lesbian" a foolish fantasy since "sex with a woman" in his case would clearly make him heterosexual. My personal response to "male lesbians" has often been a mixture of suspicion, befuddlement, and sometimes anger toward the arrogance of this appropriation. These are men who claim not merely to act like lesbians or to be lesbian-identified or to feel like lesbians, but *to be* lesbians, to take on the identity of lesbian as I have in my own existence as a genetic female. They are sometimes men who claim to be more lesbian than I am in our conflicting interpretations of lesbian writings. They are usually men who want access to lesbian-only space in all its varieties.

Feminists have struggled for years with the concept of a male feminist. While some are willing to acknowledge that there are men who are trustworthy and who can join feminist circles by virtue of sharing an ideological perspective and by giving up some power and privilege, others fall back onto body ontologies: "No, they can't really be feminists; they're not women." From this perspective, the difference of sex is perceived as an insurmountable obstacle to becoming a real feminist in some deeply authentic sense. Regarding the "male lesbian," these same sentiments bring the body even more into focus: "No, you can't be a lesbian; you're not a woman." Being a lesbian seems to require more obviously and at least minimally a certain kind of body. It is questionable whether men can be authentic feminists; it *seems* unquestionable that men can not be lesbians. Only the second possibility interests me.

Why take this seriously? I am intrigued by the chimera of the "male lesbian" and the questions posed by this construction of identity within recent postmodernist theorizing on the body. If, according to some postmodernists, the body is itself a product of discursive construction and a field of interpretative possibilities that can occupy different locations or positionalities, what prevents a male body from occupying the positionality of "woman" or "lesbian"? How does any body, even one with XX sex chromosomes and primary sex characteristics identified as female, become a woman? Is it possible to become a woman trapped in a male body? Wouldn't a preference for women in this case imply a lesbian trapped in a male body? How do lesbians know when we are with other lesbians? Are genetic males who claim to be lesbians exhibiting great pretense or denial toward the real meaning of their genitals or their sexual desires? How do genitals or desires come to mean anything? What makes any sex or gender identity real when it is possible that humans make up these meanings through the disciplinary practices of "doing gender" or "having sex"? Why should we privilege genital anatomies in defining the truth of our sex? In light of these questions, the "male lesbian" strikes me as a proverbial Trickster whose self-proclaimed identification presents an interesting philosophical puzzle.

In this essay I will explore this special case of lesbian identity through an analysis of how sex, gender, and sexual identities are established by heterosexual codes of the dominant sex culture and by similar rules informing various lesbian communities. I examine "lesbian identity" as a construction defined by normative positioning, empirical inspection, and sex-specific acts. In each of these frameworks, the "male lesbian" creates a stress on established social categories, which are further challenged by postmodernist theorizing about the body. Using the theoretical tactics of postmodernism, a male can argue his way into "lesbian-only" community as a "lesbian." "He" becomes a "she" who desires "her." Surprisingly for me, my exploration of this special case has lead to a critique of postmodernism as well as a new way of conceptualizing the cultural construction of the sexed body.

HISTORICITY OF THE BODY

Human bodies as a species form have remained relatively constant throughout Western history. What has changed more dramatically are the ways in which subjectivity has been embodied and made sense of its embodiment. Premodernist, modernist, and postmodernist modes of embodiment provide a topography for thinking about the history of these changes.

In the Western premodernist world, bodies were tightly integrated into the collectives of kinship and social wholes. In deeply internal connections, bodies belonged to larger social aggregates—the family, the manor, the church, the village, the clan or the tribe and were in a sense owned and controlled by higher social powers that determined the body's place, meaning, and use. Only with great difficulty can words such as "homosexual" be applied to isolate bodies in a premodernist world, since "individuals" who "owned their body and its sexual rights" did not exist as a possible self-construction. Bodies were woven into the tapestry of larger social aggregates. David Halperin (1990) makes this point when he argues against using the modernist concept of "homosexual" to categorize male-to-male sexual activity in Greek society. Such sex, Halperin contends, was used to reconstitute the hierarchical structure of male social relations, to solidify and honor social status roles between older and younger Greek males. Sex was not being used to constitute homosexual identities in the modernist sense.

The modernist construction of "the homosexual" awaited three important historical developments: the Cartesian separation of the body from contexts of folk and social nexus (the construction of the intelligible body), the "invention" of sexuality as a truth about the body and as such a truth about the individual (the construction of the clinical body), and, consequently, the historical emergence of shameless communities of sexual minorities (the construction of sexual identity politics). An example of early foreshadowings of a modernist homosexual politic can be seen in 1726 when William Brown responded to his arrest at one of London's Molly Houses with the claim that "there is no crime in making what use I please of my own body," a claim that reflects a new sentiment of private ownership of one's own body and a public flaunting of kinship moralism. In the modernist world, individuals would increasingly flock to networks and communities where sex attraction drew strangers together and where the organization of sexuality relied increasingly on individualization of the subject's agency in sex.

By the end of the nineteenth century, socioerotic identities were constructed by reference to preferred "object choice." This aspect of personhood was seen as a deep truth about the individual and as a resource for creating communities of affinity. In the transition into this secular world, the status of homosexuality moved from sin to pathology, as bodies were assigned a place on either side of the great homo/hetero divide. Linking sexual deviance to pathologies, whether mental or physical, required a new authority—the modern medical expert— who saw the body as a thing controlling and defining the stricken homosexual. Through a confluence of institutional changes, these discursive practices both created and discovered "the pervert" and "the invert" signified by "abnormal" object choice and gender dysphoria. Many lesbian and gay liberation movements have been built on a reversal of modernist sex discourse (Foucault 1978).

A critique of the modernist body has been recently articulated in postmodernist thinking about the body. Although postmodernism is primarily thought of as an epistemic critique of Enlightenment philosophy, its belief in the power of reason, and the autonomy of the "knowing" self, this critique of traditional epistemology also spawns a new way of conceptualizing the cultural constructedness of the body. By challenging the Archimedean ideal of disembodied knowledge, postmodernism brings into focus first of all the "locatedness" of one's body as a place from which particular viewpoints on reality can be generated. Thus, any universal reading of reality from one perspective can be challenged by the multiplicity of different selves in different locations. For some postmodernists, subjectivities can ambulate into these multiple locations, each generating a particular discursive view of the world, which in turn "constructs" the subjectivity of that location. The subject becomes a product of discourse or intersecting textualities, as the world becomes a ceaseless play of interlocking and conflicting texts, spoken from different locations and negotiated across different perspectives.

The body under postmodernist imagery can be extracted from its historically concrete daily context and "shifted" into an ever-increasing multiplicity of positionalities, a creative movement, according to Suleiman (1986), which "invents" the body itself. The simple unities and stabilities of self in the modernist world are shattered in this choreography of multiple selves, as the body loses its surety of boundary and its fixity of truth and meaning. As Susan

Bordo has suggested, "here is where deconstruction may slip into its own fantasy of escape from human locatedness—by supposing that the critic can become wholly protean, by adopting endlessly shifting, seemingly inexhaustible vantage points, none of which are 'owned' by either the critic or the author of the text under examination" (Bordo 1990, 142). Similarly, the body becomes a portable site for reinventing the meanings of flesh.

I would like to explore this idea further in my reflections on "male lesbians." The theoretical assumptions of postmodernism seem to make possible the transmutation of male to female as a matter of shifting contextual locations that "reinvent" the body. Whereas modernism considers the body to be fixed, by nature, in its sexedness, the tactics of postmodernism suggest that there are indeed more things possible on heaven and earth than we are willing to grant a rightful status of being.

LESBIAN IDENTITY AS NORMATIVE POSITIONING

A lesbian is the rage of all women condensed to the point of explosion. (Radicalesbians 1971)

In the primacy of women, of women creating a new consciousness of and with each other, which is at the heart of women's liberation, and the basis of cultural revolution. (Radicalesbians 1971)

Feminism is the theory; lesbianism is the practice. (Ti-Grace Atkinson 1974)

In the early 1970s, an effort was made by some lesbians to remove lesbianism from its sex bed. Definitions of "lesbian" were desexualized and presented as a political choice. Lesbian feminists were represented as woman-identified, in contrast to heterosexual feminists, who were considered male-identified with their energies continuing to flow "backward toward our oppressors" (Radicalesbians 1971). This downnplay of sexual stigma purified the "female deviant," whose identity was less essentially defined by how and with whom she had sex (in all its graphically, clinically, and culturally hegemonic representations) and more essentially defined as a political position in opposition to heteropatriarchy. This approach, which disembodies "lesbianism" of saturated sex and separates it from explicit genital reference to the bodies and pleasures pursued by many lesbians, allows a possible port of entry—strained though it may be—for the "male lesbian." "Lesbian" becomes a role, a positionality open to insertion.

This is especially true if "lesbian" is defined as an ideological, ethical, or political posture: a way of being in the world or relating to others, a way of seeing the world which is "woman-identified" or "woman-seeing," a special

way of loving, preferring, or "sexing" women—any number of political oppositional practices engaging or disengaging the domination of heteropatriarchy.
I take it that many males who claim to be lesbians identify with these
ideological positions as preferable to masculinist options or as more "true to
their selves." Males who claim to be inside these "lesbian" positions may
embody in their actions or character a number of principles that comply with
these ways of being, relating, or acting in the world. In lesbian reader theory,
for example, a male might read a particular text like a lesbian or with a lesbian
sensibility and come to conclusions similar to those of a number of other
lesbian readers (Olano 1992). He could be said to share a normative worldview,
occupy a position or participate in a role that constitutes a significant component of lesbian identity.

The question remains—does he read *like a lesbian* or does he read *as a lesbian?*
Our "male lesbian" is likely to claim the latter. This shift from *a similarity claim*
to *an identity claim* assumes that we know what it means to do anything "as a
lesbian," and thus to know when we are in the presence of lesbians. The claim
that there is such a way of being, seeing, and doing is minimally epistemolog-
ically separatist: there must be some way in which lesbians are different from
other human beings and that way is what it means to be a lesbian. Some
lesbians do make such claims, but others don't. Given any normative definition
of "lesbian," there will always be some self-identified lesbians who do not fit
the norm and who are categorized as "male-identified," "gay," "educable or
not," or "not real lesbians." The "misfits" are frequently able to contest the
norms used to exclude them. Can our "male lesbian" similarly decry a totali-
tarianism of the norm?

Lesbian identity as normative positioning implies an identity construction
that is prescriptive and often exclusionary. For a male to claim a lesbian identity
in this normative sense is to claim to be a particular kind of lesbian, usually a
highly politicized lesbian who sees lesbianism as anti-establishment separation
from men or as a radical directive for social change. To be "lesbian" in this
sense is to be ethically or politically postured toward the world in a particular
way. Oddly, our "male lesbian" could claim to be a "male lesbian separatist,"
separating himself from other men and from his own body in order to be
ideologically consistent. A postmodernist perspective, which construes the
subject as protean and the body as a neutral field open to interpretation or as
constructed by its contingently discursive positionality, makes plausible this
creation of identity.

From a modernist perspective, however, a genetic male who claims to be
lesbian by virtue of occupying the normative positionality of "lesbian," while
clearly having the wrong body, is mistaken. The identity of lesbian, unlike
other positionalities, is defined by explicit reference to a particular kind of
body—namely female. His body is different, in fact "the opposite sex" of female
bodies, and certainly because of that, his bodily and embodied experiences will

in some ways be different from those of women. You have "to body" lesbian in order to be one. However, what does it mean "to body" lesbian? Am I assuming that there is something deeply incommensurable between a male's acting like a lesbian and my being a lesbian? Is it a male's XY chromosomes, his testosterone profile, testicles, sperm, penis, or ejaculate—in general the distribution of substances in his body—that makes it impossible for him to be a lesbian? From a modernist perspective, the answer relies on the physical criteria that we commonly use to demarcate one sex from the other; from a postmodernist perspective, we are thrown back onto the question of why the body is given this criteria-bound interpretation from among others.

Perhaps the issue here is not one of identifying some Lesbian X-Factor in the body or of justifiying sex-differentiation criteria, but simply a question of preference or desire. A male body is not what most lesbians hope to find under the sheets or under "her" clothes. If physical sexual preference is our reference, then lesbians are customarily defined by a preference for sexual encounters generally involving four breasts, two vaginas, and two clitorides, among other things. The male body is lacking. However, we may ask, what counts as having any of this? Women who have had mastectomies, vulvectomies, hysterectomies, and other surgical operations removing body parts can still claim to be female and self-declared lesbians. Likewise, persons who for whatever reason were born without any number of these parts may claim identities as women and sometimes as lesbians. Consider, for example, an individual born with testicular feminization, with an XY chromosomal constitution, undescended testicles, a short-ended vagina, a clitoris, labia minora and labia majora, who has been raised as a female only to discover at puberty, with the absence of menses, that "she" is a genetic male. "She" may continue to think of herself as female, feel comfortable with this, and if "she" experiences deep erotic desires for other females rather than males, "she" may choose to call herself "lesbian."

The defining mark of "female" in most instances is not the presence or absence of certain female body parts but the absence of phallic genitalia or their genetic correlates, a fixation confirmed by our culture's concern about the "overly enlarged clitoris," surgically corrected at birth to its proper life dimensions, and by chromosomal tests for female and not male athletes. But how much is too much? If a body exists with a "penoclitoris" but is incapable of producing sperm, what have we here? If a body has a smaller clitoris and the capacity of producing sperm, what have we here? If a lesbian friend is given a sex reassignment after a chromosome test, what have we here? My fear is that we as lesbians too quickly subscribe to a very rigid cultural binarism by insisting that bodies fit consistently and permanently into two exclusive and exhaustive sex types, using the same genetic-gonadal-anatomical master norms of the dominant culture. Is it always the case that having nothing short of a female body is what is required before one can feel like a woman? become a woman? know that one is woman-to-woman? before one can "body lesbian"?

To further complicate the issue, lesbians who fall for men sometimes claim that they do not feel like they are any different from their former selves. In spite of community responses to their purported "backsliding," they insist on claming a lesbian identity, just as Jan Clausen (1990) has identified herself as "the dyke sleeping with a man." In this case, the experienced continuity of self-identity survives, while the naming of difference is lost. Others may be inclined to describe these phenomena as bi-phobia, acute denial, unusual sex fantasy, or just plain confusion, guilt, and cowardice. The pregnant man-loving lesbian, who claims to be a lesbian, who happens to be in love with a man, who, as luck would have it, happens to be a "male lesbian" (a "sperm-bearing lesbian," in this case), has created a miracle for *some* lesbian couples: how to get pregnant together! Not all lesbians desire this. Is there not something missing from this picture?

LESBIAN IDENTITY AS BODILY INSPECTION: A QUESTION OF EVIDENCE?

What exactly does "membership" in the queer community entail? Who makes up the rules and decides who belongs and who doesn't? (Robyn Oches 1990)

A National Lesbian Purity Board is called for in this time of wavering allegiance to the cunt. Laminated identity cards with small, colorful photographs could easily fit into one's wallet. And random vaginal smears would be helpful in culling imposters from the ranks. (Mary Wings 1990)

At first women simply undressed for "visual inspection," or what the press called "nude parades," in front of a panel of gynecologists. In 1968, the International Olympic Committee (IOC) adopted a chromosome measure. . . . It's called the buccal smear, and it has nothing to do with the way a woman looks, feels or was raised. Instead, it's based upon the sex chromosome pattern found in cells scraped from inside her cheek. (Alison Carlson 1991, 26)

It would seem that the dilemma posed by the "male lesbian" could be resolved in most cases by bodily inspection. Sex identity is understood to have clear biological criteria, measurable and countable in kind and number. Sex chromosomes, hormonal profiles, genitals, gonads, and secondary sex characteristics are traits often used, in various combinations and with different weights, to determine the male or female sex status of a given body. Since lesbians are females, the special case of the "male lesbian" can be quickly closed. However, I will explore an incident that confounds the simplicity of this procedure.

I have heard a story about a lesbian who was an active member in a metropolitan lesbian community. She defined herself as a lesbian separatist and in the late 1970s was active in a community coffeehouse that was a social gathering place for lesbians. She lived in a lesbian collective, where one day the awful truth was discovered. She had male genitalia and had over the years been "passing" as a lesbian. The community response was swift and definitive: reject, abject, exclude. Friends who had known "her" as a lesbian turned against "him." The coffeehouse was no longer a welcome space for "him."

Why did this discovery make such a difference? In oppressed communities there is obviously a fear of intruders, spies, and government agents, but in a lesbian community these will most likely be women passing as lesbians rather than "male lesbians." From all that was known, this individual was not a spy (unless considered so by definition). Understandably, male entry into lesbian- or woman-only spaces is intrusive. However, this individual felt like a woman, was attracted to women, was at home in lesbian separatist spaces and politics, was reliable and trustworthy in those relationships, and had for years self-iden- tified as a lesbian though outwardly celibate and body-shy. The community test had little to do with how "she" felt, how "she" was raised, or how "she" appeared in public. Was anatomy a justifiable reason for the community's response? Would surgical reconstruction of the body to the anatomically correct requirements of membership have resolved this problem? Or would the knife always fail to go deep enough to cut out the traces of difference disqual- ifying "him" from community membership? How does anyone successfully "pass" as a lesbian?

In both the frameworks explored so far—lesbian identity based on norma- tive positioning and lesbian identity based on bodily inspection—the "male lesbian" emerges as a figure oddly out of place. This person claims to be "lesbian" but seems to be male in somatic appearance and heterosexual in his preference for women. The challenge of the "male lesbian" reflects back onto the practices we commonly use to ascribe sex and gender categories to the body, raising some new possibilities for undoing how we have done such things.

LESBIAN IDENTITY AS DOING SEX AND GENDER

In attribution theories about gender and sexual identity, there are two starting points of reference: self-to-other and other-to-self. In the first, the attribution of gender or sex identity is ascribed to the self by the self and presented to others; in the second, it is ascribed by others to the self and presented to the self by these others. I will label the first a "self-intending attribution" and the second an "other-extending attribution." It is usually the case that self-intending and other-extending attributions are the same, as when the self sees itself as female (sex identity) as do others or sees itself as a woman (social sex identity) as do others. For the individual, the consolidation of gender and sex identity as a meaningful aspect of self is an achievement that requires this mutually reinforcing and consistent interaction between self and others. However, when self-intending attributions and other-extending attributions contradict one another, the criteria for making such attributions come into question as does the application to a specific individual. The case of a "male lesbian" claiming to be "a woman trapped in a male body" presents an intriguing example of this. Here the inner sense of self may be regarded as a deeper "figuration of the body" that rests uneasily in its externalized somatic form. In this case, self-intending and other-extending attributions of the same body may contradict one another.

A grid that is helpful in understanding the different kinds of sex and gender attributions and their relationships to one another is the following:

Identity Category	Oppositional Categories	
Sex*	Female	Male
Gender**	Feminine	Masculine
Socioerotic*** (heterosexual)	Male	Female

*Sex Identity is considered a physical category where bodies are sorted into clearly identifiable kinds, female and male, on the basis of biological criteria.

**Gender Identity is a behavioral and psychological category in which individuals are considered to fit or misfit expected behaviors, functions, and personal attributes associated with one sex or the other.

***Socioerotic Identity is a behavioral and psychological category in which individuals are differentiated from one another on the basis of erotic desire for and/or sexual acts with the same or "opposite" sex. This is also referred to as sexual preference or sexual orientation identity.

Several comments need to made about this sex/gender grid (Penelope 1990).[1] It maps the relationships and assumptions most commonly operative in the everyday world: that there are two kinds of people (male and female), that males are masculine and females feminine, and that everyone is heterosexual. Where there are misfits, there are "mistakes of nature" or "sicknesses of soul." Commonly held ontological beliefs about the body assume that these identities represent naturally determined facts about the body and the self. According to a "naturalist perspective," this order of things is nature.

There is another interpretation of the grid. Some social constructionists argue that all three of these binary categories are imposed on the continuum of human natures, forcefully dividing bodies into mutually exclusive and exhaustive types, ignoring the significance of "misfits" and pressing a relationship of entailment between these categorical levels. From a naturalist perspective, "maleness" implies "masculinity" implies "female" as object choice, implies "heterosexual"—reflecting a seeming logical and maturational order to the body's identities. In contrast, some social constructionists argue that establishing such "linear" identities is an achievement of many discursive practices and policing mechanisms that invest in the body and inspire a desire in the subject to belong unambiguously to one social sex category or the other. The grid does not reflect nature; it reflects constructions of sex, gender, and sexuality as meanings and identities made out of nature.

There is one additional composite category that combines all three of these identities into an individual's "social sex." The "social sex category" is what it means "to be a man" or "to be a woman" in the fullest culturally specific and culturally appropriate meaning of these categories—a gendered ideal. Popular belief assumes that membership in a social sex category is not completely confirmed by simple genital inspection: it requires and is further confirmed by evidence of appropriate gender and sexual orientation presentations. To be a *real man* in the fullest sense requires biological, psychological, social, and sexual evidence. Accordingly, gay men are stereotypically not seen as real men, and lesbians are not seen as real women. While both are seen as less than human (i.e., less than a real man), not being a real man demotes one to "womanly status"; not being a real woman demotes one to nonexistence, if one is really not a man. The personages of the "heterosexual stud," "reproductive breadwinner," "the pregnable wife," "the feminine faggot," and the nonexistence of lesbians are derivatives of these representational strategies.

John Stoltenberg defines "male sexual identity" as "the conviction, held by most people born with penises, that they are male and not female, that they belong to the male sex." He also notes:

> A society predicated on the notion that there are two "opposite" and "complementary" sexes, this idea not only makes sense, it becomes sense; the very idea of a male sexual identity produces sensation, produces the meaning of sensation, becomes the meaning of how one's body feels. . . . Most people born with a penis between their legs grow up aspiring to feel and act unambiguously male, longing to belong to the sex that is male and daring not to belong to the sex that is not, and feeling this urgency for a visceral and constant verification of their male sexual identity—for a fleshy connection to manhood—as the driving force of their life. The drive does not originate in the anatomy. The sensations derive from the idea. The idea gives the feelings social meaning; the idea determines which sensations shall be sought. (Stoltenberg 1990, 31)

According to Stoltenberg, in sexual activity itself there is a correlation between doing a specific act in a specific way (what, with whom, and how) and one's self-intended socioerotic attribution: "for many people, for instance, the act of fucking makes their sexual identity feel more real than it does at other times, and they can predict from experience that this feeling of greater certainty will last for at least a while after each time they fuck " (Stoltenberg 1990, 32). The repetition of sex acts is used as a partial confirmation procedure—as significant evidence for assignment to appropriate sex, gender, socioerotic, and social sex categories. Sex acts in a sense "sex" the body. The intensification of sex in Western cultures has a lot to do with maintaining the stability of these categories in a modernist world.

Using the sex-gender grid and Stoltenberg's insights into the cultural construction of the "sexed body," we can understand how the commonplace construction of lesbian identity relies on the assumptions behind this grid: a "lesbian" is someone with a female body and someone who is consistently and erotically drawn to or more regularly than other females engaged in genital sex acts with other females. When such a person claims a lesbian identity, there is consistency between her self-intended attribution and other-extending identity attributions ascribed to her. By claiming or being claimed by such an identity, she becomes a special category of person, defined by her sex and her sex acts, whether potential or actualized. As Stoltenberg points out, confirmation of socioerotic identities rests on sex-specific sex acts or, I might add, on the absence of expected sex-specific sex acts. In this commonplace construction of lesbian identity, bodies come to occupy an historically preestablished category of existence. The "male lesbian" is not saying that occupants of this category are not lesbians, but that the category needs to be stretched—not by adding men, but by adding men who happen to be lesbians.

MALE LESBIANS: THE UNDOING OF SEX AND GENDER

"Do we truly need a true sex?" This question, asked by Michel Foucault in his preface to the English edition of *Herculine Barbin: Being the Recently Discovered Memoirs of the Nineteenth-Century French Hermaphrodite* (1980), brings into focus two considerations: how do we construct a "true biological sex" for any body and, once we understand how we do this, do we truly need to continue doing this to ourselves and others? In modernist Eurocentric cultures, baseline criteria for such attribution appear to be genitocentric. Kessler and McKenna describe the criteria as follows:

> There are two, and only two, genders[2] (male and female); one's gender is invariant; genitals are the essential sign of gender; any exceptions to two genders are not taken seriously; there are no transfers from one gender to another except ceremonial ones;

everyone must be classified as a member of one gender or
another; the male/female dichotomy is a "natural" one; membership in one gender or another is "natural" (Kessler and
McKenna 1978, 113-14).

This "natural attitude" toward the sex identity is for Kessler, McKenna, and
Foucault a matter of cultural construction, achieved either through the transactions of symbolic interaction (Kessler and McKenna 1978) or through the
discursive practices of power that make "true sex" an important truth about
the body (Foucault 1978). In both approaches, sex and gender attribution are
activities, something that we do to ourselves (self-intending attribution) or to
others (other-extending attribution) within layer upon layer of institutional
controls and confirmation procedures. The challenge presented by the "male
lesbian" is whether or not we can undo how this is done. To have a sex, gender,
or sexual identity requires self-presentation and displays of behavior that are
interpreted, read, and finally judged as evidence for belonging to one social
sex category or the other, using the grid of identities and linear entailment I
discussed above. Do we truly need to go on doing sex and gender as we have
done it in the past?

The "male lesbian" usually lives in a body originally assigned at birth to the
male sex category. He was expected to take on a masculine gender identity and
to maintain an active heterosexual practice, all evidence of his membership
in and allegiance to the social sex category of manhood. Undoing this involves
two generic and any number of specific transsexing strategies. The two generic
strategies ask us first of all to reconsider the criteria we use to assign "sex
identity" (to prioritize criteria in a different manner, to overlook certain
characteristics and valorize others or to replace our fixation on a select set of
"essentialized" biological criteria) and, second, to become active "readers of
the body," implementing the new criteria into our everyday life transactions.
Specific strategies designed to match self-intending sex attribution with other-
extending attributions can be marshaled in the following ways:

1. Change the physical structure of the body to fit the genital
morphological criteria for "female"; ask that others overlook
the man-made reconstructions of these genitalia and the chromosomal traces left unaltered in your body (*a postoperative
transsexual strategy*).

2. Valorize the feeling of inner certainty of being a woman
trapped in a male body; ask that others look beyond the somatic
form of your body and look for signs of this "inner figuration"
of your body's sex or its reconstitution in deep gender identity
(*a transgendering strategy*).

3. Request a reading of your body that de-centers genital and gonadal anatomy as the essential criterion for sex identity; ask that others "overlook" these indicators in attributing sex identity to you (*a genital de-essentializing strategy*).

4. Engage in "genderfuck," taking seriously the centrality of meaning-in-sex-acts as sufficient criterion for sex category membership and construct sex scenes in which your sex acts take on the meaning of acts performed by the "opposite sex"; ask that others agree to these readings and to this criterion for sex category membership (*a special "genderfuck" strategy*).

All of these strategies allow the body to enter a conversation with others, with a request for a particular reading of the body, an acceptance into a particular group, and a respect for the subject's desire to name "her" own sex identity. Rejection of this would simply mean that the wayward "male lesbian" must search until "she" finds a community of "lesbians" ready to embrace her membership and life energies as a lesbian. Note I have not questioned the authenticity of "her" sexual desire for other females. "She" claims to be "monosexual" (rather than bisexual) and a "lesbian." What is at stake here is whether, through negotiation of behaviors, interpretations, expectations, meanings, and agreed-upon readings of the body, a genetic male, usually penis-bearing and sperm-producing, can find a community of lesbians who would welcome "her" as a "lesbian" into their community. Is anything more required? As Sarah Hoagland has suggested, the "essentialism" that we may wish to give to "lesbianism" is a product of community will, not a metaphysic threatening to pound the daylights out of our mistakes:

> I think of lesbian community as a ground of lesbian being, a ground of possibility, a context in which we perceive each other essentially as lesbians, a context in which we create lesbian meaning. This context exists, not because it has walls, but because we focus on each other as lesbians. (Hoagland 1988, 9)

If "essentializing" what it is to be "lesbian" is enacted by the way we focus on each other as lesbians in any particular community—by a consensus of community will and vision—then the "male lesbian" can be seen as requesting a certain kind of selective focus from a particular community. Strategy (1) asks that we "essentialize" external genital and primary sex characteristics (regardless of origin) as criteria of membership and acceptance. Strategies (2) and (3) ask that we *overlook* the body as we habitually read it and attend to other evidence of sex identity. In these readings, the penis is not disposed of, but its significance is deposed: it is no longer the phallus. It remains an appendage, useful perhaps, interesting perhaps, a location of pleasure like the clitoris, but a perforate clitoris with some optional functions. As Kessler and McKenna have suggested:

> Some people, at some points in their lives, might wish to be identified as sperm or egg-cell carriers. Except for those times, here need be no differentiation among people on any of the dichotomies which gender implies. (Kessler and McKenna 1978, 166)

Option (4), which challenges our "natural attitudes" toward sex identity even more, suggests the possibility of temporary or permanent travel or transformation into the body of the "opposite sex" without surgery or cosmetic reconstruction. I realize that I am using the word "genderfuck" in a special way, since most practitioners of genderfuck are not so much interested in "passing" or "becoming" the opposite sex as much as tampering with the codes of sex identity by mixing male and female, masculine and feminine, man and woman signifiers on one body. I am using the term "genderfuck" to indicate a means of passage from one sex to the other through the meanings given to sex-specific sex acts. Within this special framework of "genderfuck," a male can have sex "as a female" with another female (perhaps genetic), where "having sex as a female" might be defined as a style of erotic encounter that de-centers attention from the penis and its essentially definitive acts of intercourse. Sex acts, mutually interpreted as "female" sex acts, would establish membership for both bodies in the same sex category. In and through such sex performances, both subjects come to enjoy the sexually expressed "femaleness" of both bodies. "Genderfuck" for females can involve a female fucking another body "as a man" and in those acts claiming identity in the male sex category. When appropriated in lesbian contexts, "genderfuck" would allow two genetic females in a relationship to be different sexes. It would also allow heterosexual women to enjoy "heterosexing" with another woman or heterosexuals to have "queer sex." Sex identity becomes transitive, liminal, and momentary—a veritable riot against *un sexe véritable*.

Joan Nestle explores this unspeakable border-crossing: "I feel I am being kind to myself as I caress the false cock. No need to hide the word any more. No need to hide my desires. Let me be butch for you; I have been a femme for so long. I know what your body is calling for" (Nestle 1987, 132). Nestle's declaration of desire can be variously interpreted—as a trans*gendering* moment in lesbian sex, as a pan*gendered* exploration of lesbian erotic terrain, as role occupation in one of many erotic scripts for lesbian sex, as just another way to be a lesbian in the thrill of unspeakable passion, or as a way to do something else with your hands. However, many lesbians are loath to interpret this as "wanting to be or to be with a man." Where in lesbian erotics is there a space for female transsexual desire, however temporary or continuous, however "metaphysicalized" by roles and role-playing or by the chimeric masking of "butch" and "femme"? Why is there such hesitation to open up the possibility of a "lesbian male" trapped in a genetic female body? I am not arguing that all lesbians are this or want this or that Nestle's statement implies this, but I am suggesting that lesbian communities may house a small minority of transsexuals just as one finds transsexuals in gay, bisexual, and heterosexual communities.

The existence of a transsexual minority in lesbian communities has been highly undertheorized, a situation that is complicated by transsexual males and females "passing" as lesbians. At the 1991 Michigan Womyn's Music Festival, the following commentary was made:

> There have been transsexuals on the land for many years, mostly undetected. Many are uncomfortable about revealing too much about themselves, fearful of encountering hostile reactions from participants. . . . Some women would exclude transsexuals on the basis that they have not been socialized as women. Should we then exclude women who were raised as boys? How about men raised as girls? If we accept a person's sex at birth is immutable, should we allow female-to-male transsexuals at the festival on the basis that they are still "really" females, penises and all? (Janis 1992, 12)

Transsexuals as a sex minority in lesbian communities may desire a nonsurgical means of transsexing, in which their sex identity can be liberated from soma and respecified by sex-specific sex acts. Such an interpretation meets a great deal of opposition in some lesbian communities. I suspect that the reluctance on the part of some lesbians to embrace preoperative female lesbian-identified transsexuals is not so much a function of sex-negative attitudes as a desire to defraud the stereotype of the *man*nish lesbian that has been so abusively used against lesbians and to define lesbianism as a political and sexual positionality in opposition to men or male dominance. Perhaps this politics of opposition could be separated from the desire to engage in the erotics of "opposite sexing," a code of erotic scripts that is itself a cultural construction and arbitrary division of possible erotic terrains.

The challenge of the four transsexing strategies suggests the possibility of reversing the assumptions of our "natural attitude" toward sex and gender categories. I propose the following reversal on the ethnographic observations of Kessler and McKenna:

> There are two, and only two, sexes (male and female); one's sex can be variant; genitals are not necessarily the essential sign of sex; any exceptions to two sexes are to be taken seriously; there are transfers from one sex to another; everyone must be classified as a member of one sex or another; the male/female dichotomy is a constructed one; membership in one sex or another is

a matter of "passing" and consensus in "reading" the body one way or the other.

All that remains in place in this new schema of body travel is the binarism of the original grid. When that is abandoned, we bring into view many genders and many sexes—a thickness of contiguous diversity and individual uniqueness that escapes easy categorical theorization and provides the play of multiple transfers. The assumption of binarism and belief in the unalterable mono-persistence of one's sex and gender identities become suspect. However, the hold of this binarism and its fix on identity persists. Perhaps the desire to keep this binarism intensifies a desire to transgress constructed barriers, an erotic risk of transcategorical pleasure, rather than the risk of nonidentity in an in/different world of many genders and many sexes. Perhaps some bodies and not others really are set by this binarism at a very early age. Regardless of individual variation, the politics of this culturally specific binarism are best captured by Kate Bornstein, a self-identifed lesbian transsexual:

> Why is there gender? Why do we insist that there's this? The only thing it comes down to is that it gives roughly half the people the chance to be oppressive to roughly the other half. That's the only reason that I can see that we keep it in place. There's always an "other" for half the people to oppress. And if it were all fluid, if it were kind of rainbowy kinds of genders, who could oppress whom? Everybody would be an "other." (Quoted in Myles 1990, 49)

THE RETURN OF THE BODY

Women only.
    Lesbians only.
        Women-born women only.
            Genetic female dykes only.
                No boys over the age of twelve.

These signs that hang around the edges of what precious little lesbian space there is in the world suggest that lesbians not only would like some time to be alone together in social public spaces but that lesbians are also suspicious of males trying to invade community-defined lesbian-only space. I would agree that these suspicions are well-founded. There may be little reason to trust these maneuvers. However, the "male lesbian" presents an interesting dilemma for community standards, especially where the rights of a subject to name "her" sex seem parallel to the rights of a subject to name "her" sexuality. The "male lesbian" who feels like a woman stuck in a male body may attempt to align "her" external male body by altering the body's somatic form, by altering its cosmetic appearance, or by requesting a different read of the body's sex. All of these strategies described earlier attempt to do away with the contradiction between a self-intending sex identity and other-extending sex attribution by maintaining the original entailments of the sex-gender grid. To this extent these strategies oddly conserve and reinforce linear constructions of sex and gender identities, but they are also strategies that can be used to argue male admittance into lesbian community.

Perhaps this is seen as the path of least resistance. One might ask why "woman" and "lesbian" are arenas of contestation, rather than the culturally constructed world of "heteromasculinized maleness." For some men, feelings of identity kinship with lesbians don't require a sex reassignment as much as a space for different ways of being a man. It follows that such men need not hastily reverse the sex binarism "if not man, then woman" because of deeply felt disloyalty to masculine codes of social sex category membership. However, it may be easier to contest the meaning of "lesbian" and "woman" than to contest the normative rules for heterosexual males. In other circumstances, alleged "male lesbians" may suffer from body hatred and self-loathing that is better treated by release from sex binarism and the narrow confines of heteromasculinity than by the surgeon's knife. If there were not two sexes but many and in turn many genders and sexualities, a number of different ways to inhabit the body could be engendered (Butler 1990). A "male lesbian" could then see himself as multiply gendered and erotic. No longer needing to infuse the category "lesbian" with his maleness, he could become a "lesbian-iden-tifed-non-lesbian-hating male," who loves his own body and acknowledges his heterosexual privilege. However, challenging the norms of the heteromascul-ine world is perhaps more hazardous than gutting out a space where a man can become a lesbian. Similarly, attempts to challenge the categorical binarism of sex/gender identities seem to meet an unmovable material resistance to change. The "male lesbian" is endangered in both straight and lesbian worlds: "she" doesn't want to be a man, "she" can't be a lesbian, and "she" desires women lovers, preferably lesbians, who don't want "her." It's difficult to find a support group with others of "her" own kind.

The paradox of the "male lesbian" reveals some insights into how sex identity attributions are customarily established for all of us in our culture. Membership in social sex categories is determined through gender performance and sex acts, through meanings imposed on the body and its anatomical functions, through the uptake of community readings of the body's sex, and through the essentializing of genital anatomy as the overdetermined master text for "sexing" the body. The range of lived interpretations for the body is less determined by anatomy and more determined by the interpretations and prescriptions given to that anatomy. The perspectives of postoperative "lesbian transexuals," transgendered "male lesbians," genitally de-essentialized "male lesbians," and the transsexing practitioners of "genderfuck" suggest that

1. sex categories themselves are less unified and stable than everyday thinking admits,

2. criteria for membership in sex categories can be contested,

3. sex identity may be experienced by some as transitive and liminal, as genuinely dysphoric and discontinuous, and

4. "stability" in sex identity is an ongoing achievement in particular contexts.

Postmodernism supplies a set of ontological commitments needed for a world in which the body appears to be malleable, protean, and constructed through and within discourse. Postmodernism makes the "male lesbian" a real possibility.

However, I remain stuck in a modernist closet. My mind crawls uneasily with the question, how can a male really be a lesbian? Is there any way to reconcile my resistance with postmodernism and its marvelous insights into the constructedness of the body and the playful potentials of the flesh? Has the body all but disappeared in the wash of multivalences and multivocalities? One of the consequences of this traveling flesh as it bends in and out of categories is that there may be no such thing as lesbians. If men can become lesbians, if women who sleep with men can still be lesbians, if anybody can visit lesbian positionality or transsex it with anybody else, then what would such a category really name? Postmodernism not only makes the "male lesbian" possible; it may in addition make lesbianism, at least as we have known it, impossible. The theory seems a bit pitiful.

Perhaps we should pursue the male lesbian as "she" leaves the charmed circle of her lesbian community. It is clear that a "male lesbian" best thrives in "her" charmed circle of postmodernist lesbian friends. However, entry into the charmed circle also implies the possiblity of exit into an external world that overshadows the dear delights of the circle's warmth. When our "male lesbian" leaves this circle, outsiders will most likely not read his body in the same way or take kindly to his identity claim. He will be seen as male by assumptions regarding his genitalia if nothing else, and will be granted the full registers of meaning, privilege, history, and expectation that go with that.

What about the "male lesbian" who successfully passes in the straight world as a "female"? Isn't it the case that successful passing in that world would "make up" the sex of "her" body? The difference between the response of the charmed circle in the lesbian community and the straight world is that the request made in the postmodernist lesbian circle is to change the criteria by which the body's sex is determined, to rename the sex of the body so that the body is seen, read, experienced, and respected as the "sex" desired by the authorizing subject. This is an ontological shift into the "opposite" sex category, not a masquerade of belonging to it. The straight world may be fooled by the artifice of a passing "female" but also violent in its discovery of the "truth"—"you can get killed for this sort of thing." This is because the straight world is overly invested in a naturalist ontology supporting sex binarism and the strict linear entailments of the sex/gender grid: a man with a vagina and a woman with a penis do not (and shall not) exist. "Passing" implies pretense and lying, not a new ontological reading of the body's sex. Postmodernism with its notion of the body as an invention of discursivity makes plausible the "transsexualization" of the body, a possibility dependent on the adoption of new criteria and alternative readings of the body's sex. In this context, the subject's desire to "sex" a body of one's own becomes a defensible right. However, when our "male lesbian" fails to maintain a consistent female identity at all times, this is not a failure in postmodernist imagination but an indication of the individual's inability to control overdetermined hegemonic readings from the outside world forced on the body. When these readings numerically outnumber the less frequent "lesbian" attributions in the charmed circle, this external world definitively "sexes" his body. From this perspective, conferring a "sex" on the body is not only about meaning but also about access to gendered asymmetries of power. These privileges and points of access granted to male bodies and not to female bodies may be rejected or "disowned" later in life or variously distributed among males early in life, but they cannot be denied or discounted in the life experiences that generally mark male somatic existence. Flesh so named makes difference.

I refer to this "maleness" or "femaleness" as the historical gravity of the sexed body. It is not clear to me that the historical gravity of the male body can be completely negated in the charmed circle where the male lesbian is embraced as a legitimate member of a lesbian group qua lesbian. It is clear, however, that the hegemonically more numerous and controlling contexts that "sex" our bodies by genitocentric criteria serve the interests of heterosexual and male domination. The "male lesbian" is a strikingly odd figure in this scene, challenging the naturalness of "maleness" and "heterosexuality" by the bizarreness of his self-intending sex and gender attributions. From this perspective, the "male lesbian" is perhaps more of an imposter to the heterosexual world than he seems to be in lesbian communities.

What I am suggesting is that the stubborn return of the body's sex, its "maleness" in this case, is nothing more than a hegemonically overdetermined set of readings made apparently "continuous" and "natural" by their seriality, redundancy, and consistency that confer "a sex" on the body without regard to the will or authorship of the subject. These meanings are perhaps metaphysically and historically contingent, utterly constructed and arbitrary, but encumbering. What agency the subject has to move in, around, and against these readings in this culture is a question for exploration and struggle. What agency we have in this culture to move beyond these assigned categories, to become "unstuck" from our constructed bodies, to travel transgendering and transsexing journeys of relocation, or to deconstruct sex binarism altogether are questions left uncomfortably unanswered in my thoughts. Perhaps all is "drag" made up of cells, soma, and style marked redundantly in memory and public readings.

IN/CONCLUSION

My conclusions are tentative. Postmodernism is right in bringing into focus the contingency of sex identity imposed on and incorporated into the body's soma but wrong in supposing these to be lightweight and detachable. This body is not only a thing in the world, subject to physical gravity, but a thing that carries its own historical gravity, and this collected weight bears down on the "sexedness" of the body and the possibilities of experience. Postmodernism is right in revealing the "inventedness" of this body but wrong in supposing that this implies a protean self ambulating between "positionalities." The "male lesbian" is perhaps right in challenging the commonplace criteria of sex attribution but wrong in his conclusion. His failure to become a lesbian in all her fullness—dare I say "a real lesbian"—is not a failure of postmodernist tools but a lacuna in postmodernist ontology and a failure to recognize the individual's real powerlessness against the imposition of other-extending attributions that "sex" the flesh. In this failure is a discovery of the historically located body—a discovery of the historical gravity of a culturally constructed "sexed" body. Against the intellectual anorexia of postmodernism, this body stubbornly returns with a weight that defies the promises of postmodernist fantasy and its idealist denial. We are called on to "own" what is ours, where we sit, breathe, and theorize in the Cartesianized circles of postmodernist academia.

NOTES

1. I am indebted to Julia Penelope's development of a grid from which mine is derived. Several of the ideas developed in this paragraph were influenced by her work in (Penelope 1986, 1991).
2. Kessler and McKenna are using "gender" in a different way from my usage. This quotation aligns with my definitional system if the reader substitutes "sexes" for "genders."

REFERENCES

Atkinson, Ti Grace. 1974. *Amazon odessy*. New York: Links Books.
Bordo, Susan. 1990. Feminism, postmodernism, and gender-skepticism. In *Feminism and postmodernism*, ed. Linda Nicholson. New York: Routledge.

Bornstein, Kate. 1991. Transsexual lesbian playwright tells all! In *High risk*, ed. Amy Scholder and Ira Silberberg, New York: Plume Press.

Butler, Judith. 1990. *Gender trouble: Feminism and the subversion of community*. New York: Routledge.

Carlson, Alison. 1991. When is a woman not a woman? *Women's Sports and Fitness*. March: 24-29.

Clausen, Jan. 1990. My interesting condition. *Out/look*, Winter: 10-21.

Foucault, Michel. 1978. *History of sexuality: Vol. 1, An introduction*, trans. Robert Hurley. New York: Random House.

———. 1980. *Herculine Barbin: Being the recently discovered memoirs of the nineteenth century French hermaphrodite*, trans. Richard McDougal. New York: Pantheon.

Halperin, David. 1990. *One hundred years of homosexuality and European Greek love*. New York: Routledge.

Hoagland, Sarah Lucia. 1988. *Lesbian ethics: Toward new value*. Palo Alto, CA: Institute for Lesbian Studies.

Janis, Ashby. 1992. Festival forum. *Lesbian Connection* 14(4): 11-12.

Kessler, Suzanne, and Wendy McKenna. 1978. *Gender: An ethnomethodological approach*. Chicago: University of Chicago Press.

Myles, Eileen. 1990. Gender play. *Outweek* 5 Dec.: 48-49.

Nestle, Joan. 1987. *A Restricted country*. New York: Firebrand.

Oches, Robin. 1990. A letter to the editor. *Out/look* Summer.

Olano, Pamela J. 1992. Throw over your man, I say, and come: Reading Virginia Woolf as a lesbian. Unpublished manuscript.

Penelope, Julia. 1986. Hetersexual semantics: "Just two kinds of people in the world." *Lesbian Ethics* Fall: 58-80.

———. 1990. The partriarchal universe of discourse. In *Speaking freely: Unlearning the lies of the father tongue*, ed. Julia Penelope. New York: Pergamon.

Radicalesbians. 1971. The woman-identified woman. In *Notes from the third year: Women's liberation*, ed. Anne Koedt, Anita Rapone, and Ellen Levine. New York: Radical Feminist.

Stoltenberg, John. 1990. *Refusing to be a man: Essays on sex and justice*. New York: Firebrand.

Suleiman, Susan. 1986. (Re)writing the body: The politics of female eroticism. In *The female body in Western culture*, ed. Susan Suleiman. Cambridge: Harvard University Press.

Wings, Mary. 1990. A letter to the editor. *Out/look* Summer.

In Praise of Blame

BARBARA HOUSTON

Recent writers in feminist ethics have been concerned to find ways to reclaim and augment women's moral agency. This essay considers Sarah Hoagland's intriguing suggestion that we renounce moral praise and blame and pursue what she calls an "ethic of intelligibility." I argue that the eschewal of moral blame would not help but rather hinder our efforts to increase our sense of moral agency. It would, I claim, further intensify our __demoralization__.

I. INTRODUCTION

What ethic can best serve lesbians? What ethic best serves any group of people who are exploited, marginalized, and relatively powerless, any group of those whose perspectives, point of view, is invisible while at the same time they are stereotyped and marked as Other, any group who is subject to systematic and "legitimated" violence?[1] These are the larger questions that spawn the topic of this paper, which has predominantly to do with our sense of self and our sense of moral agency as they are shaped by the practice of blame. In particular, is blame a help or a hindrance? Should we, among lesbians, renounce it or embrace it?[2]

Many feminist writers remind us of the devastating impact oppression can have on women's daily lives. Sarah Hoagland (1988) and Kathryn Morgan (1988), in particular, have written perceptively about the implications of psychological oppression for the possibility of women's moral agency. In *Lesbian Ethics*, Hoagland highlights three aspects of the *de*moralization women experience in their position of subordination: 1) the undermining of the ability to perceive oneself as a moral agent and to make choices (as is evidenced by the underreporting of rape, sexual abuse, sexual harassment, and physical violence against women); 2) being put in the position of having to betray oneself or someone or some value one honors (for example, when a woman must choose between living with her lover and having custody of her children or between laughing at sexist jokes and giving up a job she needs); 3) an undermining of

Hypatia vol. 7, no. 4 (Fall 1992) © by Barbara Houston

one's sense of self in community with other women (as reflected in women's fear of being identified as a feminist or of being thought a lesbian or even a certain kind of lesbian (Hoagland 1988, 213). There is, as Claudia Card has noted, a powerful tension between the damage of oppression and the possibility of resistance. In her words, "If the damage of oppression is as great as they document, how is it possible for women to resist?" (Card 1986, 150).

One route to resistance embraced by several recent writers on women's morality and feminist ethics can be described as the discovery of a radically subversive potential within an ethics of women caring for one another. Hoagland develops such an ethic, which she promises will combat our demoralization. She cites three major aims an ethic must achieve if it is to serve as a basis for women's resistance and have liberatory potential: it must increase women's sense of moral agency, strengthen our sense of integrity, and develop our sense of self in community with other women.[3] The particular development of the ethics of lesbians caring for one another that Hoagland proposes is this: a reconstrual of the notions of moral agency. Specifically, she proposes that we renounce moral praise and blame and abandon a preoccupation with justification that now lies at the core of our notions of moral agency.

I think Hoagland has correctly identified what a morality needs to provide if it is to be a basis for our resistance. I think she is on the right track in insisting that feminist morality attend to these features. I also think that she, along with other writers on feminist ethics, brings to the fore some interesting observations about moral interdependency.[4] However, I am not myself persuaded that renouncing blame and simply pursuing an "ethic of intelligibility," as Hoagland calls it, will realize the radical subversive potential she thinks is inherent in women caring for each other. I doubt that we can in this way increase our sense of moral agency, develop integrity, or increase our sense of self in community with other women. Indeed, I think that renouncing blame jeopardizes those values.

Arguments for Renouncing Blame

It is easy to understand why Sarah Hoagland and others interested in feminist ethics should not want lesbians to focus on blame, especially among ourselves, for, as Hoagland notes, among oppressed groups "we find the extremes of blaming the victim or victimism":

> As it stands now, someone who is harmed under oppression is held responsible for everything that happened to her; she is responsible not only for her choices, but for the situation itself (women invite rape, slaves never resisted slavery, jews are willing victims and so on). Alternatively, she is perceived as

total victim, as if she were not trying to make choices, to survive
and go on. (Hoagland 1988, 215)

In essence, she argues that we should eschew blame because 1) it is ineffective:
people who are blamed usually simply become defensive and do not change
(217); 2) it masks the complexity of situations and persons: we tend to perceive
people as static characters, we ignore what they do that is right, we see them
as bad and ourselves as good, and once we can find someone to blame we tend
to forget about the harm that has been caused and do little to remedy it
(217-18); and 3) blaming keeps us from acquiring the knowledge we need
about how the political context affects our choices and how we affect each
other's choices: we tend to call someone a liar and neglect to ask what was our
part in the lying process (224).

Hoagland also notes that we often blame not the worst nor the most
perceptible "sinners" but the ones who irritate us the most, or the handiest, or
the ones we most dislike because they are the ones most like us. In the end,
she says, we should reject judgments of moral praise and blame as superficial
and "simplistic" (221, 217).[5] The central task for women, Hoagland says, is
not to decide whether we can be excused for what we've done or what excuses
apply but rather to determine how we persist, how we "go on to realize, to
create the values which will undermine oppression" (215).

So how are we to respond to felt or perceived wrongdoing? Hoagland adopts
a suggestion of Marilyn Frye's that we eliminate the notion of justification at
the center of our notion of agency and appeal instead to the concept of
intelligibility (221). The point of an emphasis on intelligibility is to ensure
that we acquire an understanding of our own choices, the choices of others,
and the dynamics of the situation. The aim is to perceive what others who
differ from us perceive. Paraphrasing Frye, Hoagland states that intelligibility
means "being willing to situate ourselves in such a way that others who make
choices different from ours can be intelligible" (226).[6]

In short, the trouble with blame and accountability is that they keep us fixed
on ourselves. As Hoagland puts it, our attention is "riveted on ourselves":

> justifying ourselves so that others understand that at least we
> meant well, or demanding that others justify themselves to us
> on our own terms. They do not encourage us to attend to the
> other and understand how it goes with her. (227)

II. AN EVALUATION OF THE PROPOSAL TO RENOUNCE BLAME

My interest lies in exploring certain questions Hoagland's account raises: Is
our sense of moral agency in fact undermined by renouncing blame? If we don't
blame, can we avoid sanctioning wrongdoing? And what effect does this have

on our integrity? Can we renounce blame and still retain a close connection with those toward whom we eschew blame?

I think that Hoagland is correct in claiming that often, perhaps frequently, blaming is not effective. But I think it is a mistake to assume that all blame seeks achievement or realization of ends external to our relations with one another. I think that she is right that arrogance and antagonism are often the concomitants of blame, but I don't think that they are *necessary* concomitants.

The suggestion that we renounce blame rests, I think, on too narrow a construal of the concept of blame and the practices it encompasses. There are ambiguities associated with blame, clarification of which can assist our discussion—ambiguities concerning the range of activities blame covers, the degree of publicness involved, and the emotional tone associated with it.

According to standard definitions, *blame* can mean something as neutral-sounding as "responsibility for a fault or error." It can also mean "an expression of disapproval or reproach." Common synonyms for blame include "criticize," which is the least specific; "reprehend," "censure," "condemn," which imply sharp or strong disapproval, even sentencing by a court; and the strongest, "denounce," which entails strong adverse judging, openly and vehemently, and which can also refer to a public proclamation of official criticism or repudiation. We need to note, however, that blaming *activities* can range, as one writer suggests, from dropping bombs to thinking poorly of someone (Watson 1987, 262). They needn't always involve a public denunciation.

Hoagland's use of the term "blame" seems primarily associated with the notion of public censure and the act of condemning. She speaks of "pointing a blaming finger," and "nailing so-and-so to the wall for a given act and holding her up before the community for condemnation." She speaks of "the obsession with confession and absolution before the community," of "trying to make another admit she was mean and nasty." Such blaming, she says, "doesn't move us anywhere" (Hoagland 1988, 217, 221).

Along with the wide range of activities associated with blame there are varying degrees of publicness and different sorts of sentiments. Does blaming *require* public expression? Richard Brandt (1958) thinks not. He claims that blaming is not something we do, like scowling; it is the adoption of an attitude of disapproval toward someone for something he or she has done or failed to do. But one may privately adopt this attitude and behave in an amiable way toward the person she or he blames. I think Brandt is correct in this, but we need to remember that even this private blaming presupposes a public set of expectations. I could hardly blame someone for taking what didn't belong to her or him if "stealing is wrong" were some sort of esoteric piece of knowledge.

I am interested in this sort of private blaming and it is one of the kinds of cases I want to defend. However, for the purposes of this paper, I am primarily concerned with cases that involve *some* public expression of the disapproval because these are the cases Hoagland has in mind, although I do want to draw attention to the quieter kinds of blame that fit this category. Hoagland appears to be less interested in the cases of quieter blame, but she still recommends we eschew them.

Blame suggests an attack and gets bad press because it is often misplaced and misused. For example, we may blame someone else as a way of avoiding taking responsibility ourselves. Blame also receives bad publicity because it is sometimes done vehemently. But the emotional tone of blaming can vary considerably. One can use strong, loud, angry tones in blaming another, but one can also have a quizzical or hurt-feeling tone. The point here is that we can blame in a number of ways, expressing a wide variety of sentiments ranging from vindictiveness and malice to quiet indignation. A well-placed question may be enough to imply blame: "Why did you do it?" I'm interested in blame at the quiet end of the spectrum—call it quiet blame—as well as the more vehement kind.[7]

We miss important functions that blame serves in our relations when we focus only on the blamings that are clustered at the censure end of the spectrum and are accompanied by strong retributive sentiments of vindictiveness. What has been eclipsed in Hoagland's view of blame can be revealed if we take seriously the suggestion that we renounce blame. When we consider what we would miss in the absence of blame, we will have a better clue as to its nature.

PERSONAL RESPONSES

I begin my explorations by imaging myself to be a member of a lesbian community who is asked to renounce blame. I start with my own rather strong reactions to the suggestion. My aim, in the end, is both to make sense of these reactions and to persuade you that they embody some truths that should lead us to be, at the least, skeptical of the liberatory promise of Hoagland's suggestion to renounce blame.

My initial reactions to the suggestion that we renounce blame are those of a person who might no longer be blamed. I notice first an experience of enormous relief. And this relief translates into a felt experience of freedom. I remember times when someone was understanding rather than blaming me and how I experienced overwhelming relief and felt freer as a result.

Then I remember other times when someone did blame me and it was futile because I turned stubbornly defensive. Hoagland is right: we often do simply act defensively and resort to counterblame.

There also comes back to me a strong recognition of the hurt I can experience in being blamed. We feel vulnerable, exposed by others telling us what we too vividly know about our faults, errors, and inadequacies. In remembering the hurt I also recall the gratitude I sometimes feel when someone withholds blame from me—for example, when someone says in the face of my transgression, "I know you did your best, I know you were well-intentioned."

When others in these circumstances remind me of the good things I've done in the past, when they struggle to understand my concerns rather than blame me, I can only feel this as a blessing.

These personal feelings are all powerful reminders to me of the damage blaming can do and good reasons for giving serious thought to renouncing blame. In addition, I also recognize that renouncing blame will reduce the danger of triggering the generalized shame that most women seem to experience. Many of us know how our personalities have been shaped by early shaming associated with sexual or physical abuse or as the result of profoundly disappointing our parents by not being the "daughter" they had hoped for. This generalized shame is easily invoked when we are blamed for even small, unrelated matters.[8]

When I take the vantage point of myself as someone blaming others, I have to acknowledge further difficulties with the practice of blaming. It can be tiresome; it certainly gets in the way when we want to accomplish something. Further, blaming often provokes strong negative emotions that are upsetting. If we blame in a hotheaded fashion, we do have, as Hoagland points out, the further problem of foreclosing on intelligibility. As a potential blamer, I recognize that in the past very often blaming did not get me what I wanted: in response I was often lied to and in return accused of inadequacies of my own.

However, even recognizing blaming as hurtful and as an often unnecessary indulgence that can be destructive of personal and community relations, I am not yet ready to renounce blame because I have another opposing set of strong negative responses. The strongest among these is a terrible sense of vulnerability: I feel that to renounce blame is to leave myself without recourse when I am wronged; I feel I have no way to declare my boundaries, assert my rights, defend myself when I am treated unfairly or hurt. Along with this heightened sense of vulnerability comes fear: can I trust a world in which I cannot blame?

Accompanying this fear is a sense of powerlessness. We blame not just on our own behalf but also on behalf of others. Without recourse to blame, I feel powerless to protest on behalf of others. Specifically, I feel powerless to help those who experience sexual abuse, harassment, or physical violence at the hands of others and whose psychological survival I know depends on a proper fixing of blame on the perpetrators.

I begin to experience other feelings more diffuse and difficult to identify: something like a sense of detachment from those whom I cannot blame, a sense of impending isolation from those I am close to. Even when I consider myself as someone not to be blamed, along with gratitude and relief I have a feeling of being diminished, objectified, removed. I also begin to sense some loss of moral status. I recall occasions on which I desperately wanted to be held accountable when it seemed others were refusing to blame me out of a sense of the futility of it. "It won't make any difference blaming Houston; she just can't be held responsible." Such comments can bring forth in me a passionate desire to be blamed, to be held responsible for my interactions with others.

These are the sorts of feelings that predominate when I take seriously the suggestion that we eschew moral blame and accountability. I cannot help but think that these feelings reveal a point toward a set of judgments and important insights about moral blame, accountability, and our human relationships.[9]

THE INELIMINABILITY OF BLAME

We might begin a philosophical evaluation of the suggestion to eschew blame by considering whether we *can* withhold blame. It is clear that we can *temporarily* withhold blame with respect to particular injuries done to us, and we can change the rituals and executions of blame, the emotional tone of it. But I think we cannot wholly suspend the practice in a community of connected persons and still maintain our relationships.

Whether one thinks blame is eliminable or not and with what consequences will depend on what one thinks it is to blame. Hoagland rightly acknowledges that praise and blame have been an intricate part of the practice of holding others responsible. Part of what we mean by saying someone is responsible is that she or he can (appropriately) be blamed. However, in Hoagland's discussion blame is seen primarily as faultfinding judgments with associated demands for justification. But my own resistance, and those of others, to the plea that we renounce blame suggest that there is more to blame than this.

There are competing accounts that make intelligible my resistances to Hoagland's suggestion that we renounce blame. One that I initially found quite compelling is Marilyn Frye's account of what it can mean for a white, middle-class, Christian-raised woman to want to be good, to want others to be good, to want ethics. It can mean, as she says, that one understands one's agency in terms of one's knowledge of right and wrong, to see one's agency as that of the judge, teacher/preacher, and administrator. It can mean that one is ambitious for "full personhood" (Frye 1991, 55).

I recognize myself in Frye's account. Yet I think that is not all there is to my wanting to be good or wanting others to be good to me. Trying to be good, for me, is not only a way of pursuing race and class and other privilege. It is not only a "will-binding" that keeps me bonded to our oppressors, not only a way to keep me a "dutiful daughter," although I have no doubt that it often functions, within the present social practices both within and outside lesbian communities, to do this. I think there is something more in my wanting to *be* good and in wanting others to be good. I do not conceive of my agency solely in terms of my knowledge of right and wrong, nor solely as a judge, teacher/preacher, or administrator.

For me, to *be* good, to *be* a moral agent, just *is* to (want to) be the subject of responses to others that express normative expectations. I cannot imagine myself as an agent without also imagining myself being held to some standard and being regarded as a disappointment when I fail to live up to it. The content of these standards sometimes changes, as I constantly discover that I am not good enough or that I don't know how to be good. But, unlike Frye, I am not tempted to give up ethics altogether (Frye 1991, 58).

It is at this point that I find P. F. Strawson's account of an "expressive theory of responsibility"[10] helpful in making my own position more intelligible and persuasive. According to Strawson, to hold someone responsible is to have certain feelings in response to that person, feelings such as gratitude, love, forgiveness, anger, hurt feelings, and resentment. These responses, Strawson claims, are the reactions we have "to the good or ill will or indifference of others as displayed in *their* attitudes and actions" (1974, 10).

Strawson describes three different types of what I will call responsive attitudes. First there are what we call personal responsive attitudes, such as gratitude, love, resentment, anger, hurt feelings, those we feel directly and personally about others' good or ill will to us. Second, there are responses that Strawson calls the moral analogues of the first type.[11] These are responses we may have on our own behalf but which are also "essentially vicarious" in that they are capable of being felt on behalf of another. Moral blame and moral indignation are the moral analogues of the personal reactions of resentment, anger, and hurt feelings. A third type of attitude is connected to these: feelings of being bound or obligated; feelings of compunction, guilt, remorse, and shame. These arise in response to the demands others' responsive attitudes make on us.

Undoubtedly all these responses do include appraisals and judgments of another, but to focus only on the judgments is to miss important elements in the practice of holding someone responsible. Strawson is insistent that these "participant reactive attitudes" (Strawson 1974, 10) are constitutive of responsibility. To hold someone responsible *just is* the proneness to react to that person in these kinds of ways under certain circumstances.[12]

The crucial point for our purposes is that the practice of blame, on this theory, is seen to rest on certain needs and aversions that are "not so much justified as acknowledged" (Watson 1987, 261) and that are basic to our conception of ourselves as persons-in-relation. We expect, demand, from those with whom we are in close association a measure of good will and an absence of ill will or indifference. It is difficult to see how we could have any sort of community without such a basic expectation. In blaming we are not, as Hoagland implies, mostly moral clerks recording moral faults (Watson 1987, 261); rather, we are responding in a wide-ranging way to others based on how they meet our expectation of good will.

Once we see blame in this way we realize that it is not easily extricable from other moral responses. If we give up blame, what happens to forgiveness? What happens to apology, resentment, anger? Blame as a responsive attitude is logically connected to other personal responses such as anger, resentment, hurt feelings. Blame is simply the form these responses take when we experience them on behalf of others as well as ourselves.

Notice also that these personal feelings of resentment and anger presuppose a recognition of their generalized moral analogue: moral indignation, disapproval, and blame. Anger is essentially a moral emotion. When we experience anger we judge that we have been wronged. Our personal experience of anger presupposes a background of shared norms regarding who counts as a person, what counts as acceptable treatment of and wrongful interference with persons.[13] Given their symbiotic nature, I doubt if one could renounce blame and still retain anger.

Can we imagine what it would be like to experience anger always and only on our own behalf? The expression of emotion we now recognize as anger might well lose its intelligibility under these circumstances, just as it does when another refuses to give it uptake (Frye 1983, 88). The same goes for the other personal responsive attitudes with which blame is connected: resentment and hurt feelings. If we try to imagine what it would be like to experience them only on our own behalf and never on behalf of another, we have an "eccentricity" and "moral solipsism" that is almost inconceivable (Strawson 1974, 15-16).

Hoagland's optimism that we can renounce blame and retain the other responsive attitudes depends on restricting the notion of blame to a consequentialist understanding. On this account, blaming judgments and acts are to be understood as justified only as forms of social control, tools in our quest for something we can never have—a guarantee of securing what is important to us. This understanding underlies Hoagland's chief criticism that blame is ineffective.

Certainly the efficacy, or lack thereof, of the practice of blaming is to the point, but it is not, as Strawson notes, the whole point:

> What is wrong is to forget that these practices and their reception, the reactions to them, really *are* expressions of our moral attitudes and not merely devices we calculatingly employ for regulative purposes. Our practices do not merely exploit our natures, they *express* them. Indeed the very understanding of this kind of efficacy these expressions of our attitudes have turns on our remembering this. (Strawson 1974, 25)

Blame consists of responses to others that we regard as appropriate responses regardless of their effects. The practice of blaming directly expresses certain sentiments without which the practice of blame cannot be understood. To regard another as responsible just is the proneness to react to that person in these kinds of ways. These reactive attitudes are *constitutive* of moral responsibility.

THE UNDESIRABILITY OF ELIMINATING BLAME

Given that blame, along with the other responsive participant attitudes, is the expression of our expectation of another's good will, or at the least the absence of ill will, we could presumably renounce blame by simply giving up this expectation.[14] But this expectation is essential to what it means to be in relation with another. Being in connection, in relation, requires the giving up of one's self, a responsiveness of self to another, a willingness to be to some degree vulnerable to another. But without an expectation of good will, we cannot expect any giving up of the self nor any knowledge of our self by another, for at heart the presentation of self (or selves) is an achievement that requires some minimal cooperation.[15] In the absence of the expectation of good will from others, we would need to adopt a sense of detachment and distance from them to protect ourselves.[16]

To withhold the self, to suspend the participant attitudes, is in Strawson's view

> to adopt the objective attitude to another human being . . . to see [her], perhaps as an object of social policy; a subject for what in a wide range of sense might be called treatment; or something to be taken account of, perhaps precautionary account of; to be managed, handled, or cured or trained; perhaps simply to be avoided. (Strawson 1974, 9)

Hoagland's notion of intelligibility is, of course, intended to be nothing like Strawson's "objective attitude." But what, if anything, keeps the quest for intelligibility from becoming the adoption of the objective attitude? One difference between Hoagland's intelligibility stance and Strawson's objective attitude is that for Hoagland the quest for intelligibility is to be a mutual undertaking, some shared goal we pursue, something that requires from all concerned an effort at clarity (explanation) and understanding.[17]

But what makes this more than simply the *mutual* adoption of the objective attitude? Both the quest for intelligibility and the adoption of the objective stance require the attention to others that Hoagland wants to ensure. The crucial difference between the two is captured in Hoagland's claim that intelligibility requires "an act of love."[18] It involves approaching others in "a spirit of acceptance," understanding another "in her own world," situating ourselves so that others' choices, especially those that differ from ours, can be intelligible to us (Hoagland 1988, 226). The quest for intelligibility, Hoagland claims, is a "two-way process," which suggests that it is not something one could undertake unilaterally. Further, she claims it is a process that "enables a foundation—an axis, held in place by what surrounds it—of cooperation" (227).

From her description it is not clear whether Hoagland thinks that intelligibility is what makes cooperation possible or whether she thinks that cooperation is a requirement of the quest for intelligibility. I think it is the cooperation that makes intelligibility possible. It is approaching others in "a spirit of acceptance"—that is, with good will—that makes (good) explanations and understandings possible. Intelligibility can only be kept conceptually and practically distinct from the objective stance by building good will into the concept, by making it part of the stipulative account of intelligibility. But it is precisely the presupposition of good will that gives rise to the responsive attitudes we call blame that occur when we experience acts of ill will or indifference.

The Sanctioning of Wrongdoing

Renouncing blame also risks other dangers we may not be able to avoid. Chesire Calhoun (1989) reminds us that the situation with respect to women is one in which we are at the frontiers of moral knowledge, in which we cannot be sure that our moral knowledge is shared.[19] In this context, moral ignorance in some sense can be seen as occurring at the social level and not just the individual level. In such contexts, she claims, not blaming has different effects than in other contexts in which we can rely on a shared moral understanding. In contexts where there is a shared moral understanding, not blaming is ambiguous. It can mean we either: 1) excuse the wrongdoing or 2) sanction it. But in situations where wrongdoing may not be acknowledged, not blaming gets interpreted automatically as sanctioning. Thus, to eschew blame makes it difficult to avoid sanctioning wrongdoing.[20]

The Enhancement of Demoralization

Although Hoagland urges that we relinquish blame in order to avoid our demoralization, I think renouncing blame among ourselves can intensify our demoralization in two ways: 1) it risks loss of a sense of self-worth; 2) it entails the eschewal of self-blame, and with this comes a diminishment of our own sense of agency.

The first difficulty arises because we have a history of reluctance to blame. We have been taught to forgive and accept what we should have been taught to resent and resist.[21] Gilligan writes of this in her description of the abortion study she did with Belenky (Gilligan 1977). In contrast to Gilligan's observation about women in conventional settings, one can often find such blaming and vociferous disapproval within women's feminist and lesbian communities. Some of our enthusiastic blaming activities might be explained by the fact that we may, for the first time, sense our newly acquired moral status within communities where blaming, on our own behalf and on behalf of other women, is taken seriously.

The blamings that stem from our resentment and indignation reaffirm the value we place on ourselves and others. Bad treatment by others can raise doubts about our value. As Jean Hampton puts it, an "act of defiance is the heart of the emotion" of resentment (Murphy and Hampton 1988, 57). The active resenter denies to herself and anyone else that she is low in value and she thereby defies the appearance (implicit in the demeaning and act) of low status (59-60). Thus, blaming can be an attempt to assert "the correct relative value of the wrongdoer and the victim" (125), an attempt to maintain the victim's equal worth in the face of a challenge to it.[22]

An intensification of demoralization can also occur with the loss of self-blame entailed by the wholesale eschewal of blame. Hoagland uses the case of self-blame among lesbians as a *reductio* argument against blame. However, Alice Walker, in her book *The Third Life of Grange Copeland*, sees it differently. The character Grange points out how not blaming ourselves makes us weak and can confound us. He says

> By George, I *know* the danger of putting all the blame on somebody else for the mess you made out of your life. I fell into the trap myself! And I'm bound to believe that that's the way the white folks can corrupt you even when you done held up before. 'Cause when they got you to thinking that they're to blame for *everything* they have you thinking they some kind of gods! You can't do nothing wrong without them being behind it. You gits just as weak as water, no feeling of doing *nothing* yourself. Then you begins to think up evil and begins to destroy everybody around you and you blames it on the crackers. *Shit!* Nobody's as powerful as we make them out to be. We got our own *souls*, don't we? (Walker 1970, 206-07)

I take Alice Walker's point to be this: self-blame, which is in fact parasitic on the general practice of blame, is necessary to keep us alive to our own moral agency. Our idea that we are agents is increased or developed to the extent that we engage in the practice of holding ourselves and others responsible. Thus, even for those, indeed especially for those, whose agency may be circumscribed, a social vulnerability to blame and self-blame may be one of the significant means we have to maintain a realistic sense of our own agency.

This view is challenged by Marilyn Frye, who describes herself first as someone wholly demoralized by self-blame and then released by abandoning it altogether. In counterpoint to Grange, Frye gives us a poignant description of someone at a moral loss in her efforts to respond constructively to criticisms of herself and her work as racist.

> It all combined to precipitate me into profound and unnerv-
> ing distrust of myself. All of my ways of knowing seemed to have
> failed me—my perception, my common sense, my good will, my
> anger, honor and affection, my intelligence and insight. Just as
> walking requires something fairly sturdy and firm underfoot, so
> being an actor in the world requires a foundation of ordinary
> moral and intellectual confidence. Without that, we don't
> know how to be or how to act; we become strangely stupid. . . .
> If you want to be good, and you don't know good from bad, you
> can't move. (Frye 1990, 133)

Marilyn Frye has come to welcome this sort of demoralization as a release from
the "game of 'good' and 'evil.' " She sees it as an opportunity to do without
ethics altogether—that is, to learn to do without the need to know what to do
and without the confidence that she has acted rightly.

But I think we need to remind ourselves that ethics is not just about knowing
what to do and desiring the confidence that one has acted rightly. It may be
that much has failed her—her perceptions, common sense, anger, honor,
intelligence, and insight. She claims her good will too has failed her. But this
I doubt. It is her good will that has made her listen to and hear the criticisms,
weigh them, and question herself in such a radical fashion. It is her good will
that has made her responsive to the blamings of others, that has brought on
her self-blame. And it is her good will that reminds us that ethics is about "how
we meet the other,"[23] how we meet the other even when we don't know what's
right, even when we don't have confidence that we have acted rightly, or ever
will act "rightly." Her good will reminds us that our agency is expressed in our
attitudes to others, as well as in our deeds.

THE JEOPARDIZING OF MORAL AGENCY, INTEGRITY, AND SENSE OF SELF IN
COMMUNITY

If my analysis of blame as an important and fundamental expression of our
moral self is correct, then in renouncing blame we may not be furthering the
aims of developing 1) our sense of moral agency, 2) our integrity, and 3) our
sense of self in community with others. In fact, I believe that the eschewal of
blame could jeopardize all three.

In withholding blame as an important expression of self, we would, as I have
argued, experience detachment and isolation from others in our community.
But given that our sense of self is fundamentally a relational self and that our
sense of ourselves as moral agents is formed in relation with others, this
detachment could work to diminish our sense of moral agency.

Blaming is a way others have of expressing their vision of our better selves—a
way of saying this failing or this injury was unnecessary; she can do better.

Although blame appears to be backward-looking, in these instances it is generally premised on a vision of a better possibility. This vision of the possibilities inherent in blame is something necessary to a fuller sense of moral agency.

Moreover, to withhold blame can also jeopardize one's sense of integrity. Our expectation of good will and its concomitant intolerance of ill will or indifference, of which blame is an expression, is central to our own sense of who we are: it reveals that we regard ourselves as persons of worth and dignity; as persons who are vulnerable, who can be injured, who can be hurt by indifference or contempt and can be pleased by another's expression of good will toward us; and, finally, as persons who are capable of reciprocity in these matters.

Just as shame is experienced as an exposure of self resulting from another's blaming us, so too blaming entails an exposure or revealing of the self of the person doing the blaming. In both cases persons are made vulnerable in the revelation. If you doubt that you too, in blaming another, are exposed or revealed, think of those occasions on which you have blamed someone only to have that person exclaim that she or he has no idea of what you are talking about. The exclamation is often not simply a denial of agency but also an expression of disdain at your sense of reality or of what you consider to be morally important. (Consider: "Darling, you're imagining things.")[24]

My moral disapprovals are expressions of who I am; thus blame, in the sense of public expression of this disapproval, is one announcement to others of who I am. It is one form of public expression that helps to contribute to my efforts to be to others what I am to myself. Without this as a possibility, we could be in danger of having no identity and hence no integrity. (Consider Jan Morris' remark: "I had no identity because I was not to others what I was to myself" [1973, 41]).

The kind of attention to oneself, and what one is up to, that Hoagland sees as the basis of integrity is sufficient for integrity only if we insist that the needed understanding is sought in the right conditions. Those conditions are made clear by Victoria Davion (1991). It may be we are more like the multiplicitous being María Lugones (1990) describes: we feel ourselves never wholly at home in any one community, and often living in borderlands. Even so, we can still maintain integrity, as Davion reminds us, if we "can somehow keep a connection between [our] two selves alive, as long as one can critique the other" (Davion 1991, 190). For this to be possible, Davion tells us, the selves must have certain values in common, which ensures that they do not work against each other. We could not have integrity, "if each autokoenonous self wanted the death of the other or simply wanted to undermine the fundamental projects of the other" (190).

The point is that a presumption of good will on behalf of others or even from our other selves is one of the conditions for integrity. With this presumption of good will we open ourselves to those sentiments and passions that include blame—the occurrence of which is constitutive of holding ourselves and others responsible. These responses and sentiments are, I submit, more spontaneous and more like passions than Hoagland seems to allow. Notice how often we do just find ourselves *feeling* blame.

I also think removing blame risks our sense of self-in-community. Inasmuch as blame is an expression of moral self, it is quintessentially an expression of one's self-in-relation, as in connection with others. If blame just is the generalized analogue of feelings I experience, they are feelings I recognize as experiencing on behalf of others. Then when I blame another for injury to myself, it reveals that I see myself as the same as others, insofar as we have the same moral standing; and when I express blame on behalf of others, I am seeing them as an extension of myself or as persons having the same moral status as myself.[25] In such cases blame functions predominantly as an emotion that fosters a sense of moral identification within the community. To suspend it, to renounce it, is to put at risk our sense of self-in-community.

What we need, then, is not a total eschewal of blame but rather a feminist transformation of blame. We can use blaming as a measure of our sense of responsibility for one another, as a measure of our respond-ability. Blaming as a responsive attitude can help us to clarify our political and social identities. Our expressions of moral blame can be a vehicle for us to initiate public consideration of the desirability, the appropriateness, and the reasonableness of our particular moral visions. It can create an opportunity to revise them, reform them, applaud them. Our hurt feelings, our resentments, angers, gratitude—on our behalf and on behalf of others—are the stuff out of which our community can be formed, shaped, constructed, and reconstructed.[26]

III. CONCLUSION

I have tried to indicate how much we have to set aside if we adopt Sarah Hoagland's proposal for a blameless lesbian ethic. Although I have argued that some social practices of blaming are indispensable, it is clear that not just any blaming practice will do. Hoagland's *Lesbian Ethics* can be read as a critique of certain specific forms that our blaming practice often takes. But blame plays many roles. It functions not only instrumentally to get things done, to educate, to teach others what is wrong, to remind others of their agency, but it also functions as an *expression* of our moral selves.

I want to praise blame primarily as a form of moral self-expression that functions to keep us in connection or in relation with others. The exposure of ourselves and others inherent in blaming carries great risks, but blaming is nothing less than a strong expression of our confidence in our moral agency, our integrity, and our sense of self-in-community, for the simple reason that blaming *just is* an expression of our moral agency, our integrity, and our sense of self-in-community.

NOTES

This paper has benefitted much from the careful, cheerful, critical discussions I have had with Jane Martin, Janet Farrell-Smith, Jennifer Radden, Susan Franzosa, Beebe Nelson, and Barbara Brockelman. I also want to thank Cheshire Calhoun, Susan Sherwin, and an anonymous reviewer for *Hypatia* for encouraging and useful critical commentary on earlier drafts. Special thanks goes to Ann Diller for her thoughtful comments and assistance in editing and revising the paper.

1. For a lucid discussion of oppression outlining these features, see Iris Young (1988).

2. I am aware of just how difficult it can be to say, unproblematically, of whom, for whom, and to whom one speaks. In this paper I consciously choose to speak of and to those I call women, lesbians, and feminists. As to the matter of *for whom* I speak, I speak primarily for myself. From my discussions with others whom I call women, lesbians, and feminists, I can say that some of what I write here resonates with some of them.

3. Hoagland (1988) explicates these features throughout her book, but see especially pp. 214-15 and 285-86.

4. Two points should be noted here. First, Hoagland has herself been quite critical of the ethics of care, at least as it has been articulated by Carol Gilligan and especially Nel Noddings. Nevertheless, I think it does not do her suggestions an injustice to see them as advocating one form of an ethics of caring. Hoagland's central objection to the ethics of care, as it has been described by Noddings, is to the use of the mother-child relation as the paradigm of caring. For a detailed account of her thoughts on Noddings's work, see Hoagland (1991).

Despite her critique of Noddings, Hoagland also appreciates many features of Noddings's approach to ethics and one finds many points of agreement between them. Hoagland's description of the struggle for intelligibility is very similar to Noddings's discussion of caring. And Hoagland's reconstrual of moral agency is, I think, implicit in the ethics of care as it has been advanced by Noddings (1984) and Sara Ruddick (1989). Noddings and Hoagland both want to marginalize justification on the grounds that it interferes with the main business of ethics; Noddings also emphasizes the importance of good motive attribution. Ruddick's discussion of the nurturance ethic embedded in maternal thinking tacitly eschews blame inasmuch as she insists that, at least heuristically, we should construe disagreement as evidence of *misunderstandings*. See Ruddick (1989).

However, the second point that should be noted is that Hoagland is talking about renouncing moral blame and accountability *within the lesbian community*. She, along with Mary Daly, Adrienne Rich, and Marilyn Frye, claims that the possibility and motivation for resistance to women's oppression are to be found in women loving women. These feminists see relations among women as the source of revolutionary energy, motivation, and understanding. However, there are some grounds for claiming that Hoagland thinks that the shifts in perception that she is recommending can be used as a strategy for dealing with the wider society. She cautiously claims that the values she thinks are created with this shift are also a source of empowerment for women even in the wider context. See Hoagland (1988, 22).

5. In Hoagland's case I am abstracting the argument against blame from her own larger theory, in which renouncing blame is intricately connected with giving up moral praise and what she terms accountability. Hoagland discusses accountability only in terms of a preoccupation with justification, ignoring associated notions of causal and moral responsibility. She sees justification only in the reductionistic terms of people "objectively" judging another solely in terms of their own framework, which they take to be the only framework there is. She thus associates accountability with arrogant, abusive, and superficial judgments, judgments that contribute to our demoralization. While I am sympathetic with her attempts to address the problems of arrogant judgment associated with justification, these issues go beyond the scope of this paper.

6. Hoagland is paraphrasing Marilyn Frye, "Notes for Comments on Presentations by S. Hoagland, C. Card, and M. Lugones in Honor of the *Politics of Reality*, unpublished notes from SWIP meeting at the APA in St. Louis, spring 1986.

7. There is a fine example of quiet blame in Toni Morrison's novel *Sula*. Although in this case we have a woman blaming a man, one can easily imagine the same sort of blaming of a lesbian by her lover. In this example the blame is expressed only in Nel's imagined encounter with her husband, who has run off with Sula:

> Could he be gone if his tie is still here? He will remember it and come back and then she would . . . uh. Then she could . . . tell him. Sit quietly and tell him. "But Jude," she would say, "you *knew* me. My ways and my hands and how my stomach folded . . . and how about that time when the landlord said . . . but you said..and I cried Jude. You knew me and had listened to the things I said in the night, and heard me in the bathroom and laughed at my raggedy girdle and I laughed too because I knew you too, Jude. So how could you leave me when you knew me?" (Morrison 1984, 104-5)

8. An insightful discussion of the generalized kind of shame that women experience and exhibit can be found in Sandra Bartky (1990 especially the chapter entitled "Shame and Gender").

9. For a different but related discussion of the ways in which our feelings of guilt, regret, remorse, embarrassment, and shame imply different notions of responsibility, see Elizabeth Spelman (1991).

10. Strawson's theory is named thus by Gary Watson (1987).

11. He also calls them "impersonal, disinterested or generalized analogues." See Strawson (1974, 14).

12. This is Watson's concise way of stating it. See Watson (1987, 261).

13. For an insightful discussion of anger that defends these claims, see Marilyn Frye (1983, 85-86).

14. Strawson's discussion of the "expectation of good will" leaves the phrase open to several interpretations. It could mean (a) an *anticipation* of good will on the part of others; (b) a *hope* for good will from others; or (c) a belief that others are *capable* of showing good will.

Although it may appear that there is more emotional investment on the part of the moral agent if we understand "expectation" in sense (a) or (b), it doesn't matter here which interpretation we take. My claim is that, on any interpretation, an expectation of good will is not something we can wholly jettison with respect to persons with whom we hope to remain in relation.

15. For a lucid discussion of the extent of the cooperation required, see Marilyn Frye's "The Problem That Has No Name" (Frye 1983).

16. Both Gilligan (1982) and Noddings (1984), prominent exponents of an ethics of caring, understand this presence of good will, or at least an absence of ill will or indifference, to be a necessary minimal condition for relation.

17. As I have read her, Hoagland sees the pursuit of intelligibility not as a strategy one employs prior to the practice of blaming but rather as the end in itself. She recognizes that it will not preclude judgment (that is impossible) and it does not preclude disagreement.

18. Hoagland gets this expression from María Lugones; see Hoagland (1988, 225).

19. Cheshire Calhoun calls this situation an "abnormal context." See Calhoun (1989).

20. For an elaborate discussion of this point, see Calhoun (1989). What one may want to accomplish here is a correction without blame. We might think that we can both not blame and correct inasmuch as we do this all the time, especially, as Calhoun notes, with children ("I'm not blaming you, I know you meant well, etc., but in the future you should. . . .") We can do this with children, but Calhoun claims that in adult-adult interactions it doesn't work. To not blame and correct in these interactions is perceived as insulting or as arrogant, for either you impugn the other's status as a moral adult or you appear to be claiming special moral authority (Calhoun 1989, 401).

We might think we can both not blame and correct if we mention the reasons for not blaming: for example, if we declare we women are a damaged people, given to pathological uses of morality, etc. However, there are problems with this too. First, it can simply reinforce the notion of the unalterability of our circumstances. It is likely to reinforce the notion that the damage is unalterable and mask our role in sustaining these circumstances. Further, it tends to create illusory moral identities—we are either perceived or perceive ourselves as moral heroes doing what is supererogatory if we avoid the wrongdoing or else we perceive ourselves as incapable of self-legislation.

This result occurs, Calhoun points out, because of the logic of moral language. " 'X is obligatory' means 'Unless there are exceptional excusing conditions you are blameworthy and reproachable for not doing X.' And 'X is supererogatory' means 'You are not blameworthy and reproachable for doing X and deserve special praise for doing X.' " However, as Calhoun points out, this logic breaks down in abnormal contexts when individuals are routinely rather than exceptionally exempted (not blamed) for failing to do the obligatory. Thus, "the logic of our moral language dooms any attempt to convey the obligatoriness of x while simultaneously not blaming most failures to do X" (Calhoun 1989, 404). Under these conditions, in a lesbian or feminist community, it will be difficult for women to sustain their sense of what is owed them and we will likely find ourselves feeling gratitude when merely given our due.

21. This is Fay Weldon's point and is discussed by Jeffrie Murphy and Jean Hampton (1988, 10).

22. Jean Hampton's interesting discussion of the retributive sentiments I associate with blame occurs in the context of a discussion of retributive punishment (Murphy and Hampton, 1988). Although I accept, as Chesire Calhoun has pointed out to me, that blame itself often serves as a punishment, the point I am concerned to make here is that I find Jean Hampton's account of the retributive emotions compelling, in large part, because she shows how it presupposes some theory of human worth. Hampton herself invokes a Kantian theory of human worth with which I am quite sympathetic.

23. Nel Noddings (1984) describes the point of morality in just this way.

24. Nicole Brossard used this example in a public lecture to show how women's sense of reality becomes distorted.

25. This passage shows up the striking difference between Nel Noddings's approach to an ethics of caring and this more Kantian view of our interdependency. Both Noddings and Hoagland would say that the approach here is wrong. Seeing another in terms of my own feelings cuts me off from understanding her in terms of her own feelings. It assumes similarities where there may be none, etc. The answer to this criticism has to lie in an emphasis on the similarity of *moral* standing. The work of both Gilligan and Noddings can be criticized for failing to provide an adequate basis for the independent moral worth of the person.

26. This use of blame is eloquently described by Berenice Fisher, who points out that a real danger occurs when we fail to see the feelings associated with blame, guilt, and shame as important sources of knowledge and as "tools for grasping the world and changing it" (Fisher 1984, 187).

REFERENCES

Bartky, Sandra. 1990. *Femininity and domination*. New York: Routledge.

Brandt, Richard. 1958. Blameworthiness and obligation. In *Essays in moral philosophy*, ed. A. I. Melden. Seattle: University of Washington Press.

Calhoun, Chesire. 1989. Responsibility and reproach. *Ethics* 99(2): 389-407.

Card, Claudia. 1986. Oppression and resistance: Frye's *Politics of reality*. *Hypatia* 1(1): 149-66.

———. 1991. *Feminist ethics*. Lawrence: University Press of Kansas.

Davion, Victoria. 1991. Integrity and radical change. In *Feminist ethics*, ed. Claudia Card. Lawrence: University Press of Kansas.

Fisher, Berenice. 1984. Guilt and shame in the women's movement. *Feminist Studies* 10 (2): 185-212.

Frye, Marilyn. 1983. *The politics of reality*. Trumansburg, NY: Crossing Press.

———. 1990. A response to *Lesbian Ethics*. *Hypatia* 5 (3): 132-37.

———. 1991. A response to *Lesbian ethics*: Why ethics? In *Feminist ethics*, ed. Claudia Card. Lawrence: University Press of Kansas.

Gilligan, Carol. 1977. In a different voice: Women's conceptions of self and morality. *Harvard Educational Review* 47 (4): 486-87.

———. 1982. *In a different voice*. Cambridge: Harvard University Press.

Hoagland, Sarah Lucia. 1988. *Lesbian ethics: Towards new value*. Palo Alto, CA: Institute of Lesbian Studies.

———. 1991. Some thoughts about caring. In *Feminist ethics*, ed. Claudia Card. Lawrence: University Press of Kansas.

Lugones, Maria. 1990. Hispaneando y lesbiando: On Sarah Hoagland's *Lesbian Ethics*. *Hypatia* 5(3): 138-46.

Morgan, Kathryn. 1988. Women and moral madness. In *Feminist perspectives: Philosophical essays on method and morals*, ed. L. Code, S. Mullett, and C. Overall. Toronto: University of Toronto Press.

Morris, Jan. 1974. *Conundrum*. New York: Harcourt Brace Jovanovich.

Morrison, Toni. 1974. *Sula*. New York: Alfred A. Knopf.

Murphy, Jeffrie, and Jean Hampton. 1988. *Forgiveness and mercy.* New York: Cambridge University Press.

Noddings, Nel. 1984. *Caring: A feminine approach to ethics and moral education.* Berkeley: University of California Press.

Ruddick, Sara. 1989. *Maternal thinking.* Boston: Beacon Press.

Spelman, Elizabeth. 1991. Virtue of feeling and feeling of virtue. In *Feminist Ethics*, ed. Claudia Card. Lawrence: University Press of Kansas.

Strawson, P. F. 1974. *Freedom, resentment and other essays.* London: Methuen.

Walker, Alice. 1970. *The third life of Grange Copeland.* New York: Harcourt Brace Jovanovich.

Watson, Gary. 1987. Responsibility and the limits of evil. In *Responsibility, character and the emotions*, ed. Ferdinand Schoeman. New York: Cambridge University Press.

Young, Iris. 1988. Five faces of oppression. *Philosophical Forum*, 21 (4): 270-88.

Realizing Love and Justice: Lesbian Ethics in the Upper and Lower Case

KATHLEEN MARTINDALE and MARTHA SAUNDERS

This essay examines two tendencies in lesbian ethics as differing visions of community, as well as contrasting views of the relationship between the erotic and the ethical. In addition to considering those authors who make explicit claims about lesbian ethics, this paper reflects on the works of some lesbians whose works are less frequently attended to in discussions about lesbian ethics, including lesbians writing from the perspectives of theology and of literature.

> What is real? What is feminist? What is inside? What is out-
> side?
> All are false distinctions, something I've known all along.
> There
> is no inside or outside. I do not live in two worlds. I live in
> one.
> —Irena Klepfisz, "The Distances Between Us: Feminism,
> Consciousness and the Girls at the Office," (1990, 45)

Lesbian ethics can be seen as an ethics for the lesbian community, an ethics for lesbians' treatment of each other. Or it can be seen as an ethical orientation to justice that begins in lesbian identity but moves from this starting point to a sense of solidarity with groups and individuals whose self-articulations may embrace a variety of histories, including experiences of oppression as well as experiences of joy and pleasure, strength and empowerment. Differences between the two tendencies in lesbian ethics can be understood as different visions of community, as well as contrasting ways of figuring the relationship between the erotic and the ethical. While the two tendencies are not neces-sarily mutually exclusive and ought not to be constructed as oppositional, they have manifested themselves differently in lesbian writing and activism.

Hypatia vol. 7, no. 4 (Fall 1992) © by Kathleen Martindale And Martha Saunders

MAPPING LESBIAN ETHICS

When we began to teach and write about feminist and lesbian ethics seven years ago, we encountered primarily surprise and resistance from many of our feminist colleagues and students. Our militant feminist and lesbian students thought ethics was a trap; our feminist colleagues were unsure that feminist or lesbian ethics was a legitimate field of study. While these colleagues became most excited when they read articles appropriating Hume or Rawls for feminism, we were left cold because we felt that the intellectual energy put into that sort of appropriation was largely misspent.

Lesbian ethics seemed more exciting, but it also excluded us to a certain degree because of our political and disciplinary allegiances. Perhaps because we were located in departments of religious studies or women's studies/English, we traced our lineages in feminist and lesbian ethics differently than did our colleagues who were philosophers. In this article, we map a field of lesbian ethics, not so much because we think that doing taxonomical work is always valuable or necessary in itself, but because we construct the field differently and more inclusively than those who work in what we call "upper case" or self-styled Lesbian Ethics.

By initiating a critique of that work from within another site, a less well-known and less "disciplined" area that writes itself as lesbian ethics in the "lower case," we hope to begin a dialogue badly needed among lesbians working in ethics but starting from different disciplinary and political locations. We believe that the work of elaborating how the erotic and the ethico-political are related is the primary task of a lesbian ethics, but that it has just begun. We find the relationship generally passed over in Lesbian Ethics in the upper case and asserted but not carefully or fully argued in the homiletic and inspirational writing of Carter Heyward, who advances, as do we, a nonseparatist and multisystems approach to a lesbian ethics of justice. The nomenclature, "lower case" and "upper case," is borrowed from the lesbian literary theorist Elizabeth Meese's usage in her book (Ex)Tensions: Re-Figuring Feminist Criticism, where it functions to name, investigate, and refigure the different ways feminist literary criticism has identified, institutionalized, or contested its own construction and ownership of what has become a "field" (1990, 3-7). The apparent hierarchy of her terminological typography is, if anything, rejected in her analyses, as in our own here. Nonetheless, neither Meese nor we want to set up a new central proprietorship of "the" discipline of literary criticism or lesbian ethics. Moreover, though her views, like our own, are throughout passionate and sometimes even polemical, she does not want to claim a new space of correctness or closure, but to open the field to questioning. The refiguring Meese wants to do is endless, provisional, and requires on her part, if not that of her and our readers as well, an unusual blend of "love, [and] contestatory workings out" (181).

The two of us have been engaged, both together and separately, in feminist study groups and collaborative writing projects, which have made us aware of the ethico-political meanings of our construction of inside/outside feminist and lesbian ethics. The impetus for this article, like that for our coedited journal, originally called the *Canadian Journal of Feminist Ethics* and then, more simply, *Feminist Ethics* (1986-90), can be traced back to our experiences of feminist collaboration, which raised a variety of ethical questions.

We have found it necessary to construct a lesbian genealogy that would allow us to place ourselves and our work, which centers on the establishment and meaning of justice for lesbians in particular, but not exclusively, in an ethico-political tradition. Voluntary exiles from the United States as well as from heterosexuality, we realize that most of the choices we've experienced in our lives relate to our white skin privilege. But we connect our feelings of ambivalence and wariness about the desire or expectation of ever being completely at home in the world with our ways of being lesbian in a hostile world. Our thinking about lesbian ethics primarily focuses on working through the ethical implications and consequences of inclusivity and exclusivity, for those whom María Lugones calls "world-travellers" and "outsiders" (1990b) and Gloria Anzaldúa has called lives lived on "la frontera" (1987, preface, 194-95).

Martha, who is, like Kathleen, an ex-Catholic and a convert to Judaism, finds it ironic and sometimes difficult to explain why she, an ex-nun, feels her strongest connections with feminists and lesbians working in a religious tradition she abandoned because of its misogyny. Martha's work has focused on developing a feminist and lesbian critique of ethics and an ethical critique of feminist and lesbian theory and politics. She has been "doing ethics" in the context of religious studies and finds an orientation to justice to be central to the work of feminist and lesbian theologians but often missing from other approaches to feminist and lesbian ethics (Saunders 1989, 1990). Although Kathleen is also impressed with the writings of lesbian liberation theologians, she finds herself most frequently "writing with" the work of lesbian and materialist feminist writers and cultural theorists whose work has significant ethical implications.[1] Kathleen became intrigued by the different ways feminist theorists map the traditions that enable and sustain their intellectual work when she collaborated with four Canadian feminist philosophers, two of whom were lesbians, on the process of writing ethically (Code et al., "Some Issues in the Ethics of Collaborative Work," forthcoming). In a monograph titled *Is Feminist Ethics Possible?* (Code et al. 1991) Kathleen and the other contributors all write in their own voices, because no one register could express the writers' differences about ethics or its relationship to language, subjectivity, and ideology. Kathleen's writing has attempted to probe the ethical agenda underlying feminist literary theorizing (Martindale 1987, 1988, 1988-89). Because an intellectually moribund liberal humanist "ethical criticism" based on demonizing Otherness has had remarkable staying power in mainstream literary criticism, feminist and lesbian critical theorists have, understandably enough, not been keen to study how their own work is fundamentally "moved by a desire" for justice (Spivak, quoted in Martindale, forthcoming).

We believe that, without an ethic, feminist and particularly lesbian theory does not make sense logically or politically. While in our opinion lesbian ethics could not have developed without feminist analysis and critique, there are significant differences between feminist ethics and lesbian ethics. The former is, one could argue, older, and the community of participants is bigger. Feminist ethics is by now a somewhat more credible institutionalized academic discourse; and the literature, conferences and academic journals that support it are greatly enabled by the involvement of established groups such as SWIP (Society for Women in Philosophy) and, in Canada, C-SWIP. Writing about feminist ethics could help the writer to get tenure; we doubt that the same is true of lesbian ethics. Many contributors to lesbian ethics are not credentialed philosophers, nor would they want to be. Their writing has an authority in the community that does not derive from the writers' academic credentials. In comparison with feminist ethics, lesbian ethics is a far more marginalized and clearly counterhegemonic, even rowdy, enterprise. Its concerns are not meta-ethical, and there will most likely never be any attempt to construct "grand theory." Lesbian ethics is homespun, even when the writers are academic philosophers. For example, Sarah Hoagland offers helpful advice in *Lesbian Ethics* (1988) for readers who might want to skip the denser, more technical parts, and she lightens the book's tone by incorporating animal designs into the chapter headings. This work invites the reader in; it is frequently personal and dialogical to the point of urging direct response. Kathleen remembers exactly where she was when she first read Jeffner Allen's essay "Looking at Our Blood: A Lesbian Response to Men's Terrorization of Women" (1986, 27-60). It forever changed her understanding of the ethics of nonviolence as they concern lesbians. Lesbian ethics treats ethical concerns as fundamentally contextual; contributors are unusually involved with the development of the discourse. Lesbian ethics is emphatically a localized and historically and culturally specific discourse, though some writers, the ones we most depend on, speak out of a commitment to global politics. Perhaps because lesbian ethics is more obviously radical in its subject matter and institutional affiliations than is feminist ethics, it is still angry after all these years, and proud of it.

Elaborating how the erotic and the ethico-political are related is the primary task of a lesbian ethics, and, in our opinion, it has not yet been attempted. The lesbian Episcopal priest and theologian Carter Heyward asserts their oneness but without fully theorizing their relationship. We find it instructive to compare her approach, as articulated in her recent book *Touching Our Strength: The Erotic as Power and the Love of God* (1989), with that of Teresa de Lauretis (1990b). Heyward writes:

> Anger at injustice is essential to sexual ethics because sexual
> relationships do not occur in social vacuums. Our erotic capac-
> ities are formed and deformed by our alienation from one
> another and from ourselves. It is enormously difficult to make
> love in contexts of poverty and despair, injustice and fear, but
> it may be, in a given moment, all that people can do to share
> even a glimmer of hope. (Heyward 1989, 144)

While Heyward sees the erotic and the political as identical for lesbians, Teresa
de Lauretis sees them as mutually contradictory but necessary. Though we see
the underlying binary and its elaboration differently, we find her claim enor-
mously evocative for understanding the history of feminist and lesbian theorizing about ethics: an erotic, narcissistic drive . . . enhances images of
feminism as

> difference, rebellion, daring, excess, subversion, disloyalty,
> agency, empowerment, pleasure and danger, and rejects all
> images of powerlessness, victimization, subjection, acquies-
> cence, passivity, conformism, femininity; and an ethical
> drive . . . works toward community, accountability, entrust-
> ment, sisterhood, bonding, belonging to a common world of
> women. . . . Are these two drives together, most often in mutual
> contradiction, what particularly distinguishes lesbian femi-
> nism, where the erotic is as necessary a condition of the ethical,
> if not more? (de Lauretis 1990b, 265-66)[2]

In the context of American lesbian ethics, we see two different approaches
to those concerns, and we think it potentially helpful to clarify the similarities
and differences between them. We are characterizing these two tendencies as
"Lesbian Ethics" (or "upper case") and "lesbian ethics" (or "lower case"). The
journal Lesbian Ethics and Sarah Hoagland's book Lesbian Ethics exemplify the
first sort. The other work in this field is more varied and inscribes a lesbian
ethic in the lower case. The first sort is far more visible among lesbians and
focuses on lesbian ethical concerns of identity and community specific to those
it regards as insiders. Each sort has a different relationship to outsiders, and
this is one of the main issues we will consider in this paper. Which set of
tendencies lesbians choose to adopt as foundational to a lesbian ethics is really
a function of the kind of community with which lesbians want to identify—is
it the smaller, intimate community of those with whom one feels relatively safe
and protected in an otherwise hostile world? Or is it a larger, or at any rate
more broadly conceived, community of all those who are struggling for justice?
We believe that this set of options is more than simply a matter of personal
preference; rather the choice is a political and ethical choice about to whom
lesbians will be accountable. It is a question of making a commitment to justice

or to safety and retrenchment.[3] That an orientation to justice is a compelling demand for lesbian ethics will be argued throughout this paper.

INCLUSION/EXCLUSION AND COMMUNITY: TENDENCIES IN LESBIAN ETHICS

Lesbian Ethics in the Upper Case: Separatist

Most of what is called "lesbian ethics" is separatist, but what exactly lesbians who name themselves as such are separating from and what "world" or "worldlessness" they inhabit as a result remain open to clarification (see Card 1988). A separatist orientation gives lesbian ethics its meaning as an ethics for how lesbians should treat each other within their communities. If we use the journal *Lesbian Ethics* as exemplary, inclusion/exclusion primarily concerns the establishment and maintenance of community boundaries. The most important question is, who is inside (who counts as a lesbian) and who is out there (that is, part of heteropatriarchy)? This is the ethics of a strict separatism, which begins and ends with an unproblematized notion of lesbian identity. The journal *Lesbian Ethics*, edited by Jeanette Silveira, originally had guidelines indicating it was a "forum for lesbian feminist ethics and philosophy with an emphasis on how lesbians behave with each other." In later years, the wording changed slightly but significantly to read "radical lesbian feminist ethics." This feisty and antitheoretical publication is characterized by heated discussion of lesbian experience and refuses to rely on the support of the Western philosophical tradition, especially as it concerns metaethics. Even more striking is the absence of feminist and lesbian theories. Since the journal is more preoccupied with establishing standards of correctness for lesbian social and sexual behavior than with ethics per se, a more accurate name would be "Lesbian Etiquette."[4]

As a separatist publication, the journal's chief concern is with keeping lesbianism pure. The writers are vigilant about the dangers of backsliding among lesbians. The outlook of *Lesbian Ethics* is oddly similar to that of Christian sectarian ethics. Separatist lesbian ethics takes its place in a long line of world-denying, in-group sectarian ethics that is mostly concerned with developing an etiquette for relating to each other within the society of the elect. Early twentieth-century sociologists of Christianity Max Weber and Ernst Troeltsch saw the ethics of sectarian groups as world-denying and inward-turning; their point was to keep group members pure and uncontaminated in anticipation of the (imminent) day of judgment and delivery. Sectarian movements often arose as a protest against injustice (e.g., in the Middle Ages against the wealth and corrupt power of the church), but their solution to injustice was not to change the world but to withdraw from it and improve themselves instead. Rather than engage with and battle injustice, they attempted to escape it by creating little egalitarian communities of the just (Troeltsch 1960, 331-43).

As nonseparatist lesbians, we recognize that the easiest critiques of separatism are cheap shots that do little more than valorize the discourse and the ethical terrain of "larger struggles." We also admit that any mapping narrative, such as our own, will repress certain features of a story and exaggerate others. Like Heyward, we believe that coming out into lesbian feminism constitutes at least an implicit epistemological, ethical, and political break with heterosexism. Because it must be articulated and defended against continual attack, even from friends, the decision to live as a separatist makes that break explicit and therefore has profound ethical consequences. There are, nonetheless, several problems with a lesbian separatist ethics. One is that separatist communities judge their moral standing only intramurally. Since the rest of humankind is outside the kingdom of the saved, behavior toward them is not a matter for ethics. Sectarians forfeit any possibility of influencing world events through their insistence on withdrawal from as much of it as possible or necessary. They thereby also abandon all moral responsibility for anyone other than their own members. And since there is little concern for wider issues of justice, sectarian ethics does not provide moral analysis of the relationship of community members to injustice except as victims. Because one element of identity is prioritized, differences among lesbians that can be traced to systemic injustices such as racism or class oppressions tend to be individualized and interpreted as moral failures of sensitivity to others' feelings, rather than as complicity in oppressive social structures that are much larger than individuals. Rather than seeking change in these social structures, a separatist ethics aims only at the transformation of individual attitudes.

In a separatist ethics, the relationship between the erotic and the ethical is not itself theorized; rather, the erotic is a matter for ethical reflection primarily in terms of right and wrong kinds of sexual behavior, such as s/m, or right and wrong kinds of social/relational behaviors such as butch/femme. The relationship between the erotic and power is articulated only in terms of heterosexuality and heteropatriarchal models of relating, and the assumption is that whenever power differentials manifest themselves between lesbians, lesbians are simply mimicking heterosexist patterns.

Another problem with sectarian ethics is that it leads to moral absolutism: sectarians tend to set themselves up as judges of the saved and the damned. Evil is easily identified; in this case, it is men and patriarchy. The absolutism defines community boundaries, since any issue related to membership is clearcut. However, there is also a moral relativism concerning issues within the community and between community members; efforts are made not to decide who is right or wrong, but rather to determine ways of doing the least harm and promoting the greatest well-being.

A profound contradiction operates in this view of lesbian ethics: lesbian feminism as presented is so compelling a vision, as providing an implicit if not explicit value system for all lesbians, that living by it would seem obvious. Paradoxically, however, this vision has to be fought for and scrupulously maintained by an iron force of will in order not to be recuperated back into heteropatriarchy. The imaginary of Lesbian Ethics is fixed on the immediate past of American lesbian feminist separatism, in particular the 1970s, rather than the present or the future. We believe that this preoccupation of a small subgroup of lesbians with the immediate past to the extent of being unconcerned for the longer past of lesbian cultures as well as lesbian futures is a serious problem for upper case Lesbian Ethics. Like Heyward, we believe that lesbian ethics must shape itself, as a process of creation and re-creation, in relation to the historical moral dimensions of our lives. While not as ahistorical or as ethnocentrically oriented as most canonical feminist ethics, which is preoccupied with defining and privileging a white, classist and heterosexualist notion of caring, the journal *Lesbian Ethics*, in its attention to the paradise lost of lesbian feminism, fails to take up justice issues, which are most concerned with bringing us into a future that is not only feminist but lesbian.

Hoagland and Lesbian Communitarian Ethics

A more moderate tendency in "upper case" Lesbian Ethics is represented by Sarah Hoagland's book *Lesbian Ethics: Toward New Value*. Although Hoagland is a separatist, she explicitly refuses to define "lesbian" and "lesbianism" and to draw the boundaries of the community (Hoagland 1988, 8). Hoagland recognizes that community is a process, not an entity that simply needs to be protected from encroachment by heteropatriarchy. This position perhaps implies that separation itself can never be total and final.

While Hoagland's ethics share some of the assumptions of communitarian ethics (see Friedman 1990), in other ways her work departs from those assumptions because her ethics is lesbian. More than most communitarians, Hoagland is implicitly critical of assumptions about an "inherently social self" (Friedman 1990, 279). Bringing a feminist critique to individualist concepts of self, Hoagland then develops the critique further by addressing the problems that a caring and nurturant, relational self—that is a feminized, heterosexualized self—would face in living up to the moral demands of living as a lesbian (Hoagland 1988, 82-100).

Hoagland is also more aware than communitarian ethicists that communities and their members, even lesbians, can make inappropriate moral demands on members. Hoagland departs most clearly from communitarian ethics in her concept of autokoenony, a concept that reflects the complexities of relationship between self and community:

> "Autokoenony" is "the self in community." The self in commu-
> nity involves each of us making choices; it involves each of us
> having a self-conscious sense of ourselves as moral agents in a
> community of other self-conscious moral agents. (145)

While community is essential to her ethics, it is not, as in communitarian
ethics, merely a given. Recognizing that women too easily lose themselves in
community, she admonishes readers to remember that the separateness or
specificity of each lesbian self must not be lost. That uniqueness is located in
what each lesbian focuses on, and the quality of this focus is the moral moment
(cf. Frye's metaphor of attention, in Frye 1983, 167-70).

Lesbian community is both Hoagland's moral starting point—"without it
no individual lesbian could make any of the changes that are taking place here"
(Hoagland 1988, 290)—and the context that allows lesbians to create meaning.[5] Hoagland's refusal to define "lesbian" or to police the borders of lesbian
community makes her analysis unique within the tradition of separatist ethics
and, in particular, far more optimistic about the possibilities for moral growth
(9).

Hoagland is concerned not with moral reform but with, following feminist
philosopher Kathryn Pyne Addelson, a "moral revolution" in the creation of
moral values. Nonetheless, she does not claim as much as Heyward does for
the ethical foundations of lesbian subjectivity; it "holds *a certain possibility
which can effect* a transformation of consciousness: the conceptual/material
possibility of female agency not defined in terms of an other" (6; italics added).
Hoagland's lesbian community is a context of possibility, of interaction and
relation in which, unlike heterosexuality, dominance and subordination are
not the normal pattern of relating (7). Since Heyward also believes that the
possibility of mutuality or right relations is unique to lesbian (and gay male)
relationships, it's unfortunate, for this and for other reasons, that neither
lesbian thinker, as far as we know, has addressed the other's work.

Heterosexualism becomes the primary contradiction for Hoagland, the
foundation of "social concepts which validate oppression" (8). While for her
lesbian separatism has revolutionary moral authority, we think the most
original contribution in her thinking about a lesbian subject is her notion of
"moral agency under oppression." Ethical existence under oppression involves
making judgments and choices—that is, exercising agency—in coercive and
oppressive situations not of our making.

While Hoagland has some very useful insights on the nature of lesbian
relationships (164-77) and avoids idealizing them as some separatists do,
discussion of sexuality (she rejects the term's usefulness for lesbians) and the
erotic (she prefers "lesbian desire") occupies very little space in her large work.
The reader can get the impression that "sexuality" is too bound up with
"heterosexualism" to merit much attention in lesbian ethics. While her

argument of this point is valid (and draws heavily on both Claudia Card and Marilyn Frye), it tends to leave lesbian eroticism again somewhat disembodied and ethereal. This disembodiment is at the root of her lack of concern with issues of justice in the world (see Saunders 1990, 36-37). She never does address global injustices, except as they relate directly to justice for lesbians, as in her critique of heterosexualism. She ignores the power of the internalization of relations of domination and subordination within individuals in reducing all such relations to "heterosexualism."

The Ethics of Worldly Lesbians: lesbian ethics in the Lower Case

The other tendency is found in concentrated form in the lesbian theological ethics of Carter Heyward; though not so often claimed as "ethics," it is also scattered throughout the work of some lesbian materialist writers and cultural theorists. This work is in principle nonseparatist. While the ethics of these lesbians insists on a lesbian starting point, the moral concern is not primarily who is inside but who is excluded from their communities of concern and why. For some, the inside/outside binary is deconstructed; for others, exclusion is unjust, and justice is the primary ethical concern of these lesbians who inhabit several intersecting communities of accountability. Lesbianism is one facet of identity, an important one, and, for many relatively privileged women, the entry point into awareness of oppression. But it is the entry point only, not the end point. These writers' ethical passion comes out of their lesbianism, and their lesbianism is basic to their subjectivity but is not sufficient in establishing it. Only if lesbian identity is singular, clearcut and easily definable can we always know who we are and are not. But many lesbians do not experience identity so unproblematically. They do not believe that they cease to be lesbians when sharing a world with non-lesbians, for none of us can live consistently, or for long, in a single world (Lugones 1990a, 1990b).

Confusion, complexity and ambiguity are fundamental to this lesbian worldview. Minnie Bruce Pratt, poet, essayist, and activist against racism and anti-Semitism, explains the ethical motivations propelling her toward inclusivity in her writing and her life in community: "Now I know that in order to keep hoping, and living, and writing, I need work from other women that is rooted in the messy complexity of our daily lives, work in which we upset the predictable ending" (Pratt 1991, 163). Pratt cannot totally dissociate herself from the evil she names and battles, but rather acknowledges various evils as continuing parts of her own history and identity—racism, anti-Semitism, class privilege, internalized homophobia and sexism. Perhaps it is the acknowledgment of the continuing power of this evil not only over her but within her that makes her refuse a simple ethics. It is not so easy to label the enemy and sever connections with it if it continues to live within you. It is also not possible ever to be safe from evil; there is no place to which to retreat, and therefore the only way to live is to live in the midst of the danger. Pratt talks about how her childhood white southern home was defined not so much by what was inside as by what was kept out:

> Raised to believe that I could be where I wanted and have what I wanted, as a grown woman I thought I could simply claim what I wanted, even the making of a new place to live with other women. I had no understanding of the limits that I lived within, nor of how much my memory and my experience of a safe space to be was based on places secured by omission, exclusion or violence, and on my submitting to the limits of that place. (Pratt 1991, 25-26)

But from whence comes this need for a "messy complexity"? For those we call "worldly lesbians," the conscientizing process of analyzing our varied experiences of oppression as women and lesbians is the entry point into solidarity with, and accountability to, other oppressed peoples whose oppressions are different, and even, perhaps, in whose oppression these lesbians have in some ways been complicit. This process is a refusal of victimhood; it involves moving from one's own experience of oppression to something beyond it.

This movement insists on an ethics of interconnectedness, stressing the interrelation of different forms of oppression and the connections among all the oppressed. It is grounded in historical specificity; there are many possible starting points and many overlapping communities, of which lesbian is one, or several, for not all are lesbians with the same meanings (see Lugones's critique of Hoagland, 1990a). It also consists in the recognition that there can be no safe place for some women until all oppressions have been overcome, to paraphrase Audre Lorde (1984). It is a recognition that ultimately the good of lesbians is interdependent with the good of all oppressed people, and that the struggle to overcome a particular form of oppression depends on the overcoming of all forms of oppression. This is why this tendency stresses justice rather than safety and sees community in larger terms.

Carter Heyward and Lesbian Theological Ethics of Interconnectedness

If separatism is comparable to the ethics representative of the sectarian tendency in Western history, the ethics of Carter Heyward is also anomalous in relation to the mainstream Protestant tradition that represents her starting point. She characterizes herself as a

> white anglo southern christian lesbian priest and academic with class roots in middle-strata United States of America. I am teacher and learner, activist and theorist, well educated by life as well as by school in classical and feminist western culture. I

am interested in multicultural and global realities, and hope someday to better understand them. (Heyward 1989, 8)

For many, perhaps, "christian lesbian priest" would be an oxymoron. Yet, if the voice of sectarianism, or separatism, is a voice speaking to an inner community of the elect, there is also a tradition of prophecy—that is, a voice crying in the wilderness of corruption and misuse of power, a voice speaking to the oppressive institutions out of the conviction that those institutions can change, that social structures can be transformed. The position of remaining within these institutions in the hope of transforming them is a dangerous one, as the separatists warn, and the critique of unjust power structures that it entails can be turned backward to uphold those very structures. There is also always the danger of compromise and co-optation, which can lead either to action in bad faith or to total despair.

However, this position is also a grounded one: it recognizes the real power of the institutions, power that is internalized in the minds and hearts of all, including even those who would rebel against the power. Unjust power cannot be escaped by locking it out in the cold; rather it must be faced head-on and struggled with. Heyward, Pratt, and the others we discuss below will not give up their own power-in-relation with which they can struggle for social transformation with all the risks that this entails.

Heyward's approach suggests how much separatist ethics loses when it fails to be interested in elaborating a notion of justice. Hoagland's discussion of justice is limited to a few liberal theorists such as Mill and Rawls and leads her to conclude that " 'justice' is a concept that exists to sort out competing claims within a system that has as its axis dominance and subordination. The function of justice is social control" (Hoagland 1988, 264). Given that in Hoagland's thinking desire for control is heterosexualist, justice is eliminated as a concern for lesbian ethics.

Although Heyward's conception of justice is more original and materialist than that of other openly lesbian ethicists, it is also apparently less well-known to lesbians. We think her work needs to be cited somewhat more extensively than the writing we have discussed so far. She claims a different meaning for justice than Hoagland does, and Heyward's meaning makes justice the foundation for a different notion of community:

> But what is justice? I invite you to think beyond the images of jurisprudence and legalism often associated with justice in patriarchal, androcentric society into a realm of radical relationality. In this realm, justice is right relation, and right relation is mutual relation. In a mutual relationship both (or all) people are empowered to experience one another as intrinsically valuable, irreplaceable earthcreatures, sources of joy and love and respect in relation to one another. To experience

ourselves genuinely as friends: This is justice. (Heyward 1989,
22-23)

This is a universalist kind of vision, but Heyward presents it precisely as a
vision of what might be, not as a present reality. It is the goal toward which
political and ethical life is directed, but it is never fully achieved.
Heteropatriarchal ethical conceptions of the "just society" function as though
the good society were already achieved—they lack an analysis of the actual
workings of injustice in the world, a realization of the way power structures
impede the achievement of justice and the ways in which every individual is
to a greater or lesser degree complicit in those power structures.

It is here that we see the relationship between the erotic and the ethical.
According to Heyward, it is through our bodies that we know relationship,
that right relationship which is justice. Justice is not an abstract universal social
principle but the condition of possibility of relationship. Justice and love are
not identical, but they are inseparable: "Justice is the actual shape of love in
the world" (191). All relationships involve a struggle to achieve mutuality,
which is not the same as equality. Mutuality is growth toward shared power
and must be struggled for in relationships that are not equal, as well as in those
that appear equal. The erotic is "our desire to taste and smell and see and hear
and touch one another . . . our yearning to be involved . . . in each other's
sounds and glances and bodies and feelings" (187). The erotic is the precon-
dition of our connectedness with others, of relationship, rather than a particular kind of connectedness or relationship.[6] Thus the erotic is much more than
the sexual, although it includes it. Heyward is not clear on how this process
works, and her argument suffers from an idealism that is not always easily
translated into strategies for action. She needs to be read along with lesbians
like Pratt, Lorde, Anzaldúa, and others who give very concrete articulations
of the working out of the erotic in the ethical. Heyward presents the vision;
these other writers show us some of the concrete ways the vision has to be
realized. We will return to this later on.

Community includes both the microsociety of friends and the global
macrosociety. For Heyward, the community of friendship is the source of her
power and strength in working for justice in the larger society, even though
injustice is found also within the smaller community, as well as within ourselves. This is the refusal of a separatist or sectarian position, although it affirms
the ethical importance of the small community. But establishing justice or
right-relation between individuals within our small community is only a
prerequisite in our work for justice in the world. Moral purity is something
none of us, nor our communities, can ever attain (contrary again to the
separatist ethic).

Lesbians as lesbians have a calling to actively realize love and justice in
human life as sacred (89). Claiming lesbian sexuality and defying the system

of domination known as heterosexuality creates the possibility (not the guarantee) of relations of mutuality. Following Lorde, Heyward defines the ethical meaning of lesbianism as centered in our sexuality, "*our embodied, relational response to erotic/sacred power*" (Heyward 1989, 193-94, italics in original), which creates in lesbians a passion for justice.

Coming out is an ethical act because it marks a "commitment to *do something* about what we have experienced, to celebrate the just and change the unjust" (Heyward 1984, 128). By suggesting what the ethico-political consequences of claiming lesbian identity are, Heyward indicates how to affirm notions of identity, community, and home-coming derived from lesbian identity politics while connecting them explicitly with political action. This is especially helpful because of the unhelpful way that identity/politics has been analyzed in feminist and lesbian critical theory as if it were always a binary.[7] By struggling to "live our values" (128), we nurture and cultivate the "goodness in our lives" (Heyward 1989, 18).

Heyward is not a theorist but a preacher; her writing is not academic, not even theological, but homiletic and exhortatory. But this is true, to a certain extent, of all writing on lesbian ethics—it is not detached, calmly reasoned, but passionate with the urgency of living in an unjust world. Thus many of Heyward's statements that we have cited are, in her books, assertions that are made without argumentation. This is not to say that her work contains no theory. She theorizes heterosexism, for example, adequately if not with originality, in a way that would satisfy any separatist. However, having established heterosexism as a "*foundational resource of alienated power*" (Heyward 1989, 51, italics in original), she refuses to regard it as the only resource or even as more foundational than any other. Rather, heterosexism is one of the learned survival mechanisms that are based on "symbols and acts of domination and violence" (55) that humans begin to assimilate at a very early age. But heterosexism is not simply something that exists out there, in society or in other people; rather, it is something that even lesbians and gay men have internalized and live with intimately, even among themselves. Thus it is not escaped by separating from the world.

It is from this conviction that Heyward moves courageously into a discussion of sadomasochism, certainly a very controversial issue among lesbians. Heyward theorizes sadomasochism in such a way that it becomes impossible to view it as a practice that some "others" engage in but I don't, or that I engage in with my partners and "others" don't. Heyward argues that we all live in an abusive society, in which all efforts toward mutuality are punished. We have all learned at an early age to associate love and intimacy with domination and subordination. Sadomasochism is not a set of practices individuals engage in but a characteristic of societies, and of each person and each attempt at relationship:

> But can sadomasochistic eroticism be a relational conduit through which we move toward mutuality not only with each other but also with God, the source of our liberation? The answer is that it must be, because we can reach one another and God only from where we are here and now. (108)

Sexuality that is claimed against a body-denying Christian spirituality, that is defined over against the sanctification of heterosexual coupling oriented toward "procreation," sexuality whose raison d'etre is its own self, not some end beyond—this is the basis of a materialist, world-affirming ethics that is oriented toward the creation of justice; that affirms the place of lesbians in the human community; that insists on lesbian connection with all who suffer, who are oppressed, and all who live life and celebrate it in the midst of oppression. This is an ethics for those who are immersed in the world, not cut off from it.

A multivocal ethics, as the basis for the struggle of many differently identified communities, enables individuals as well as each group to recognize that they are not solely responsible for justice—therefore, such an ethics avoids a demoralizing sense of helplessness in the face of evil. But it does not thereby solve the conflicts of interest that may arise between different communities of identity; rather, it recognizes that these must be struggled through as members of each group own their own participation and complicity with unjust social structures. It may not always be practical, telling us how to act in each specific situation. It has a utopian cast to it perhaps, or, to use the theological term, it is eschatological—it is about bringing about a different kind of reality.

DOMESTICATED AND WORLDLY LESBIANS: FINDING THE ETHICAL DOMAIN IN LESBIAN LITERARY CRITICISM AND THEORY

Like lesbian ethics, lesbian literary criticism and theory of the 1980s has been concerned chiefly with issues of identity, especially as they relate to questions of representation, subjectivity, desire, and community. Though neither discipline seems to read the other, each, in its apparent unawareness, seems to offer an implicit commentary on the other. In this section, we suggest how different understandings of key lesbian ethical questions are figured in a variety of lesbian critical texts.

As de Lauretis (1990b, 266) has suggested, lesbian feminism during this period developed as a tension between inside and outside, as an erotic performance that simultaneously enacts and requires an ethical quest. Her claim relates the ethical to the erotic in the ways they have been conceptualized within one tendency within lesbianism in terms of mutually contradictory "drives," whereas, as we have previously indicated, Heyward perceives them as interconnected, if not identical, when seen from her lesbian liberation theological viewpoint.

We cannot nor do we want to argue which of these rather dazzling and grandiose claims is the correct one. Both seem as problematic as they are suggestive—Heyward's for her utopianism and de Lauretis's for desiring to transcend polarization by cutting the Gordian knot through her own sheer cerebral hyperlucidity. While many of the tendencies in feminism that de Lauretis links to the erotic drive we would argue should be linked to the ethical one and vice versa, her tying of the history of conflicts in feminist theory and practice to their source in ethics is illuminating and useful. Her mapping of relationships between the erotic and the ethical provides a necessary first step to understanding the recent history of lesbian theories and current debates about the institutional ethics and politics of lesbian and gay studies, especially in relation to other "minority discourses" such as African-American, Native, and women's studies. (The earliest and perhaps still the finest piece on the exclusion of lesbianism from women's studies is Marilyn Frye's "A Lesbian Perspective on Women's Studies" [1982]; see also Thomas Yingling's [1991] more recent raising of similar ethical questions with regard to the place of lesbians in lesbian and gay studies.)

As with lesbian ethics, lesbian literary criticism and theory could be divided into that written in the upper case and the lower case. Admittedly, the terms of distinction between "criticism" and "theory" can be and often are as invidious and hierarchical as the differing typographical treatments. Recently, though, typographies have been used in apparently "inverted" fashion to entitle and to claim territories for two rather different anthologies edited by lesbians. Karla Jay and Joanne Glasgow's *Lesbian Texts and Contexts: Radical Revisions* (1990), all in caps, is a collection of critical essays written almost entirely by lesbians on lesbian writers and themes.[8] Diana Fuss's *inside/out: Lesbian Theories, Gay Theories* (1991), with its mixed typography and mixed lesbian and gay writership, is a collection that rejects that cultural and critical past. The blurb claims its originary status: "the first collection that specifically features the new theoretical work in lesbian and gay studies." In this comparison, the lower case marks the higher theory.

Like lesbian ethics in both cases, lesbian literary criticism and theory can be mapped into separatist and nonseparatist varieties, but the terms are far less applicable, since separatism has never been particularly prominent in the discipline. (See, for example, the literary critic Lillian Faderman's explicit rejection of separatism, in Faderman 1991, 293). The language used to distinguish among various forms of nonseparatist lesbian criticism has tended to distinguish essentialists from nonessentialists or cultural feminist from materialist or poststructuralist lesbian writing. The hyphen typically used with prefixes like "non" and "post," rather than the lower case, tends to mark the higher theoretical position. The hybrid, rather than the pure, garden variety, domesticated lesbian, is the new improved version.

Whatever language we use to mark the differences, the terms used will be contentious, even obnoxious, to many readers. Whatever we name the differences, whether they are called essentialist and nonessentialist or, as we have named them because of our emphasis on the ethical dimension of this work, domesticated and worldly, we stress that we did not invent the distinction but are only foregrounding it in order to question some of its possible implications for how the lesbian ethical domain has been mapped and how we desire to remap it more inclusively.

Lesbian literary criticism and theory that focuses exclusively or largely on lesbian identity and its relation to questions of representation, desire, and community as if identity were unitary and nonproblematic we term "domesticated," with all the etymological implications of living or being at home underscored. That which takes lesbian identity as nonunified and intensely but sometimes pleasurably and usefully problematic, we term "worldly," with all the etymological implications of being somewhere out of "the" or "a" house, whether in the sense of living in a larger more capacious space or of being without a home.

The terms have nothing to do with being in or out of the closet but refer to how different lesbian critics situate themselves with respect to other marginalized discourses and groups. Some lesbians, by necessity or by choice, live in what Audre Lorde has called "the house of difference," while others seek or want a more exclusive kind of home. Diana Fuss's important first book, *Essentially Speaking: Feminism, Nature and Difference*, which is categorized in women's or literary studies but is actually largely concerned with lesbian and gay studies, suggests why. Fuss argues that while it's not fair to say that lesbian theory is less sophisticated than gay male theory, it has been in general more essentialist, more concerned with securing identity rather than deconstructing it, because lesbians have suffered greater cultural oppression and invisibility and therefore have been less secure in their subjectivity than gay men (Fuss 1989, 98).

For example, in the work of many lesbian literary critics, distinctions between what is unique to lesbians and what is not are assumed but not theorized, let alone deconstructed. In *The Safe Sea of Women: Lesbian Fiction 1969-1989*, Bonnie Zimmerman mentions poststructuralist critiques of essentialism, of home and identity, but rejects the rejection of discourses of center and margin by merely adding on discussion of lesbians of color and ethnic lesbians to her central focus on "us," white, middle-class lesbian feminists and their texts. On the last page, she acknowledges that she has recentered them (Zimmerman 1990, 175-77, 186, 232).

In her first book, *Surpassing the Love of Men*, Lillian Faderman (1981) studied and valorized a notion of middle-class white women's powerful but domesticated tradition of romantic friendship and its demise at the hands of the Victorian sexologists. They originated the modern concept of lesbianism but contaminated forever the perceived sexual innocence of these couples by labeling them lesbians. Unlike those lesbian critics we call worldly, for whom no position is innocent, Faderman sees the loss of innocence as a fall from grace, an ethico-political decline to be recuperated by becoming socially respectable. Faderman's romantic friendships were and possibly still are firmly located in the homes of relatively privileged women.

In *Odd Girls and Twilight Lovers: A Study of Lesbian Life in Twentieth-Century America*, Faderman studies what she admits has been a "class war" between older or middle- and upper-class lesbians, on the one hand, and working-class and younger lesbians, on the other (Faderman 1991, 181-83). Faderman shows how the conflict plays itself out in the private space of those who can afford homes and prefer to use them as social space, and in the public spaces, such as bars, of those who must or prefer to use less controlled and exclusive places. Faderman's narrative is a teleological one tracing the trajectory from same-sex love through romantic friendship to what she sees as the current destigmatizing of lesbianism and achievement of greater social neutrality (6-7). As she draws her conclusion about the building of "community" in the conservative 1980s, Faderman indicates that she regards middle-class white lesbians—domesticated lesbians, if you will—as the mainstream of lesbian culture (273). Faderman seems to undercut her argument and her notion of a clear teleology by claiming that a shift to political moderation has taken place among lesbians but offering as evidence the rise of lesbian involvement in outsider groups such as Queer Nation and ACT UP.

For the domesticated lesbian critics as well as the upper case Lesbian Ethicists, the high point of lesbian culture remains the 1970s, the period of greatest visibility of lesbian feminism before the sex wars and struggles over racism and anti-Semitism split the lesbian feminist consensus, as well as, though Faderman does not mention it before, issues of representation, subjectivity, and language became the intense preoccupation of critical theorists who are also lesbians.

In contrast with the domesticated lesbian critics, the worldly lesbians look outward, in ways that resemble Carter Heyward's viewpoint. Prominent exemplars of worldly lesbianism include both theorists such as de Lauretis, Biddy Martin, and Elizabeth Meese, and poets, novelists, and autobiographers, such as Minnie Bruce Pratt, Audre Lorde, Gloria Anzaldúa, Cherríe Moraga, Joan Nestle, Irena Klepfisz, and Sarah Schulman, whose work frequently transcends generic boundaries and becomes a form of autobiographical theorizing.[9]

Sarah Schulman, the novelist, journalist, and gay and lesbian film festival coordinator, works with ACT UP and has recently written *People in Trouble* (1990), a novel about AIDS that relates personal homophobia to artists' apathy about poverty and homelessness in New York. Joan Nestle, whose book *A Restricted Country* (1987) combines autobiography with lesbian theory, is the founder of New York's Lesbian Herstory Archives and sex radical who works with socialist and gay groups. Irena Klepfisz, the poet and Yiddish translator, whose essays have been collected in *Dreams of an Insomniac* (1990), is now executive director of the progressive group New Jewish Agenda. By being involved with many diverse groups composed largely of nonlesbians or non-feminists, these worldly lesbians enact an ethico-political theory and practice of elaborating problems and allegiances that are messy and complex and whose ethical implications are confusing.

Their notion of lesbian community reaches out to include other, even more stigmatized women, such as lesbian prostitutes, housewives, "passing women," butch-femme women, sex radicals, urban punks, artists, and lesbians who do not feel "at home" within what one domesticated lesbian defines as the "safe sea" of the lesbian feminist/women's movement. They prefer to interrogate the present moment of lesbian culture rather than to produce a chronological narrative of the lesbian tradition in Western culture. They are more open to experimental and especially genre-blending writing than the domesticated lesbians are.

The critique they offer admits its own complicity and cannot take in the whole truth. Their subjectivity is permanently fractured according to race, class, ethnicity, and political allegiances, but they do not regard it as tragic or look to a state of unity with nostalgic longing. Their polyvocalic language delights in using many registers, dialects, and mother tongues. Their writing takes into consideration the gender of race, the race of class, and the class of sexuality rather than simply analyzing gender or sexuality as the primary contradiction.

More than the domesticated lesbians do, they find limitations in feminist theories of sexuality. For some, such as Nestle, the 1950s offer other possibilities of writing a narrative of resistance to sexual and political repression. The 1970s represent a contradictory situation that allowed them respectability as lesbians and feminists but also demanded policing and self-censorship. Lesbian feminist exclusivity stigmatized them as sometimes less than desirable members of the lesbian community. Klepfisz was made to feel guilty because, in spite of the fact that she was an immigrant, a Holocaust survivor, and working-class, she attained a Ph.D (Klepfisz 1990, 46). Nestle was intimidated at work because she insisted on being flamboyantly femme and sexual (Nestle 1987,146). More recently, in a seemingly unrelated way, some worldly lesbians who are also high theorists have come to treat sexuality as separable entirely from gender and as a result have become entranced with considering its permutations as entirely voluntarily chosen and in free play from material conditions, even or especially of embodiment (see the work of Sedgwick—a queer, not a lesbian—1990; Fuss 1989, 1991; and Butler 1990, 1991).

Unlike the domesticated lesbians, lesbian literary theorists who work deconstructively produce symptomatic readings of what is dangerous but sometimes enabling in the theorizing of inside/outside or home/not home. For example, in her first book, *Crossing the Double-Cross: The Practice of Feminist Criticism* (1986), Elizabeth Meese's use of deconstruction with and against lesbian feminist theory is inspired by an ethical vision of relationship between women (see the similarities with Lugones and Spelman 1986). Her second book, *(Ex)Tensions: Re-Figuring Feminist Criticism* (1990), written from an explicitly lesbian position, is not exclusively concerned with "lesbian" writing. Mediating between radical intellectual communities who are largely ignorant and suspicious of each other, Meese argues that feminist criticism will be at an impasse unless and until we engage each other with mutual respect about the differences in, between, and among us. Both she and Carter Heyward would agree that "tension" in doing this work of mediation is neither escapable nor resolvable, since it is a necessary condition for taking it up (see Heyward 1989, 31-36, on the relation between coming out and erotic-ethical tension).

Meese's discussion of the moral psychology of our "othering" other feminists and lesbians is especially illuminating of the dynamic between insiders/outsiders:

> "The Other" (re)presents itself either as something to be destroyed, subjugated, or assimilated in the very fundamental human interest of reducing tension (in an economy of desire), that is, seeking pleasure through some perhaps only illusory but nonetheless comforting sameness. (Meese 1990, 79)

Deconstructing this binary is risky. For lesbian ethicists who value moral clarity and certainty above all else, it is too dangerous. For others, it is necessary, either intellectually or ethically: it must be done if we are to theorize the subject of lesbianism responsibly—that is, in a way that acknowledges the hybrid state of the lesbian-as-agent who struggles to escape ideology but can never be entirely outside it. (Compare Hoagland's [1988] section on the moral agent under oppression with de Lauretis's [1990a] discussion of the difficulties of producing lesbian subjectivities.)

Ethical choice is perhaps never easy, but is made possible by negotiating between and among subject positions. Writing, especially on the borders between lesbian autobiography and theory, offers the most useful and inspiring examples of lesbian ethics in practice. For example, the essays of Minnie Bruce Pratt, particularly "Identity: Skin Blood Heart" (in Pratt 1991), in their concrete and compelling focus on the temporal process by which a lesbian desiring and ethical subject constructs herself show positively that such a thing can occur and negatively that interpellation can be resisted and fail to deliver up another compliant subject (see Martin 1986, 1988). What motivates this politicized choice of a new and stigmatized identity, in which self-interest is in conflict with something else, is a desire to direct ethico-political interests effectively.

We believe that what we need to do on the basis of our having made an ethical decision to struggle for life as lesbians who are accountable to a lesbian community-in-process, among others, is to find a way of working through the relationship between the erotic and the ethical that keeps the nature of the relationship open to greater and perhaps different questions than does de Lauretis's formulation of it as necessarily contradictory but enabling, and open to hope that some day the vision of Heyward, in which the erotic and the ethical are more affectionately interconnected, will cease to seem utopian:

> In the context of mutuality, [lesbian] sex is an expression of a commitment to right relation; . . . because such sexual expression generates more energy (rather than less, apologies to Freud) for passionate involvement in the movements for justice in the world. Lovemaking turns us simultaneously into ourselves and beyond ourselves. In experiencing the depths of our power in relation as pleasurable and good, we catch a glimpse of the power of right relation in longer, more complicated configurations of our life together. Good sex involves us more fully in the struggle for justice—as, or with, people of color, women, differently abled people, ethnic and religious minorities, elderly people, and other earthcreatures. (Heyward 1989, 4)

NOTES

1. For example, Adrienne Rich (1986), Monique Wittig (1992), Audre Lorde (1984), Biddy Martin and Chandra Mohanty (1986), Elizabeth Meese (1986, 1990), Teresa de Lauretis (1986, 1988), Sue-Ellen Case (1988/89), Cherríe Moraga (1983), Gloria Anzaldúa (1987), Minnie Bruce Pratt (1991), Sarah Schulman (1990), Joan Nestle (1987), and Irena Klepfisz (1990).

2. For a related but very different way from de Lauretis's and our own of imagining these tensions, see Janice Raymond's "Putting the Politics Back into Lesbianism" (1989).

3. See Jeffner Allen (1986, 104-5) for an example of the notion of community as a haven of safety and comfort for lesbians.

4. The *Oxford English Dictionary* defines etiquette as follows: "The prescribed ceremonial of a court; the formalities required by usage in diplomatic intercourse. The order of procedure established by custom in the army or navy (especially with reference to promotion) in parliament, etc. The conventional rules of personal behaviour observed in the intercourse of polite society, the ceremonial observances prescribed by such rules. The unwritten code of honour by which members of certain professions (especially the medical and legal) are prohibited from doing certain things deemed likely to injure the interests of their brethren, or to lower the dignity of the profession."

5. Compare the attempt to theorize and practice an implicitly if not explicitly lesbian social-symbolic that recognizes rather than effaces differences in power and ability among

women, in the Milan Women's Bookstore's collectively produced *Sexual Difference* (1990).

6. Heyward's discussion of the erotic borrows heavily and explicitly from Audre Lorde's essay "The Erotic as Power" (Lorde 1984, 53-59), as the title of Heyward's book indicates.

7. The Canadian lesbian feminist political theorist Mary Louise Adams, writing on identity politics, argues that political strategies focusing on identity and those focusing on coalition are not mutually exclusive. She quotes June Jordan's questions: "What is the purpose of your identity? What do you want to do on the basis of that?" (Adams 1989, 29).

8. An article by Elizabeth Meese is distinctively different from all the others, not only in its theoretical allegiances, but in its punning and self-conscious typography.

9. While these writers do not explicitly mention their engagement with lesbian theory, their work, rather than that of the domesticated lesbians, is frequently cited as at least illustrative, and sometimes as even exemplary, by worldly lesbians who also happen to be lesbian high theorists.

REFERENCES

Adams, Mary Louise. 1989. There's no place like home: On the place of identity in feminist politics. *Feminist Review* 31: 22-33.

Allen, Jeffner. 1986. *Lesbian philosophy: Explorations*. Palo Alto: Institute of Lesbian Studies.

Anzaldúa, Gloria. 1987. *Borderlands/la frontera: The new mestiza*. San Francisco: Spinsters/Aunt Lute.

Butler, Judith. 1990. *Gender trouble: Feminism and the subversion of identity*. New York: Routledge.

———. 1991. Imitation and gender insubordination. In *inside/out: Lesbian theories, gay theories*. See Fuss 1991.

Card, Claudia. 1988. Female friendship: Separations and continua. *Hypatia* 3(2): 123-30.

Case, Sue-Ellen. 1988-89. Towards a butch-femme aesthetic. *Discourse* 11(1): 55-73.

Code, Lorraine, Maureen Ford, Kathleen Martindale, Susan Sherwin, and Debra Shogan. 1991. *Is feminist ethics possible?* Ottawa: Canadian Research Institute for the Advancement of Women.

———. 1992. Some issues in the ethics of collaborative work. In *Explorations in feminist ethics*, ed. Eve Browning Cole and Susan Coultrap-McQuin. Bloomington: Indiana University Press.

de Lauretis, Teresa. 1986. Feminist studies/critical studies: Issues, terms, and contexts. In *Feminist studies/critical studies*, ed. Teresa de Lauretis. Bloomington: Indiana University Press.

———. 1988. Sexual indifference and lesbian representation. *Theatre Journal* 40(May): 155-77.

———. 1990a. Sexual indifference and lesbian representation. In *Performing feminisms: Feminist critical theory and theatre*, ed. Sue-Ellen Case. Baltimore: Johns Hopkins University Press.

———. 1990b. Upping the anti (sic) in feminist theory. In *Conflicts in feminism*, ed. Marianne Hirsch and Evelyn Fox Keller. New York: Routledge.

Faderman, Lillian. 1981. *Surpassing the love of men: Romantic friendship and love between women from the Renaissance to the present.* New York: William Morrow.

———. 1991. *Odd girls and twilight lovers: A history of lesbian life in twentieth-century America.* New York: Columbia University Press.

Friedman, Marilyn. 1990. Feminism and modern friendship: Dislocating the community. In *Feminism and political theory*, ed. Cass R. Sunstein. Chicago: The University of Chicago Press.

Frye, Marilyn. 1982. A lesbian perspective on women's studies. In *Lesbian studies: Present and future*, ed. Margaret Cruikshank. Old Westbury, N.Y.: The Feminist Press.

———. 1983. *The politics of reality: Essays in feminist theory.* Trumansburg, N.Y.: Crossing Press.

Fuss, Diana. 1989. *Essentially speaking: Feminism, nature and difference.* New York: Routledge.

———, ed. 1991. *inside/out: Lesbian theories, gay theories.* New York: Routledge.

Heyward, Carter. 1984. *Our passion for justice: Images of power, sexuality and liberation.* New York: Pilgrim Press.

———. 1989. *Touching our strength: The erotic as power and the love of God.* San Francisco: Harper and Row.

Hoagland, Sarah Lucia. 1988. *Lesbian ethics: Toward new value.* Palo Alto: Institute of Lesbian Studies.

Jay, Karla and Joanne Glasgow, eds. 1990. *Lesbian texts and contexts: Radical revisions.* New York: New York University Press.

Klepfisz, Irena. 1990. *Dreams of an insomniac: Jewish feminist essays, speeches and diatribes.* Portland: Eighth Mountain Press.

Lorde, Audre. 1984. *Sister outsider: Essays and speeches.* Trumansburg, N.Y.: Crossing Press.

Lugones, María. 1990a. *Hispaneando y lesbiando: On Sarah Hoagland's Lesbian ethics.* Hypatia 5(3): 138-46.

———. 1990b. Playfulness, "world"-travelling, and loving perception. In *Making face, making soul: Haciendo caras*, ed. Gloria Anzaldúa. San Francisco: Aunt Lute Foundation.

Lugones, María, and Elizabeth Spelman. 1983. Have we got a theory for you! Feminist theory, cultural imperialism and the demand for "the woman's voice. " *Hypatia* a special issue of *Women's Studies International Forum* 6(6): 573-581. Reprinted in *Women and values: Readings in recent feminist philosophy*, ed. Marilyn Pearsall. Belmont, CA: Wadsworth.

Martin, Biddy, and Chandra Mohanty. 1986. Feminist politics: What's home got to do with it? In *Feminist studies/critical studies*, ed. Teresa de Lauretis. Bloomington: Indiana University Press.

———. 1988. Lesbian identity and autobiographical difference(s). In *Life/lines: Theorizing women's autobiography*, ed. Bella Brodzki and Celeste Schenck. Ithaca, N.Y.: Cornell University Press.

Martindale, Kathleen. 1987. On the ethics of voice in feminist literary criticism. *Resources for Feminist Research* 3: 16-19.

———. 1988. Power, ethics and polyvocal feminist theory. *Tessera, Contemporary Verse* 2: 54-65.

———. 1988-89. Interview with Rachel Blau Du Plessis on ethics, rhetoric and discourse. *Feminist ethics* 3 (1): 44-66.

————. 1992. Fredric Jameson's critique of ethical criticism: A deconstructed Marxist feminist response. In *Feminist Critical Negotiations*, ed. Elizabeth Meese and Alice Parker. Amsterdam: John Benjamins.

Meese, Elizabeth. 1986. *Crossing the double-cross: The practice of feminist criticism.* Chapel Hill: University of North Carolina Press.

————. 1990. *(Ex)tensions: Re-figuring feminist criticism.* Urbana: University of Illinois Press.

Milan Women's Bookstore Collective. 1990. *Sexual difference: A theory of social-symbolic practice,* trans. Patricia Cicogna and Teresa de Lauretis. Bloomington: Indiana University Press.

Moraga, Cherríe. 1983. *Loving in the war years: Lo que nunca paso por sus labios.* Boston: South End Press.

Nestle, Joan. 1987. *A restricted country.* Ithaca, N.Y.: Firebrand Books.

Pratt, Minnie Bruce. 1991. *Rebellion: Essays 1980-1991.* Ithaca, N.Y.: Firebrand Books.

Raymond, Janice. 1989. Putting the politics back into lesbianism. *Women's Studies International Forum* 12(2): 149-56.

Rich, Adrienne. 1979. *On lies, secrets, and silence: Selected prose 1966-1978.* New York: Norton.

————. 1986. *Blood, bread and poetry: Selected prose 1979-1985.* New York: Norton.

Saunders, Martha. 1989. Mothers are our sisters: Agency, responsibility and community. *Resources for Feminist Research* 18(3): 47-50.

————. 1990. Sexuality, justice and feminist ethics. *Resources for Feminist Research* 19(3-4): 33-39.

Schulman, Sarah. 1990. *People in trouble.* New York: Plume.

Sedgwick, Eve Kosofsky. 1990. *Epistemology of the closet.* Berkeley: University of California Press.

Troeltsch, Ernst. 1960. *The social teaching of the Christian churches* vol. 1, trans. Olive Wyon. New York: Harper and Row.

Wittig, Monique. 1992. *The straight mind and other essays.* Boston: Beacon Press.

Yingling, Thomas. 1991. Sexual preference/cultural reference: The predicament of gay culture studies. *American Literary History* 3(1): 184-97.

Zimmerman, Bonnie. 1990. *The safe sea of women: Lesbian fiction 1969-1989.* Boston: Beacon Press.

Mother: The Legal Domestication of Lesbian Existence

RUTHANN ROBSON

The legal category "mother" operates restrictively and punitively to "domesticate" lesbian existence. Our domestication is the reason that we have difficulty thinking beyond the category "mother." I explore how "mother" is used by both lesbians and nonlesbians within the legal system. In order to ensure lesbian survival on lesbian terms, we must strategize theories that do not preserve the dominant legal paradigm that codifies "mother," even if that category is expanded to include "lesbian mother."

"Mother" is a legal category. Like all legal categories, it has the potential to domesticate lesbian existence and thus interfere with lesbian survival. By lesbian survival, I mean two things. First, I mean a daily individual survival that depends on food, shelter, and love—including, for some of us, love relationships with children. Second, I mean an individual and collective survival that depends on some sort of identity as lesbians.

The law can interfere with both the tangible and intangible types of survival in many ways, one of which is a process I call domestication. Domestication is similar to other political processes that have been named colonization and imperialism. Yet both imperialism and colonization describe concrete historical processes that have resulted in slavery, death, and destruction,[1] and I have come to prefer the term "domestication" to connote the law's hegemony over lesbian survival. Domestication is connotatively gendered. It connotes the relegation of women to the domestic sphere, a private place that can facilitate being dominated and inhibit collective action. It also connotes the circumscribing of one's potential to the service of another, as when animals are domesticated for human use.

Domestication also describes a process of substituting one way of thinking for another. Domestication has occurred when the views of the dominant culture, in this case the legal culture, are so internalized they are considered common sense. The barbed-wire enclosures seem to exist for our protection

Hypatia vol. 7, no. 4 (Fall 1992) © by Ruthann Robson

rather than restriction.[2] We attempt to argue ourselves into legal categories so that we can be protected, not noticing how such categories restrict our lesbianism.

The category of mother is such a legal category. While mother is certainly a category in the nonlegal world, a category with biological, affectional, cultural, and religious implications, its legality is pervasive. One example is especially telling. At the National Lesbian Conference in Atlanta last year, I participated in a workshop discussing lesbian parenting. During a small-group discussion, lesbians—ever practical—began talking about what our children should call us. The lesbians in the group did not know each other. No one knew I was an attorney, and I was not thinking about the law. My suggestion was that a child call both mothers simply by their first names. This suggestion was vigorously objected to by another lesbian, who said, "The law gives me twenty-four-hour-a-day responsibility for that child. Me—and me only, not my lover and not anyone else. I deserve to be called something special; something that no one else calls me; something like mother." What surprised me was not this lesbian's disagreement with my particular proposal but her appeal to the law. Where I expected the birth pangs of biology, I got the legal rule of parental responsibility. The other members of the small group took up her point, not only agreeing with the special nature of the word "mother" but also appealing to its legal force.

When we talk about the legal rules as the basis for lesbian choices, I believe we are domesticated. At stake is not whether the children who live with us call us "Alice" or "Mama Alice" or "Mom"—the range of choices is as wide as the range of lesbians. However, what is at stake is our process. We can appeal to equality models in which no mother would be "other," antihierarchical models in which children are not deferential to adults, historical models in which children are property, and even personal models based on our own childhoods. Or we can simply like the way something sounds. But when the reasoning for our lesbian decisions is predicated on an uncritical adoption of the rule of law, I believe this is problematic. It marks lesbian domestication by law.

In seeking to move beyond our domestication by the rule of law, a specifically lesbian legal theory is important. The first step in this lesbian legal theory is to examine critically the rules of law and legal categories and assess them in regard to lesbian survival. Thus, I seek to center lesbian concerns rather than legal ones and to examine the ways in which the rule of law employs the legal category of mother with reference to lesbians.

Legal decisions have real effects. The extent to which a lesbian is a legally recognized mother is the extent to which a lesbian's relationship with a child might be protected. Yet even if this relationship is legally defined as mother-child, this does not guarantee absolute protection. The law may determine that a particular lesbian is not within the category of mother as the law defines it.

In such a case, the law denies the lesbian custody or visitation and places the child with another person or with the state. In this essay, I explore the state of the rule of law with regard to lesbian motherhood and examine particular cases in which the rules of law domesticate individual lesbians. However, I also make the claim that the very category of mother domesticates our own thinking about our relationships with children.

Lesbian motherhood has received much attention, including attention to its legal ramifications.[3] However, much of the law-related attention has focused on manipulation of the rules of law to achieve desired results and not on challenges to the underlying premises of law. Much of this attention has been by legal reformers and scholars who are responsible for many of the changes in the rule of law that benefit lesbians who seek to maintain relationships with children. It must be stressed at the outset, however, that any lesbian legal theory cannot assume that lesbian custody is the preferable outcome. As always, the emphasis must be on lesbian choice. By centering lesbians rather than law, a lesbian legal theory might be able to confront more directly the power of the rule of law to domesticate our lesbian lives.

I. LESBIAN MOTHERS AND NONLESBIAN CHALLENGES

Lesbians' relationships with children are subject to legal interference by two general categories of nonlesbians. (Disputes between lesbians are considered in the next section.) The first category is the other parent, the father. The mother-child-father relationship is a legal one. For lesbians who share parentage of a child with a man, regardless of whether they have been married or not, the law dictates that the man has parental rights. The rules of law determining men's parental rights have fluctuated throughout legal history. At one time the father had an absolute right to sole custody (of legitimate children), an obvious result given the man's ownership of both the wife and the children. The more recent American rules of law generally employed a maternal preference, especially if the child was of "tender years." This so-called tender-years doctrine gave the mother a presumption of custody, unless the father could prove the mother was unfit. Under this standard, many lesbians could be proven unfit. However, the tender-years doctrine did not change because of lesbian legal reform but because of the relatively recent feminist legal reform that led to the establishment of gender-neutral laws. Thus, the present rule of law in all states provides that in any custody litigation between the mother and father, the court must determine the "best interests of the child." This gender-neutral rule supposedly allows the parents to start off in equal positions. The court then applies numerous factors depending on the particular state statute or case law in order to weigh the relative merits of the parents. Factors considered include economic, educational, social, and cultural ones; and given women's disadvantage in these areas relative to men, it should not be surprising that current statistics reveal that fathers who litigate for custody have substantial chance of prevailing. Not surprisingly, the best-interests-of-the-child test is often applied as if it is the best-interests-of-the-state test, especially when judges disclose reasons such as it is in the best interests of a child to grow up in a conventional state-approved family.

When lesbianism is raised in a case between a mother and a father, whether it is in an original custody case or in a suit seeking a change of custody because of the discovery of the mother's lesbianism, courts employ three different approaches. The first and most limiting approach is that living with a lesbian mother cannot be in the best interests of the child. The second or middle-ground approach is that living with a (lesbian) mother can be in the best interests of a child as long as the mother is a mother and not a lesbian who flaunts her lesbianism, lives with a lesbian lover, or engages in lesbian politics. The third and presumably most enlightened approach is the nexus approach. Courts use what they call the nexus test to determine whether the mother's lesbianism actually harms the child. The application of this harm principle in practice often makes the nexus test indistinguishable from the first, per se approach or the middle-ground, mother-first/lesbian-last approach. The types of harm that courts often consider under this nexus test include the harm of molestation (although this is usually more likely in a gay father's case than a lesbian mother's case), the harm of a potential gay or lesbian identity in the child, the harm of stigmatization to the child because of having a lesbian mother, and the harm of living in an immoral and illegal environment.

For example, in a 1989 Missouri appellate court opinion, the court specifically adopted the requirement that there must be "a nexus between harm to the child and the parent's homosexuality" but considered evidence of harm that the

> mother admitted on cross-examination that she had slept with friend while the children were in the house. She was also unable to "say for certain" that she had not kissed friend on the lips or touched her affectionately in front of the children.

The court also noted that

> even if the mother remains discreet about her sexual preference, a number of experts at the trial testified and Missouri case law recognizes that a parent's homosexuality can never be kept secret enough to be a neutral factor in the development of a child's values and character.[4]

The appellate court affirmed the trial court's award of custody to the father and his new wife, despite the fact that each child told the trial judge that he or she wished to remain with the mother.

Not all courts have applied the nexus test, or even the middle-ground approach, as homophobically as the Missouri court. Many courts, including appellate courts in New Jersey, Alaska, Massachusetts, South Carolina, and New York have specifically found that a mother's lesbianism did not constitute a harm to the child.[5] However, underlying even these relatively liberal opinions filled with fact-specific reasoning is the assumption that having a lesbian mother could be harmful to a child and thus considered to be not in the best interest of the child, that future citizen of the state.

Lesbian relationships with children are also subject to legal interference by nonlesbians who are not parents to the child. These third parties can include nonparents, such as interested relatives, foster parents, or the state. In these cases, the third party must generally prove the mother unfit. The rule of law does not impose equality on the mother and the nonparent, and these third parties have a greater burden than simply proving that it would be in the best interests of the child to remove the child from the lesbian mother. Courts do not generally consider lesbianism alone proof of unfitness, but this does not mean courts do not consider it or even rely on it. For example, in a 1990 case the Supreme Court of Mississippi affirmed an award of custody to the paternal grandparents of the children of a lesbian mother, An(drea) White.[6] Mississippi's highest court noted that even though the trial court "may have relied almost exclusively" on the mother's lesbian relationship, there was enough evidence in the record—including some conflicting testimony about the children being outside in cold weather without adequate clothing—to support the trial court's removing the children from An White's custody as well as not allowing the children to visit with her in the presence of her lover. The mother in this case is not a middle-class model of respectability, but what is interesting is that she was not that model when she was married; in fact, her conditions had apparently improved since she separated from her husband and began living with her lover. No one claimed that the children's father should be awarded custody "given his financial situation and his drinking problem." Yet when An White became involved with a woman, her husband's parents decided that she should be denied custody. The courts of Mississippi agreed.

The per se rule of law that "lesbian" and "mother" are mutually exclusive legal categories is in disrepute. The enlightened view, subject to many permutations, is that lesbianism alone cannot satisfy the requirement of a mother being unfit should third parties attempt to gain custody, or even the requirement that custody be awarded to the parent who best comports with the best interests of the child should a father attempt to gain custody. This enlightened view has been forced on the courts by many brave lesbian mothers who engaged in painful litigation with the advocacy of many hardworking and clever lesbian legal workers. It is certainly an advancement.

Nevertheless, this enlightenment can be merely the patina of privilege. Like the specter of lesbian marriage, these liberal custody rules of law contribute to a division between bad lesbians and good ones: good lesbians are white and from a professional class, monogamous and discreet, and self-sacrificing mothers. These exemplary lesbians "deserve" custody despite their lesbianism, assuming that their children are also "above-average." Two examples are illustrative. First, there is Jane Doe, so good that she keeps her real name out of the court records. Jane does not have sole custody of her son, the eleven-year-old "well-adjusted and above-average" Jack, but he visits her for eight weeks in the summer and on alternate Easter and Christmas vacations. Ann Smith Doe, the father's new wife, wants to adopt Jack and thus terminate Jane Doe's parental rights. A Virginia trial court agrees, terminates Jane's status as a mother, and allows the adoption. But when Jane appeals to the Supreme Court of Virginia, she prevails. The court's opinion sounds like she is winning the Miss Congeniality contest rather than a custody appeal:

> Although there was testimony that her relationship with the woman with whom she lives is unorthodox, the testimony is also that Jane Doe is an exceptionally well-educated, stable, responsible, and sensitive individual. Witnesses described Jane in various ways, but always in a highly complimentary manner. They referred to her as a conscientious and creative parent, friendly by nature, who instills in the boy a love for other people and for animals. It was testified that Jane's love for Jack was a nurturing love, and that she exercised a selfless wisdom in caring for him. Jane Doe has apparently earned the respect of her peers . . . because of her civic work and active interest in the community and her relationship with the people with whom she comes into contact.[7]

I do not mean to belittle Jane Doe or the accomplishment of her attorney for putting together such impressive evidence. But factors such as being well educated and engaging in civic work can be a bit daunting to someone like An White, who lived in a trailer and who had most recently worked at a convenience store. Also daunting, besides class considerations, are lesbian-identity considerations. As the Supreme Court of Virginia specifically noted, it was not "approving, condoning, or sanctioning" Jane's "unnatural lifestyle," which was proper for the court to consider but was found to be outweighed in her particular circumstances, a resolution that the court warned might be temporary:

> Further, in determining her fitness as a mother and the future welfare of her son, we are not unmindful of her testimony that should it become necessary, for her son's sake, she would sever the relationship with the woman with whom she now lives.

There may come a time when the welfare and best interest of her son require that she honor this commitment.

For women who are not willing to separate from their lesbian lovers, courts are less lenient. They are especially prone to less leniency if the mother in question is less than congenial, a little too "dykey," and the child is less than perfect. In a Pennsylvania case, the mother appealed the state's taking away of her preschool son who had a speech problem. The appellate court upheld the removal, writing an opinion containing the following:

> Joey was exposed to a chaotic and harmful home life. The mother is a lesbian who effects a masculine appearance, wears men's clothing, and has a masculine oriented mental status. At the time of the hearing, she lived with Nancy M . . . and two of her children in a two bedroom apartment. . . .
> [The caseworker] also found the mother to be uncooperative. The mother took notes throughout her meetings with the caseworker and responded in an adversarial manner that her attorney, "knows about this."[8]

When the mother refused the condition that she not live with her lover, the court found that this "revealed forcefully her true feelings and attitudes regarding Joey's [speech] therapy." The appellate court disingenuously rejected the mother's claim that the court was unnecessarily interfering in her lesbian relationship absent a causal connection between the lesbianism and harm. The court noted that the order to exclude the lover from the home was not meant to interfere with the lesbian relationship but only to establish order and foster the close relationship between the mother and son.

When conflicts over a child arise between a lesbian and a heterosexual man or state agency, our lesbian loyalties are undivided. Any lesbian legal theory must center the lesbian and privilege her position to choose custody. In most cases, a lesbian in a custody dispute has not chosen to be within the rules of law. There must be legal reform to afford lesbians who find themselves within that legal system their choices. A liberal nexus test that states that harm must be proven or else lesbianism will not be considered is not liberal enough: "harm" must not include a child being exposed to lesbian expression or a child's potential lesbianism or gayness. Exclusion of a lesbian's lover from her home is asking a lesbian to choose between her lover and her child. This is not the type of lesbian choice that any lesbian legal theory would seek to promote.

Yet a lesbian legal theory must stress lesbian choice rather than lesbian custody. An assumption that custody is what should be chosen by any lesbian is detrimental. A lesbian legal theory puts lesbians at the center, even to the exclusion of the children of lesbians. It is difficult to disagree with the legal standard of "best interests of the child," but a lesbian legal theory has a different focus. Its central focus is lesbian.

II. LESBIAN MOTHERS AND GAY/LESBIAN COPARENTS

When conflicts over a child within our communities arise, our lesbian loyalties can be divided: when two lesbians who are raising a child together separate, centering lesbians does not necessarily solve the problem. However, before considering this scenario, I think it should be distinguished from another scenario, one in which lesbian loyalties can be falsely divided and centering lesbians does reorient our perspectives. The scenario involves the gay sperm donor.

Under the rule of law, contribution of sperm is an entitlement to the benefits and burdens of fatherhood. Many states do have statutes that alleviate this rule somewhat, but importantly these statutes protect the rights of infertile fathers by severing the sperm donor's father right when insemination is performed by a licensed physician on a married woman. This severing is consistent with the rule of law's limitation of parentage: a child has one father and one mother, no more and no less. In the case of a woman married to an infertile man, the rule of law declares that the husband is the child's father and not the sperm donor. In the case of an unmarried woman, there is no husband to assume the role of father. A court, ever eager to promote fatherhood, allows the donor the appellation "father" and awards him visitation.

Illustrative of this scenario is the California case of *Jhordan C. v. Mary K.* [9] Although the court never tells us that Mary K. is a lesbian, the opinion does reveal that Mary decided to have a child by "artificial insemination" jointly with "Victoria, a close friend." After making that decision,

> Mary sought a semen donor by talking with friends and acquaintances. This led to three or four potential donors with whom Mary spoke directly. She and Victoria ultimately chose Jhordan after he had one personal interview with Mary and one dinner at Mary's home.

Without discussing Jhordan's sexuality, the court affirmed the award of Jhordan's visitation. The court also rejected Mary's constitutional challenges to the insemination statute, raised on her behalf by her attorney Roberta Achtenberg of the Lesbian Rights Project.

The result in Mary K's case is troubling. While the court did not award Jhordan the joint custody he sought (which would have allowed him to participate in day-to-day decisions about the child), it did grant him father status and generous visitation. However, what I find more troubling is a shift in lesbian legal strategies since the mid-1980s when Mary K. came before a California appellate court. In the past year, I have heard of numerous cases of gay men who have been sperm donors now seeking court-ordered visitation of three-, four-, ten-, and thirteen-year-old children. The lesbians defending themselves against these lawsuits have often been denied representation and support from the organized gay/lesbian legal community. The gay/lesbian legal reform agenda is devoted to an expansion of the legal concept of family. This may include visitation for gay men who have been sperm donors and now decide to establish father-right. With the rule of law in their favor, gay men who have been sperm donors can most often win an award of visitation. It does not matter whether visitation is desired by the lesbians who have been caring for the child since birth. And it matters little whether visitation is desired by the child, for courts will presume and court-ordered psychologists will declare that a child should have contact with a "father."

If we center real lesbians rather than gay/lesbian concerns, this controversy demands a different result. The rights of men, whether gay or not, are not the focus of any lesbian legal theory. Just as marriage has a legal history of dominance of men over women, so too does father-right. What needs to be preserved is lesbian choice, not father-right. Likewise, if we center lesbians rather than law—even law as expressed by the lesbian/gay legal reform movement—our loyalties are undivided. Again, what we must preserve is lesbian choice, not the legal category of family, however alternative or expansive.

The centering of lesbians is more difficult when the dispute is between two lesbians. In a situation in which two lesbians have a baby, the biological mother is the legal mother. The other lesbian is profoundly "other": she is a legal stranger to her child, just as she is a legal stranger to her lover. As in the case of lovers when no child is involved, centering lesbians requires a distinction between situations in which third parties are involved and situations between lesbians. In situations involving third parties, legal tools may prevent the operation of laws that privilege the legal category "family" in the event one of the lesbians dies or becomes incapacitated. The death or incapacitation of the biological/legal mother can interfere with the relationship between the "other" mother and the child. The biological mother can express her desires in a will or other document, but although the law at times regards children almost akin to property, in fact they are not property and cannot be willed. However, a court can consider the biological mother's statement in the event of a custody dispute. A medical guardianship is another document which can allow an adult to make medical decisions for a child. Like the wills and powers of attorney, these documents are outer-directed and not intended to give the lesbians rights against each other.

As in relationships without children, many suggest the solution of contract. A contract cannot have as its subject the child (this would be baby-selling and considered illegal), but a contract could give the adults rights against each other. However, the contract solution suffers the same problems in this context as in a childless context. The danger is that lesbians adopt the assumptions of contract and that particular lesbians may be disempowered by the operation of those assumptions.[10]

The legal solution most often posed has been adoption, a recognized legal procedure that allows a nonbiological parent to become a legal parent. How-ever, until very recently courts have been unanimous in their conclusion that parents are limited to a mother and a father: a child cannot have two mothers by adoption or otherwise; and a female parent must be a mother. Lesbian legal reformers have argued this point in impressive scholarship and in the courts. A 1991 District of Columbia opinion is apparently the first to allow one lesbian to adopt the child born to her lover.[11] The court was troubled by the statute that provided that an adoption terminated the rights of the biological mother. The court decided, however, that the statute's language was only directive; the biological mother's rights did not have to be terminated. In this same case, the court also allowed a previously adopted child to be adopted by the other lesbian parent as well, and there have been a few cases of two lesbians simultaneously adopting one child.

Absent an adoption, there are legal theories that might support a lesbian parent being awarded custody of a child should the biological parent die or become incapacitated. Such theories include de facto parenthood (also called psychological parenthood), equitable parenthood, and in loco parentis. In all these theories, the adult's actions that emulate parenthood are adjudicated by a court to determine whether or not the adult will be legally deemed a parent. In many of these cases, the adult's actions are judged not only against an ideal parent but also against any other parentlike adults in the child's life. At times, formal legal rights would be in direct conflict with these creative theories. For example, should a biological mother die, custody of the child might be awarded on the basis of the recognized father status of a sperm donor rather than the less formal psychological-parent status of the lesbian parent. If the parents of the deceased lesbian seek custody of the child from the surviving lesbian parent, their grandparent status is entitled to some weight but is less compelling than father status.[12]

All of these theories, including adoption, can serve as tools to forestall the effect of the rules of law that would otherwise operate. In that capacity, I think they can be useful. Using these tools in a prospective way as much as possible is also good practical advice. Thus, to the extent any tool can dissuade third parties from seeking custody of a child, the more useful the tool. However, when these theories are the basis of a contest waged between lesbians in the legal arena, we turn the tools and rules of law on each other.

If two lesbians decide to have a child together, do so, and then decide to separate, the child's future becomes uncertain. In the best of all possible lesbian utopias, the two lesbians would exercise their lesbian choices in a way that honored themselves, each other, and the child. There would be no need to resort to the rules of law. But one lesbian can decide that she is the true and only mother, and if she is the biological mother (and there is no adoption), the rule of law will enforce her decision. And the other lesbian can sue her ex-lover for visitation of the child, utilizing theories to persuade the court that she should be accorded at least some parental rights. She will be represented by gay/lesbian legal reform organizations, arguing for recognition of the lesbian family as analogous to the nuclear family. Other gay/lesbian rights organizations will file briefs as interested parties urging the court to expand the legal category of family to include both lesbian parents (and perhaps even the gay male sperm donor). In the courts that have considered this scenario, the nonbiological lesbian parent will lose. Despite the courts' opinions, there is a ground swell of liberal popular support for expanding legal concepts of parenthood and family to include the nonbiological lesbian parent.

The case of *Alison D. v. Virginia M.* is an example.[13] Decided in 1991 by New York's highest court, the decision rejects a claim for visitation from a lesbian nonbiological mother, deciding that she is not a "parent" within the meaning of the statute. Represented by Paula Ettlebrick of Lambda Legal Defense and Education Fund, and supported by briefs from the NOW Legal Defense Fund, the ACLU, and the Gay and Lesbian Parents Coalition, Alison D. argued that she was a de facto parent entitled to visitation. Although the same court had the year before given an expansive reading to the term "family" in a rent-stabilization case involving a surviving male lover, the court here declined to give a similar expansive reading to the term "parent." Judge Judith Kaye, the only judge on New York's highest court who could even remotely be called a feminist, was the sole dissenting judge.

Judge Kaye's dissent and many reactions to the case from heterosexual feminists and liberal nonlesbians are telling. Although a few feminists worried about the consequences for violence should de facto parent visitation include an abusive boyfriend of a battered woman, most sought to bring lesbians within preestablished legal definitions. Liberals extended their sympathies that lesbians were once again excluded.

Because Alison D. and Virginia M. are in conflict, it is difficult to center the concerns of both lesbians and not be inconsistent. Yet this inconsistency—and the dispute itself—are constructed by the rule of law. To the extent that the biological mother Virginia M. supports her denial of visitation to her ex-lover with her superior position within the rules of law, she is domesticated by the legal regime. And to the extent that the nonbiological mother Alison D. believes she is entitled to visitation because she can fit herself into legal theories like in loco parentis, she is also domesticated by the legal regime. And to the extent that both lesbians appeal to the legalism inherent in categories like "parent" and "family" as they attempt to settle their problem, they import the law into their lesbianism. Lesbianism is limited by legalism.

III. CONCLUSIONS

I am less concerned with the legal positions of Alison D. and Virginia M. than with how they came to make their claims in courts of law. This is not squeamishness about public revelation of lesbians disagreeing but concern that we are being used by the law rather than using it. My concern is the same whether Alison D. wins or loses; my concern is even more pronounced if Virginia M. merely appeals to her superior legal status to resolve disagreements with the woman she once loved. When we use the law against each other, we are ultimately being used by the law: to sustain its own (nonlesbian) power. We sustain the law's power when we appeal to its categories rather than empowering our lesbian selves by appealing to lesbian categories.

We must decide whether or not "mother" (or "parent") is a category that can be lesbian as well as legal. Just as I do not find convincing the argument that as lesbians we can enter the state-created marriage contract and transform it by our very existence, I do not think that as lesbians (either singly or in pairs) we can enter the state-defined parent role and transform it. Perhaps I am not optimistic enough. Or perhaps I am too intimidated by the rules of law that operate in the parent-child relationship to give parents virtual ownership over their children unless the parents are not model state citizens. I am intimidated by the class and antilesbian model of the well-educated and well-liked Jane Doe and her summers with her well-adjusted and above-average son. And I am intimidated by judicial disapproval profound enough to take a child away if a mother does not dress her children correctly in the Mississippi cold or does not dress herself correctly in feminine attire. Even absent a lesbian mother, the legal category of mother operates restrictively and punitively.

Ultimately, I think that the legal category of mother (or even parent or family) is too stifling for our lesbian imaginations and relationships. The category of mother domesticates us. We have difficulty thinking in other than its terms. While I am not abandoning its strategic use, I am suggesting we recognize strategic uses of the legal category of mother in litigation, even as we attempt to develop lesbian categories for the complex relationships between lesbians and children. If we are ever to move beyond our domestication and ensure lesbian survival on lesbian terms, we must theorize against the dominant discourse of the legal regime, including the legal regime that codifies the category mother.

NOTES

This article has benefitted immeasurably from the research assistance of Rebecca Baehr, as well as from comments by S. E. Valentine, Claudia Card, the anonymous reviewers at *Hypatia*, and the invaluable assistance of Leslie Thrope. Portions of this article appear in Robson (1992).

1. The term "colonization," however, has been used metaphorically to describe a process of overlegalization. For an extended discussion of the concept of the "colonization of the life-world," see Habermas (1984, 1985). I employed the term "colonization" in an earlier form of theorizing about this process; see Robson and Valentine (1990).

2. Yet domestication also has within it the idea of its opposite. To have been domesticated, one must have once existed wild, and there is the possibility of a feral future. To be feral is to have survived domestication and be transformed into an untamed state. Post-domestication lesbian existence is one purpose of a lesbian legal theory: if we can confront the ways in which we are domesticated, we can begin to challenge our domestication.

Despite the domestication metaphor, I am not conceptualizing lesbians as women who have been trapped in little houses on the prairie by mean men or as wild animals who have been harnessed to plow the soybean fields. While these are tempting images that foster an idealized version of our innocence and victimization, such images conflict with my experience. To use the postmodern phrase, we are "always already" domesticated. We are born and socialized with reference to the dominant culture. However, I do not believe that we are necessarily so constricted.

3. Among the many fine pieces of legal scholarship on lesbian motherhood issues, the following are especially noteworthy: Polikoff (1990); Sella (1991); Sheppard (1985); and Dooley (1990). Also especially noteworthy is an anthology of lesbian parenting issues: Pollack and Vaughn (1987). Essential reading for anyone considering lesbian mothering issues is Allen (1986).

4. T.C.H. v. K.M.H., 784 S.W.2d 281, 284-5 (Mo. Ct. App. 1989).

5. S.N.E. v. R.L.B., 699 P.2d 875 (Alaska 1985); Doe v. Doe, 452 N.E.2d 293 (Ma. 1983); M.P. v. S.P., 404 A.2d 1256 (N.J. 1979); Guinan v. Guinan, 102 A.D.2d 963, 477 N.Y.S.2d 830 (3rd Dep't 1984); Stronman v. Williams, 353 S.E.2d 704 (S.C. 1987).

6. White v. Thompson, 569 So. 2d 1181 (Miss. 1990).

7. Doe v. Doe, 284 S.E.2d 799 (Va. 1981).

8. In re Breisch, 434 A.2d 815 (Pa. Super. Ct. 1981).

9. 179 Cal. App.3d 386, 224 Cal. Rptr. 530 (1st Dist. 1986).

10. The assumptions of contract include equality expressed in terms of bargaining power. Historical, cultural, and personal feelings of entitlement to bargain or lack of entitlement are irrelevant. For further discussion, see Robson and Valentine (1990) and Robson (1992).

11. In re Adoption of Minor T., D.C. Super Ct Fam. Div. Nos. A-269-90 and A-270-90 (August 30, 1991).

12. See, e.g., In re Pearlman, Florida Circuit Court Broward County, No. 87-24926 (March 31, 1989) 15 FAMILY LAW REPORTER 1355 (1989).

13. 77 N.Y.2d 651, 572 N.E.2d 27, 569 N.Y.S.2d 586 (N.Y. 1991).

REFERENCES

Allen, Jeffner. 1986. Motherhood: The anniliation of women. In *Lesbian philosophy: Explorations*, ed. Jeffner Allen. Palo Alto, CA: Institute for Lesbian Studies.

Dooley, David S. 1990. Immoral because they're bad, bad because they're wrong: Sexual orientation and presumptions of parental unfitness in custody disputes. *California Western Law Review* 26: 395-424.

Habermas, Jurgen. 1984. *The theory of communicative action* I, trans. Thomas McCarthy. Boston: Beacon Press.

———. 1985. *The theory of communicative action* II, trans. Thomas McCarthy. Boston: Beacon Press.

Polikoff, Nancy. 1990. This child does have two mothers: Redefining parenthood to meet the needs of children in lesbian-mother and other nontraditional families. *Georgetown Law Journal* 78: 469-575.

Pollack, Sandra, and Vaughn, Jeanne, eds. 1987. *Politics of the heart.* Ithaca, NY: Firebrand Books.

Robson, Ruthann. 1992. *Lesbian (out)law: Survival under the rule of law.* Ithaca, NY: Firebrand Press.

Robson, Ruthann, and Valentine, S.E. 1990. Lov(h)ers: Lesbians as intimate partners and lesbian legal theory. *Temple Law Review* 63: 511-41.

Sella, Carmel. 1991. When a mother is a legal stranger to her child: The law's challenge to the lesbian nonbiological mother. *UCLA Women's Law Review* 1: 135-64.

Sheppard, Annamay T. 1985. Lesbian mothers II: Long night's journey into day. *Women's Rights Law Reporter* 8: 219-46.

Jewish Lesbian Writing:
A Review Essay

NAOMI SCHEMAN

Recent writing by Jewish lesbians is characterized by challenging and evocative reflection on themes of home and identity, family and choice, tradition and transformation. This essay is a personal journey through some of this writing. An exploration of the obvious and troubling tensions between lesbian or feminist and Jewish identities leads to the paradoxical but ultimately unsurprising suggestion that lesbian identity and eroticism can provide a route of return to and affirmation of Jewish identity.

> With whom do you believe your lot is cast?
> From where does your strength come?
> —Adrienne Rich
> "Sources," IV (1986b, 6)

As I was growing up, in a very progressive, secular, Jewish home, my parents' message about intermarriage was that relationships were difficult enough even between people with a great deal in common; trying to span differences that were too great could make them nearly impossible. There was nothing *wrong* about such relationships; one just needed to be aware of how difficult they would likely be, and the message was a discouraging one. We (my two sisters and I) were to take it to apply not only to men of other races and religiously observant men of other faiths, but also to observant Jews. More recently, that message has come to seem to me more an argument against heterosexuality: the difference that was, of course, taken absolutely for granted—that of gender—seems to me, as a feminist, to be perhaps the most daunting.

As Audre Lorde has noted, it's the one difference Euro-American culture is not committed either to ignoring or to obliterating; rather it's eroticized, made the defining *sine qua non* of the erotic. As such, it has had the power of conscripting other differences and eroticizing them, through the construction of mythologically sexy "others," fantasy figures that haunt the dreams of the

Hypatia vol. 7, no. 4 (Fall 1992) © by Naomi Scheman

privileged with pleasure or terror or both. The actual human beings who have been so conscripted live with the consequences, in the world and in our own psyches, of being the exoticized, eroticized Other. We are taught our own desire as a response to theirs; we are taught, depending on who we are, complex amalgams of longings for the powerfully dangerous "seducer" and the hypernormalized paragon of acceptability, who have in common only their power over us. As feminists, we have inherited these dreams and nightmares, and they thread their way through our attempts to redefine, equally in our politics and our desires, the meaning of difference.

In *The New Woman's Broken Heart* Andrea Dworkin tells "the simple story of a lesbian girlhood," in which Bertha Schneider learns sexual passion as danger and difference: she and S. spend a long sweat-drenched night taking turns "being Barry Greenberg" and later fall out over their rivalry for Mary, who "wasnt like us. we were both brilliant. Mary wasnt. . . . we were both Jewish. Mary wasnt. we were both too smart to be popular. Mary wasnt" (Dworkin 1980, 3). Only much later does Bertha recognize S. as her first lover, a lover in whom she saw herself, at a time when she could name desire only as for the Other: men—dangerous or redemptive—or the women she could never be.

In reading the work of Jewish lesbians over the past few months, I have been repeatedly struck by the ways in which, for so many of them, the discovery or affirmation of their lesbianism has meant a (re)discovery and (re)affirmation of their Jewishness, not, as one might expect, a new or heightened estrangement from it. For some, the coming home to a lesbian community has meant the pain of confronting anti-Semitism in a place where one couldn't just walk away or close one's eyes and ears; for others, the whole-hearted commitment to community and to building a home has meant attending to the traditions and tradition-laden objects that furnish a home; for still others, the connection to women has transfigured the meaning of Judaism through a new appreciation of maternal labor and love.

As a bisexual woman currently living heterosexually, my immersion in these books—chosen in part through the recommendation of friends, in part from earlier familiarity, in part through the vagaries of what I found on the shelves of the local women's bookstore—has felt like a homecoming. Which is to say it has felt warming, exhilarating, awkward, challenging, frightening, claustrophobic, heartwarming, and heartbreaking. It is an experience I recommend, perhaps the closest most of are likely to get these hectic days to the consciousness-raising groups of the early seventies.

As in those groups, I was struck by the power of recognition, by seeing myself, my family, my friends mirrored in these pages. It has become a commonplace to decry the focus on similarity in CR groups, and in the feminism that took root there, and to find in them the difference-denying tendencies that so flawed much of feminist theory and practice. The flaw was, and is, profoundly important, as are the attempts on the part of a healthily more diverse group of theorists to account for the ways in which gender is always inflected by race, class, sexual identity, and other institutionalized identifications. But I'm less convinced that consciousness-raising was the culprit. The women, actual and fictional, in whose stories I found myself mirrored are, in fact, quite different from me, in myriad ways. But the differences were played out within a frame of identification, of familiarity, grounded not in some transcendent, content-less humanity but in historical specificity: in seeing myself, I was also seeing another, as she actually is, not as the Other. Many of us in the seventies found ourselves and each other in CR groups, when the only common identity we knew to name was Woman. We overgeneralized, both about the lives, thoughts, and feelings of the women who were not there and about the grounds of the similarity among those who were, but we had found a way of getting to know self and other in collaborative intimacy that we ought not to lose.

One of the things we learned is that such a route to knowledge cannot be static; we were changed, we changed each other, by knowing and being known; we expanded the range of each other's possibilities, by imagination and by example. Face-to-face with these books I am flooded with the same unsettling joy: my identity is neither given nor fixed; I am presented with, confronted by, choices.

The two most salient identities here are, of course, lesbian and Jewish. Only relatively recently has lesbianism been, for me, consciously, a possible choice; before then heterosexuality seemed both inevitable and, on the whole, unproblematic.[1] The possibility of choosing to be a lesbian has both stirred and terrified me. And in its light I live heterosexuality differently, as, in part, a refuge from the stirring and the terror. As Melanie Kaye/Kantrowitz puts it, in recounting a heterosexual interlude, "Most important he was not and never would be me. Or my mother. No blurring" ("Dance on the Face of the Earth," Kaye/Kantrowitz 1990, 69). As different as my present choices are from hers, she evocatively maps the emotional terrain, including, marvelously, its urban-ness ("Natural," Kaye/Kantrowitz 1990, 13-16), from which I come and through which I still move, terrain that shapes the complexity of meanings and emotional resonances, the tugs and the terrors, of "blurring."

Jewishness, on the other hand, I have never experienced as a matter of choice. It has been a given of my life, it is where I come from: whatever significance I choose to give it or how I choose to live it, I could not choose not to be Jewish. Lee Knefelkamp, writing as a Jewish convert under her Jewish name of Chaya Shoshana, says, "I choose to be a Jew every day. So does every other Jew I know. We are all Jews by choice" ("Living in the In-Between," Beck 1989, 98). This has not been my experience, nor that of many Jews I know, and I resist the idea that someone could choose to be the kind of Jew I am. I don't think that that resistance is a matter (or, anyway, not wholly a matter) of "fear of the 'other' and . . . internalized anti-Semitism" (Beck 1989,

97). It feels to me rather like my uneasiness about male to female transsexuals. It isn't internalized misogyny that makes me dubious about the possibility of someone's becoming a woman: I have no problem with the *wish*, any more than I have a problem with wishing one were born in Paris; I just don't believe one can realize it.

Part of why I have trouble honoring the experience of transsexuals is that they dont just wish to become women; they believe they really are women, a belief I have trouble grasping. But I also feel reluctant to acknowledge that either being or becoming a woman is a possibility for someone who has grown to adulthood in a male body, treated by the world as a boy and a man. Converts to Judaism don't raise for me the same conceptual puzzles, nor do I feel the same need to protect Jewish identity from appropriation by raised Christians as I do to protect female experience from raised men: I don't think of conversion to Judaism as necessarily an act of arrogant appropriation (though I can imagine cases in which I would feel just this, much as American Indians respond to the New Age appropriation of their spirituality). But there is a troubling kernel of similarity nonetheless. Many (not all) transsexuals locate their supposed womanhood in femininity, in ways of being that are either no part of my experience or are parts I want to reject. If what they want to be is what it is to be a woman, then I am less of one than they. Now, at least if done officially, conversion to Judaism requires considerable attention to the aspects of Judaism—namely, Judaism as a religion—that are a minimal part of my own experience, and it requires, or at least typically involves, a degree of learning far beyond mine and in the face of which I feel awkward and insecure. And while I don't feel about religious belief quite as I feel about femininity, I am and always have been a deeply committed atheist. So it can feel to me that if what converts to Judaism are what it is to be Jewish, then I am less of a Jew than they, and that feels wrong.

Part of Lee Knefelkamp's point is precisely that she and I are "different kinds of Jews" (Beck 1989, 99), neither one more or less than the other; I can't blame her for my awkwardness and insecurity. But part of why I feel awkward and insecure is that her kind of Jewishness is more intelligible in contemporary America than mine; more intelligible even *to me*. My own feels ineffable; but one thing I know about it with certainty is that it is my birthright, that it is not something I chose, nor is it something I could cease to be. The particular contours of my inheritance, my identity—Eastern European, secular, progressively political—I have learned with a new clarity from Irena Klepfisz to call *Yidishkayt*. I could certainly understand the wish to share such an identity, and as with the wish to be a native Parisian or to be a woman, I know there are things one can do to move closer to it, to learn about it, to empathize with it, to partake, even to participate, in the culture it defines. But it doesn't seem to me that one can really choose it, imbued as it is with history: one would have to change the past.

Looming over that past, problematically shaping my Jewishness and the
Jewishness of most of these authors, whether from secular or religious families,
is the Holocaust. Born in 1946, I am part of the first generation that the
architects of the Final Solution intended never to exist. For most of us that
has meant growing up under both a shadow and an umbrella; sheltered from
the full extent of the murderousness directed against people like us, we bore
the hopes and dreams of those who survived, in the name of those who
perished.

For some of us, daughters of upwardly mobile, intellectually serious parents,
those dreams focused on the sort of academic achievement that had traditionally been the domain of men. Feminists have long been exhorted, in Virginia
Woolf's words, to "think back through our mothers," which is how, lawfully,
Jewishness is transmitted. But for many of us our Jewishness comes in important
ways through our fathers; it was his studiousness or ambition or independence
of mind we inherited. We were the favored daughters, the ones who in the
liberal atmosphere of America could grow up to be sons. Turning our backs on
the culturally dominant images of Jewish women, we vowed to become neither
smotheringly self-sacrificial Jewish mothers nor "frigid," materialistic "JAPS."
In the heterosocial world we were "exceptional" women; the "lesbian in us"
(Adrienne Rich) is a route to self-acceptance, away from the entwined
self-hatreds of internalized misogyny and anti-Semitism.

As lifelong lesbian Anemone explains to "baby dyke" Liza in Lesléa
Newman's novel Good Enough to Eat, it is important not to confuse hating men
with loving women. Certainly anger at men appears in these books (Newman
has some powerful poems about incest and the abuse and harassment of women
and girls in Love Me Like You Mean It and Sweet Dark Places), but I was
repeatedly struck by the ways in which the love between and among women,
the creation of lesbian relationships and community, mended the frayed fabric
of Jewish life, including families of origin, fathers and brothers as well as
mothers and sisters. (I'm reminded of the in-gathering of men into the
women-centered world created around Celie and Shug's love at the end of
Alice Walker's The Color Purple.) Such inclusion is by no means part of the
lives of all these women: Elana Dykewomon is the most explicitly separatist of
the writers, and she included in Nice Jewish Girls—reluctantly when she
learned that the book would not be distributed "for womyn only"—an extraor-
dinarily moving story, "The Fourth Daughter's Four Hundred Questions"
(Beck 1989, 176-88), about the painful splits and contradictions at the heart
of a separatist life for lesbians who share a continuing form of oppression with
the men from whom they most urgently need to separate, the men who had
the power most intimately and deeply to harm them and the women they love.

In different ways such tensions thread through all these writings. As the
more religiously focused pieces in Twice Blessed make clear, Judaism can be
obdurate for women, lesbian or straight, and for homosexuals, women or men

(though, as Judith Plaskow and Annette Daum remind us in their essays in *Nice Jewish Girls*, it is symptomatic of the anti-Semitism in the women's movement to blame Judaism for the death of goddesses or the birth of patriarchy). And families of origin have rarely been able easily to take joy in the knowledge that their daughter is a lesbian; as in the African-American community, homophobia is joined with the understandable pronatalism of a community come face-to-face with genocide, and lesbians are caught in the double bind of being seen as unlikely to choose motherhood and as unfit for it when they do.

Paradoxically, the resistance of many natal families to a daughter's lesbianism can bring into that paradigmatically unchosen set of relationships the element of choice: that which was initially obdurately given can, under sufficiently drastic circumstances, come to seem optional—children can be disowned, parents and siblings can be rejected—and, if then they are not, if the choice is made, often with pain and difficulty, to keep or to reestablish the relationship, what emerges is something new, neither the wholly chosen nor the absolutely given, but the accepted, acknowledged, affirmed. (Shades of Spinoza, the excommunicated Jew.)

Thus, though I never chose to be a Jew, and it seems to me that I would remain one no matter what I chose (even, wildly improbably, conversion to some other faith), I can embrace that identity, make it mine, struggle with it, make it fit; or I can ignore it, reject its relevance to what I think matters about me, find myself elsewhere. So it is with being a woman—Jews are the people the Nazis round up; women are the people misogynists target for rape: in either case I can claim an identity informed but not determined by those who define it by their hate, or I can disown the identity and find other ground on which to stand. If social ontology were up to me, I don't think there'd be either Jews or women: I don't think I'd have constructed religion or gender. But the supposition doesn't make sense: social ontology couldn't be up to me, or even us; it's a matter of history. And, in the light of history, it is a matter of honor not to walk away from the people with whom history has given me "a shared fate" (Evelyn Torton Beck, "Naming Is Not a Simple Act," in Balka and Rose 1989, 175).

Honor is not always easy. Walking away from women is what heterosexist society tries to teach us all to do. That we share a fate can, in fact, seem like the best reason to walk away, either to separate ourselves from it, to be the token exception; or to hook up with someone who, not sharing that fate, can protect us from it. Over and over in these stories, poems, and essays, women are home for each other, with all the ambivalence that implies. Over and over walking away is morally and emotionally impossible. I think the emphasis in so many of these works on *Yidishkayt* and on the homely, secular texture of Jewish family life is no accident. (Even the essays on the search for Jewish religious community and appropriate forms of observance focus largely on the rhythms of the year and of a life, the importance of community, and the role of ritual in tying those together.) Over and over grandmothers are evoked: the comfort of their bodies; their generosity with love and praise, food and stories; the sound of their voices, often speaking Yiddish, which so many of our parents used only: "*az di kinder zoln nisht farshteyn*, so the children won't understand" (Klepfisz 1990, 173).

We were never meant to understand. That is the terrible truth. As important as it was that we survive and thrive and remember that we are Jews, the terms of that thriving and of that memory have not been ours. Choosing to remember, to thrive, to identify *differently* has meant reinventing, in the act of rediscovering, what it is to be Jewish. And it is not just that being Jewish and lesbian has required, even more acutely than just being Jewish and a woman, reinvention, that heterosexism as well as sexism has to be confronted. Rather, what emerges from the astonishing world of this writing is the gynocentric eroticism at the heart of (one form of) Jewish identity. Loving women; loving oneself as a woman; bringing one's body, heart, and soul to one's relationships with women; sanctifying the daily, the ordinary—all are as deeply Jewish as are a commitment to the political struggle for social and economic justice, the passion for argument, the love of learning. And we find in these writings a long tradition of women who, even if deprived of the study of Torah, were intelligent, brave, and passionate theorists and activists: the stereotypes of the Jewish mother and the JAP are reactions to recent American assimilationism. (Even many of our mothers, caught in the most intense pressure to find safety in conformity, resisted. My own mother recently returned to address her fiftieth reunion class at Brooklyn College—in 1939 she had been the first woman student body president—to urge her classmates not to abandon the radicalism that had marked them as "premature anti-fascists.")

Adrienne Rich has written movingly of being "split at the root" (Rich 1986a, 100-23), raised as a gentile Southern lady, claiming an identity as Jewish (inherited from her father, who distanced himself from it, never intending it to be hers) first through her husband and his family, the sorts of Jews she had been taught to shun. Later, after both her husband and her father are dead, she claims her Jewishness on her own, lesbian terms—not as something wholly new but as a telling of her history, a matter of honor and truthfulness. (Rich's poetry and essays are one of the best resources for charting a middle course between Archimedean objectivism and nihilistic relativism.) She writes of her father:

> After your death I met you again as the face of patriarchy, could name at last precisely the principle you embodied, there was an ideology at last which let me dispose of you, identify the suffering you caused, hate you righteously as part of a system, the kingdom of the fathers. I saw the power and arrogance of

the male as your true watermark; I did not see beneath it the suffering of the Jew, the alien stamp you bore, because you had deliberately arranged that it should be invisible to me. It is only now, under a powerful, womanly lens, that I can decipher your suffering and deny no part of my own ("Sources" VII, Rich 1986b, 9).

A few years ago I attended a seder, the only one that has really moved me since the socialist ones of my childhood. A friend had recently come here from the San Francisco Bay area. Like Rich she is a lesbian from the South with a Jewish father and a gentile mother. She had not grown up Jewish-identified; her father had not had a seder in his own home since his marriage. In San Francisco many of her friends were Jewish, and many of them could not return home for seders because, as Lesléa Newman puts it, "even though this woman means more to me / than all the *kreplach* in Nassau County, / Tel Aviv and Brighton Beach combined, / this woman is not welcome" ("Seder Poem," Newman 1987, 73). This community had created a lesbian seder service, which had become part of what Rebecca now meant by home, part of what she brought with her to Minnesota. And so we all assembled, bearing foods recreated, with or without recipes, from the kitchens of our childhoods, for a seder to which Rebecca's parents had traveled a thousand miles. Forty years later, her father remembered the Hebrew prayers. Accepting his daughter's lesbianism was the improbable route back to his own Jewishness.

That improbability is at the heart of my reading of these books. At a time when the mainstream images of American Judaism are profoundly problematic (I'm thinking particularly of the increasing visibility of what still seem to me oxymoronic: Jewish Republicans, and the morally and politically troubling questions of Israel and our relationship to it; Irena Klepfisz and Melanie Kaye/Kantrowitz are especially eloquent on the latter), it is "the lesbian in us" who can reconnect us with alternative images, ways of being Jewish that can move, in bell hooks's terms, "from margin to center."

NOTE

1. On the meaning of lesbianism as choice, see Claudia Card's 1992 essay. "Lesbianism and choice," in the *Journal of Homosexuality* 23(3): 39-51.

BIBLIOGRAPHY OF JEWISH LESBIAN WRITING

Balka, Christie, and Andy Rose, eds. 1989. *Twice blessed: On being lesbian, gay, and Jewish.* Boston: Beacon Press.

Beck, Evelyn Torton, ed. 1989. *Nice Jewish girls: A lesbian anthology*, 2nd ed. Boston: Beacon Press.

Dworkin, Andrea. 1980. *The new womans broken heart* . East Palo Alto, CA: Frog in the Well.

Hacker, Marilyn. 1990. *Going back to the river* (poems). New York: Vintage.

Kaye/Kantrowitz, Melanie. 1990. *My Jewish face and other stories*. San Francisco: Spinsters/Aunt Lute.

Klepfisz, Irena. 1982. *Keeper of accounts* (poems). Watertown MA: Persephone Books.

———. 1990. *Dreams of an insomniac: Jewish feminist essays, speeches and diatribes*. Portland: Eighth Mountain Press.

Newman, Lesléa. 1986. *Good enough to eat* (novel). Ithaca, NY: Firebrand Books.

———. 1987. *Love me like you mean it* (poems). Santa Cruz, CA: HerBooks.

———. 1988. *Letter to Harvey Milk* (short stories). Ithaca, NY: Firebrand Books.

———. 1990. *Secrets* (short stories). Norwich VT: New Victoria Publishers.

———. 1991. *Sweet dark places* (poems). Santa Cruz, CA: HerBooks.

Rich, Adrienne. 1981. *A wild patience has taken me this far: Poems 1978-1981*. New York: Norton.

———. 1986a. *Blood, bread, and poetry: Selected prose 1979-1985*. New York: Norton.

———. 1986b. *Your native land, your life: Poems*. New York: Norton.

———. 1991. *An atlas of the difficult world: Poems 1988-1991*. New York: Norton.

Zahava, Irene, ed. 1990. *Speaking for ourselves: Short stories by Jewish lesbians*. Freedom, CA: Crossing Press.

Why *Lesbian* Ethics?

SARAH LUCIA HOAGLAND

This essay is part of a recent version of a talk I have given by way of introducing
Lesbian Ethics. *I mention ways in which lesbian existence creates certain conceptual*
possibilities that can effect conceptual shifts and transform consciousness.

Lesbian Ethics (Hoagland 1988) is a work that emerges from and acknowledges a context of oppression. It patterns a moral agency that presupposes not
privileged agency but rather agency under oppression—agency emerging in
contexts in which one is coerced, in which one has developed modes of
acquiescence and resistance, in which one might use one's strategies of survival
against one's own kind, in which one might even be demoralized by those who
oppress.

Thus, in embarking on *Lesbian Ethics* I did not begin with traditional
Anglo-European ethics, because I felt that if I started there, I would never get
out of its conceptual framework. Instead, I focused on what was actually going
on in lesbian communities. As my work proceeded, it became clear why a
concept from Anglo-European ethics, such as duty, was inadequate—indeed,
undermined rather than promoted community.

I also began to realize that distinct, and in some cases unique, concepts were
emerging through lesbian interacting.[1] In claiming a lesbian focus, I began to
notice things I had not noticed when my focus was on men or on women. And
I found that at this point in time, at least, lesbian existence creates certain
conceptual possibilities that can effect conceptual shifts and transform consciousness; what follows mentions a few of them.

I. Political Influences[2]

In addressing the context of oppression out of which our lesbian agency must
emerge, I drew on three political influences: radical feminism, lesbian separatism, and radical lesbianism. Ideas from radical feminism include (1) that
motherhood, marriage, prostitution, and the family all function to support

Hypatia vol. 7, no. 4 (Fall 1992) © by Sarah Lucia Hoagland male domination; (2) that there is a declared war against women from rape to poverty to child sexual abuse to sexual harassment; (3) that femininity is a means by which women's resistance to male domination is obscured; (4) that women can work to uncover a wild Original Self (which does not involve appealing to a "Western" essentialized self); (5) that forced sterilization, economic restrictions on a woman's ability to care for children, treatment of orphans, loss of abortion, "concern" about unwed mothers, and other U.S. policies and practices, like wires forming a cage, are systematically related barriers that serve to maintain male domination, monitor class divisions, and ensure white supremacy.

Radical lesbianism (from French-speaking lesbians) has also informed *Lesbian Ethics*, including the ideas that (1) while one is not born a woman, lesbians *are not* women; (2) the category of men cannot exist without the category of women; (3) focusing on compulsory heterosexuality focuses on problems surrounding something being compulsory and thus undermines critiques of heterosexuality itself; (4) the institution of heterosexuality is a political regime that legitimates (a binary, hierarchical form of) difference; (5) feminism is simply a release valve on the pressure cooker of patriarchy.[3]

Lesbian separatism certainly informs my work, including the ideas that (1) separatism is a no-saying to male parasitism and a withdrawal from the dominant/subordinate, man/woman relationship; (2) protectors are not essentially different from predators; (3) a feminist agreeing to defend women's rights is actually coerced into solidifying status quo values that make women's, but not men's, rights debatable in a democracy; (4) heterosexuality provides a legitimation of all forms of domination, most especially the exploitative and paternalistic justification of imperialism; (5) separatism is a focusing on lesbians and a lesbian conceptual framework from which new values can and have emerged.

II. HETEROSEXUALISM

One can note that the problematic category when combining these influences is not "men"; "men" is fairly transparent. What is problematic is "women,"—in particular, the consequences of identifying "lesbian" within or without the category of "women," a category from which emerge those values that many academic men and women consider "women's values," usually with no reference even to sexism.[4]

Focusing not on sexism, homophobia, or even heterosexism, I consider hetero*sexualism*—a relationship between men and women. "Heterosexualism is men dominating and deskilling women in any of a number of forms, from outright attack to paternalistic care, and women devaluing (of necessity) female bonding as well as finding inherent conflicts between commitment and autonomy and consequently valuing an ethics of dependence" (Hoagland 1988, 29). This undermines female agency.

Further, "heterosexualism is a particular economic, political, and emotional relationship between men and women: men must dominate and women must subordinate themselves to men in any number of ways. As a result men presume access to women while women remain riveted on men and are unable to sustain a community of women" (Hoagland 1988, 29).[5] This undermines women's community.

Thus, two serious problems of heterosexualism for women are female agency and community. By not trying to fit ourselves into a (heterosexual) women's framework and instead recognizing our own, lesbians can discover that from lesbian lives come different conceptual possibilities.

III. FEMALE AGENCY

The values assigned to women are the feminine virtues: self-sacrifice, altruism, vulnerability (Hoagland 1988, chap. 2). As a consequence, the healthy and normal woman's actions are to be toward others. If we try to fit that model, it means our actions are away from ourselves, with the result that our ability to act is located in others. And that means that the primary mode of female agency is manipulation.

Under oppression one learns survival skills, including means of manipulation. I have argued (Hoagland 1988, chap. 1) that stereotypical feminine behavior is indicative of sabotage and resistance (as is stereotypical slave behavior). And I mean for us to herald these actions for what they are, as indications of resistance to domination. Concomitantly I object to academic women's attempt to claim "the feminine" as a balance to the masculine when the feminine was conceived by ecclesiastic and academic men to legitimate male right and was developed by women in resistance and sabotage. Simply championing femininity doesn't change or even acknowledge the fact that men still own the scales.

I think from lesbian lives we can find another model of female agency. I once had an argument with a heterosexual feminist friend over a "Take Back the Night" march in which we both participated back in the days before such political actions turned into police-sanctioned events. She was chastising us lesbians, saying, "It's fine to go out and have a good time for one night, but you still have to go back to reality." For the longest time I could not figure out what she meant, until I realized that she meant she still had to go home to her husband. Now her husband is one of those "sensitive feminists" and likely he was at the march. But if so, he did not belong there as she did. For it was "take back the night" not just from predators but also from protectors. Thus, in going home to him she was going home to a different reality; apparently that night of women for women was not real for her. As I thought about this, I also realized that she understood her political action as taking her away from her center and that she considered her political work a sacrifice.

And I thought about myself and my friends. We did not consider our political work a sacrifice (even though one could note many sacrifices); it was how we made our lives meaningful. We did not consider our work away from our centers; and on nights like those, as well as others, we were taking the reality we were creating in our homes, collectives, bars, consciousness-raising groups, and other meeting places, and extending it to the streets. In considering actual lesbian lives, I found that our actions were not sacrificial but creative.

There is another aspect to this. Under U.S. ideology, if one has to choose between two things, one has sacrificed something. Thus, lesbians may avoid choice because it seems to mean that we lose something. However, this idea of choice comes from an imperialist focus—it presupposes that everything that exists is ours, or should be, such that when we have to make choices between things, we have lost something. Aside from the masculine power of imperialism suggesting that everything is ours, there is also the feminine power of manipulation: namely, that if I have lost something as a result of choice, then someone owes me something (loyalty, or at the very least, acknowledgment that I am a martyr). There are conceptual consequences of the way we approach choice—from the masculine, that I've a right to it all (whatever that means); and from the feminine, that while I must sacrifice, I am owed.

From lesbian lives, I think we can find another way of approaching choice. For from our lives we realize that nothing that exists is ours (not even a subordinate position of service). What exists that is lesbian we've created out of nothing (with not even seed nor sperm as catalyst). What exists that is lesbian exists because we've made it happen—we've been reclaiming skills, we've created festivals and bookstores and coffeehouses and political actions and on and on. As a result, lesbians can realize from the material context of our lives that choice is the possibility of creation. That we choose to focus here, that we move in this direction, that is the meaning we create.

I once asked Karen Thompson if she considered what she was doing for Sharon Kowalski a sacrifice.[6] Her response was "No, I did this to make my life meaningful." She was acting within oppressive circumstances, circumstances that she could not control, and she created meaning.

Thus, I am suggesting that by considering the category "lesbian," not "woman," we discover a different sense of female agency. In lesbian lives we find that choice is creation, not sacrifice. As a result, we can revalue female agency, developing it independently of the manipulation and control from the position of subordination of heterosexualism. Female agency becomes not a matter of sacrifice but a process of engagement and creation. And if we regard choice as creation, not sacrifice, we can regard our ability to make choices as a source of enabling power, rather than as something to avoid because it appears to mean loss.[7] All that is lesbian exists only because we've created it. And realizing this, we can realize that our power lies in choice.

IV. COMMUNITY

The second problem of heterosexualism is community. As I began writing *Lesbian Ethics*, my initial stress was on sabotage and feminine manipulation. And while unraveling it and honoring it for what it is, I also wanted to move away from it (for sabotage doesn't strictly challenge the system that gave rise to its need, and we too often use manipulation against each other). However, I found that in moving away from feminine agency, I was moving toward its complement, masculine agency, involving those who are egoistic, isolated, aggressive, competitive, and antagonistic.[8] Thus, the ethics of duty and of justice are designed to coerce antagonists into "cooperation" (Hoagland 1988, chap. 6). While from femininity we get an ethics of dependence, from masculinity we get an ethics of independence. And I think that from lesbian lives we can find another possibility.

Now while lesbians know all the methods of the feminine, lesbians have also proven quite capable of the masculine, of being arrogant, aggressive, antagonistic, and so on. Just by coming out in a world that says we do not exist, just by breaking away from the central message of heterosexualism, we have needed considerable egoism and aggression, and we have traveled this road in isolation. However, what is interesting to me is that while we broke from heterosexualism and at least to some extent its proponents, we did not break to isolation and independence; we broke to each other—in the bars and the collectives, on the baseball and hockey fields, at the demonstrations. Our desire for and attraction to each other is part of the glue that holds us together.

We have not sought to remain isolated, etc.; we have sought each other out; we have sought community at this level.[9] As I wrote the first draft of *Lesbian Ethics*, an important change washed over me—the importance of our communities and our sense of sharing in creating meaning. Being a lesbian is not a matter of remaining isolated (and thus pursuing masculine agency); it is a matter of recognizing and sharing things with other lesbians, from oppression to recipes, from resistance to outrageousness. That is, considering lesbian lives, we can notice that finding each other in communities is an important part of our lives, a central part of developing and maintaining our sense of our selves.[10]

Now if, as I am claiming, community is an important part of lesbian identity and existence as well as a significant part of the means by which we change and develop as lesbians, what does community mean? Certainly I don't mean by community a lesbian state. I mean something like a context or a place of reference. A context is a source of meaning. And how we understand our lives is affected by the context to which we refer for meaning. This is true of how we understand even our most inner feelings (Hoagland 1988, chap. 4).[11]

For example, before the women's liberation movement began, women's anger was madness. When a woman got angry, men would discount the anger by saying, "You're so cute when you get angry" or "The bitch is crazy." After the women's liberation movement got under way, women's anger became a righteous response to male domination. Men went right on saying the same things, but by coming together in a movement and focusing on each other, women as a group created a different context and stopped referring to men's values and perceptions of women. (A similar phenomenon occurred as Blacks as a group focused on each other, ignoring white definitions/perceptions of blackness.) Tragically, that women's anger has become once again taboo or psychological (therapized, especially among women), which suggests that the context of the movement has been co-opted and patriarchal disciplinarians and professionals have reasserted their control.

Or another example: before the lesbian activism of the late sixties and seventies, and within the conceptual framework of Freud and his buddies, lesbian love was a perversion. And that affected how we understood even our most private feeling—one can find this in novels such as *The Well of Loneliness* (Hall 1928). However, once lesbians undertook activism, lesbian love became a political act, a celebration; it became many things, and it ceased being, for many of us, a perversion. And this too can be perceived through the novels, particularly with the need for a happy ending. Or again, lesbian sexuality: if we continue to refer to male sexuality, we will continue to understand our responses within a context of sadomasochism—that is, sadomasochism (not by any means essential as portrayed, surprisingly, by many postmodernist thinkers) will continue to color the explorations of our desire.

In other words, by focusing on ourselves, we have created a different context, and that affects how we understand even our most private feelings. The context is crucial, and if there is no lesbian context—that is, no lesbian community—then we will once again have only the society of the brothers[12] as a reference for understanding the meaning of our lives. Without lesbian focus there is no lesbian context, and without lesbian context, there is no means to understand and develop the meanings of our lesbian lives. This is what I think about when I think of lesbian community.

One of the devastating effects of heterosexualism has been the erasure of lesbian meaning. It stifles imagination and blocks memory. When we as lesbians decide we cannot prioritize lesbian visibility and lesbian projects, when we as lesbians attempt to undermine the efforts of those lesbians who do prioritize lesbian contexts, we are displaying continued effects of that erasure. This is one of the reasons I'm a separatist. If we keep focusing on men's meanings, we'll keep focusing on men's meanings. And lesbian imagination and memory dissolves.

Of course, I do not mean that within lesbian communities there is accord or harmony. There isn't, nor should there be. But it is to say that with the festivals, the books, the music, the coffeehouses, the gatherings of all sorts, there is another place of reference, and this place has the possibility of not replicating so readily the values of the brothers. Lesbian spaces, though hardly free of the dregs of heteropatriarchy, are different, are obviously different. And from them emerge the possibility of lesbian agency and the possibilities of lesbian communities.

V. DIFFERENCE

So what are the possibilities of lesbian communities? One is diversity, for we emerge from everywhere—Palestine and Israel, Argentina and Cherokee Nation, China and India. We have the ready-made possibility of developing concepts of "difference" in a way available to few, if any, other communities.

Under heteropatriarchy, difference is binary, hence oppositional, hence yields dominance and subordination, and hence is a threat: Hegel's master/slave thesis implies that men's interaction is a one-on-one mortal battle for acknowledgment that rationally becomes instead a fight for domination. Behind this argument is the idea that another's perception of me, if through that person's own values and not through mine, is capable of destroying me. Therefore one major message of Hegel's thesis is that difference is a threat (Hoagland 1988, chap. 5).

And, in fact, in community another's perceptions have been capable of threatening us, and so we shut out her world, her values.[13] For example, if I, as a white lesbian, come to know a Latina lesbian and begin to enter her world and understand her life, I begin to understand many things differently. But should I then perceive myself through her values, I might notice something I did as racist. Trying to maintain my sense of self as having integrity against the patriarchal message that I, as a female, was never any good anyway, I shut out her values. Her difference becomes a threat. (We also tend to fear that if we admit differences in our relationships, the relationships will end.[14]) And when we perceive difference as a threat, we try to negate it or deny it exists.

However, this way of thinking is not inevitable. There is another way of gaining identity, indeed character. Instead of perceiving ourselves in a one-on-one aggressive relation, we can perceive ourselves in community, one among many. If I consider myself, not in isolated competition with another, but one among many in community, then very different results are possible. I am one among many, and I get reflections of myself from many (Hoagland 1988, chap. 5). And no one set of reflections need destroy or even threaten me. Of course, because I was raised white in a white supremacist society, elements of racism still emerge, despite my best efforts. But gaining this knowledge from others' reflections of me, rather than undermining my integrity, gives me feedback I need to consider change—information I don't get from within my own framework. In addition, there are other parts of me reflected back through others' values: respected thinker, not a real separatist, cute dyke, elitist academic, picks her nose like everyone else, etc.

In perceiving ourselves as one among many, we realize we are not destroyed (nor created) by another's reflection, but we also realize that we are not the whole picture. I am suggesting that one's self in relation to others need not be a matter of a polarity. Further, in dealing with differences, no one of us lesbians is purely a dominator, purely from the privileged classes, and no one of us is purely from the subordinate classes. How we live in resistance or acquiescence to any of these classes provides crucial information in community.[15] Thus, as we pursue the work we are doing, we begin to realize that difference is not only not a threat and that difference is more than a gift: difference is at the center of our survival.

Most communities strive to be culturally homogeneous. As lesbians we have the possibility of developing difference in new ways if we consider the reality of our lives.[16]

VI. AGENCY UNDER OPPRESSION AND IN COMMUNITY

Now while we have challenged patriarchal politics, we have not challenged patriarchal ethics, fraternal agency. We want the power and control that reside in patriarchal ethics: we want a rule to tell us what to do so that when we act we can rest comfortably in the certainty that we did the right thing no matter the consequences (an ethics of imperialists). We also want rules so we can try to force others to conform. But rules don't tell us when to apply them, and they don't help when all else fails. If we aren't already acting with integrity, then the rules won't guarantee it (Hoagland 1988, introduction).

More significantly, lesbians are an obnoxious, unruly bunch—that's partly how we became lesbians. So any ethics that tries to keep us in line and make us into ladies is not an ethics that suits us. Much of *Lesbian Ethics* involves approaching ethics, including challenges to each other and efforts to change harmful behavior, outside the focus of rules and obligation and duty.

In addition to an obsession with rules and principles, fraternal agency focuses on free will, and we are encouraged to think that to be moral agents we must have free will. Thus, when in understanding ourselves as oppressed we find we don't have free will, we are tempted to think we can't be moral agents and consequently to think of ourselves merely as victims. We get the idea that either we can control a situation or we are helpless victims. Lesbians exist within a context of oppression. Any moral or political theory useful to anyone under oppression must not convince us that either we must be in complete control or we are total victims. While we don't control situations, we do affect them. It is crucial to understand ourselves not as mere victims but as participants who are oppressed. Part of the possibility of lesbian ethics is the possibility of developing ways to act within situations without trying to control them. Sometimes I think about (lesbian) mosquitoes.

I was fired, essentially, from two jobs before I received tenure (after a dogfight) at my present university. I chose to bring a discrimination suit against the second one (together with the other woman in the department who was also dumped). I chose to bring that suit not because I thought I was going to get my job back, and I did not, and not because I thought I was going to get financial compensation and I did not, but because I had to say, "Fuck you, you will not go on as if I never existed; you may fire me, but I'm going to cause you a lot of trouble," and I did.

During the process of the suit, I nevertheless became cynical. Lesbians and heterosexual women were organizing for me and fund-raising. But they couldn't get my job back. And so, still operating in the mode of thinking that either one is in control or is helpless and of no use, I began to wonder what good these lesbians and women were, since they couldn't make a difference. (Luckily, I kept this to myself.) When we find another cannot control a situation, we can turn on her: "You are no good to me." From the other direction, when we find we can't make it all better for others we can declare: "This is not my responsibility" (Hoagland 1988, chap. 3). Thus, we can come to feel that lesbian community is worthless, has accomplished nothing.

Had I continued on that path, I would have turned to focus on those who, in my mind then, could make a difference and asked, "What do I need to do to be acceptable?" And their answer would have been the usual, "Lie down and let us walk all over you." I never got that far; soon I began to realize that these lesbians and heterosexual women did a great deal for me. For when someone is discriminating against you, they don't say, "We're discriminating against you," they say, "You're not good enough." And if one's only point of reference is oppressor values, one can become demoralized. What these lesbians and heterosexual women were saying, with all their organizing, was "Bullshit, this is discrimination." They were attending me (Hoagland 1988, chap. 3); they were helping to maintain my reality so that it would not be co-opted. Thus, rather than become de-moralized, I could make choices. In this instance I chose to fight.

Lesbian community, as a point of reference, made all the difference. No, we have not ended the Reagan/Bush administration. But we have done a great deal in terms of lesbian lives. By considering lesbian community, we find ways to not become demoralized under oppression, we learn what agency under oppression and in community can mean.

If from the reality of our lesbian lives we realize "lesbian" is a category that creates some distinct values and also some distinct possibilities—choice as creation not sacrifice, community as a context of values in which we are one among many, and community as the possibility of difference—then we may approach ethics differently: not trying to control situations but acting within them. Moral agency then becomes a question, not of how am I going to stop all the injustice, but rather what is my part, and what are we going to do next?

NOTES

This essay is part of a recent version of a talk I have given by way of introducing *Lesbian Ethics* in lesbian communities and at universities in the United States, Canada, Quebec, Argentina, Aoteoroa (New Zealand), Australia, France, Belgium, Spain, Italy and Germany (where the book has been translated and published by *Orlanda Frauenverlag*). Thanks to Claudia Card for patience and helpful comments, to Julia Penelope for helpful comments, and to Anne T. Leighton for persistent support, feedback, and ideas.

1. Lesbian community is not the only source of new value. Katie G. Cannon provides an ovular study articulating the distinctive moral character of the African-American women's community in *Black Womanist Ethics*. For example, she states: "The focus of this dissertation is to show how Black women live out a moral wisdom in their real-lived context that does not appeal to the fixed rules or absolute principles of the white-oriented, male-structured society. Black women's analysis and appraisal of what is right or wrong and good or bad develops out of the various coping mechanisms related to the conditions of their own cultural circumstances. In the face of this, Black women have justly regarded survival against tyrannical systems of triple oppression as a true sphere of moral life" (Cannon 1988, 4). One might note that Cannon's point is not about how Black women reason differently but about how circumstances yield different contexts for the development and meaning of moral value.

2. I make direct reference by means of well-known phrases to the work of Simone de Beauvoir, Kate Millett, Mary Daly, Monique Wittig, and Marilyn Frye.

3. Note, for example, Wittig (1992) along with Turcotte (1992).

4. Possibly this is because when focusing on sexism, many often focus primarily on women's victim status; and that appears, at first, to preclude discussion of moral agency. But whether or not this is the reason, some works on "women's values" simply ignore altogether the contexts of oppression (including sexism, but also racism and classism and heterosexism) out of which those values have emerged.

5. I continue to find that gay men also presume access to lesbians and lesbian space in similar manly ways; gay men still identify as and behave as men first. Whether in a modernist or postmodernist mode, gay, straight, or transsexual, men still intrude, penetrate, insert themselves, presume access, remain parasitic, attempt to dominate, and work to remain in the center of attention.

6. In 1983 Sharon Kowalski suffered brain-stem injury after being hit by a drunk driver. Following the accident, Karen Thompson, Sharon's lover, worked with Sharon to help her recover. Despite overwhelming evidence that Sharon wanted and improved with Karen's help, Karen soon found herself fighting a losing battle to retain access to Sharon against the prejudices of Sharon's father and the medical and judicial communities whose members testified and ruled against Karen's petitions. The courts gave guardianship of Sharon to Sharon's father, who proceeded to bar Karen from even seeing Sharon, much less helping her, and who switched Sharon to a lesser facility. Karen quit her job to fight the decision and to educate gays and lesbians on legal ways to protect our relationships. The story of the first five years of the ordeal is told in *Why Can't Sharon Kowalski Come*

Home? (Thompson and Andrzejewski 1988). This book is a central contribution to questions of both human rights and professional ethics, among other things exposing the vulnerability of those who are disabled and are confined to nursing homes. Since the book's publication, the saga has continued, with Karen and Sharon ceaselessly battling to have Karen gain guardianship of Sharon. Recently, Karen and Sharon won the final stage in that battle.

7. I am making a conceptual point about choice. In our actual lives, because patriarchy limits our choices, we have to scramble. My point is that we might regard choice differently, not as facing loss, since that presupposes an imperialist's stance of believing everything ought to be ours, but as creating meaning. And because of the creativity of lesbian choices, we have been experimenting with ways that allow community choices to become available to all lesbians—for example, sliding-scale fees, work-exchange, outreach, accessibility. I am *not* saying our strategies are always or even often successful. I am saying, however, that lesbian creativity is ever at work and yields new value.

8. No wonder one finds a call for the feminine virtues, and not surprisingly these virtues are demanded from subordinates—women, children, employees, students (Hoagland 1988, chap. 2).

9. Many lesbians don't have access to a community, actually *are* isolated, have to strain to find *Sinister Wisdom* or the magazine *Lesbian Ethics*, or *Common Lives, Lesbian Lives*, or *Lesbian Connection*, for example. But that effort is precisely my point.

10. Some women and many lesbians find other communities, such as the communities of nuns. However, one can be part of such communities only at the expense of developing one's lesbianism.

11. Challenging the idea that our emotions and feelings are private, Naomi Scheman (1983) argues that they are not individual states and that, in any depth and complexity, they only make sense relative to a framework.

12. I am using the phrase "society of the brothers," rather than the phrase "society of the fathers," following Carole Pateman's argument that in social contract theory the men making the social contract were doing so not as fathers (nor as husbands) but as brothers (Pateman 1988, 78).

13. María Lugones (1987) explores the idea of traveling to others' worlds.

14. Audre Lorde explores this problem in *Zami* (Lorde 1982, e.g., 203-4).

15. In April 1990 María Lugones offered a powerful workshop at the Horizons Conference in Chicago that involved locating ourselves on the map of oppression and considering how we live in resistance or acquiescence at our locations.

16. Conversation, Anna Lee.

REFERENCES

Cannon, Katie G. 1988. *Black womanist ethics*. Atlanta: Scholars Press.
Hall, Radclyffe. 1928. *The well of loneliness*. Garden City, NY: Garden City Books.
Hoagland, Sarah Lucia. 1988. *Lesbian ethics: Toward new value*. Palo Alto, CA: Institute of Lesbian Studies.
Lorde, Audre. 1982. *Zami: A new spelling of my name*. Watertown, MA: Persephone Press.
Lugones, María. 1987. Playfulness, "world"-travelling, and loving perception. *Hypatia* 2(2): 3-19.

Pateman, Carole. 1988. *The sexual contract*. Stanford, CA: Stanford University Press.

Scheman, Naomi. 1983. Individualism and the objects of psychology. In *Discovering reality: Feminist perspectives on epistemology, metaphysics, methodology, and philosophy of science*, ed. Sandra Harding and Merrill Hintikka. Boston: D. Reidel.

Thompson, Karen and Julie Andrzejewski. 1988. *Why can't Sharon Kowalski come home?* San Francisco: Spinsters/Aunt Lute.

Turcotte, Louise. 1992. Changing the point of view. Foreword to Wittig (1992).

Wittig, Monique. 1992. *The straight mind and other essays*. Boston: Beacon Press.

Lesbian Ethics and the Journal *Lesbian Ethics*: A Review

CLAUDIA CARD

Lesbian Ethics, a U.S. journal of lesbian culture, has offered highly readable philosophical essays, reviews, discussions, and other nonfiction since late 1984 (twelve issues to date). It provides a forum in which the meaning of "lesbian" takes shape from self concepts formed in cooperative interaction and thus lays the groundwork for lesbians becoming publicly recognized as the foremost interpreters of lesbian identity and history.

One of a small number of extraordinary journals of lesbian culture in the United States, *Lesbian Ethics* (hereafter, *LE*) has published highly readable philosophical essays, reviews, discussions, and other nonfiction since late 1984 in twelve issues (four volumes) to date.[1] Edited in New Mexico by Fox (formerly known as Jeanette Silveira), *LE* advertises itself as "a journal of radical lesbian ethics and politics, with an emphasis on how lesbians behave with each other." Its guidelines for authors state that "contributions should be based on lesbian experience." In practice, *LE*'s contributors tend to understand lesbian experience as experience in lesbian community and in relationships with other lesbians—following *LE*'s stated emphasis on "how lesbians behave with each other"—including the experience of coming to terms with oneself (or one's selves coming to terms with each other).

Although a number of academics and former academics have published articles in *LE*—including Jacqueline Anderson, Susan Cavin, Chris Cuomo, Marilyn Frye, Sarah Hoagland, Julia Penelope, Lori Saxe, Joyce Trebilcot, Jacqueline Zita, and yours truly—contributions come at least as frequently from lesbians outside the academy whose occupations and situations are very diverse. Some *LE* essays are reprinted in such anthologies as Jeffner Allen's *Lesbian Philosophies and Cultures* (1990); some are advance chapters of books, such as Julia Penelope's *Call Me Lesbian: Lesbian Lives, Lesbian Theory* (1992);

Hypatia vol. 7, no. 4 (Fall 1992) © by Claudia Card

at least one is a collage of newspaper articles; at least one, a collection of documents.

A frequent and absorbing *LE* feature is the "Readers' Forum," offering short pieces by many contributors on special topics set in advance. Memorable topics have been "Non? Monogamy?" (1: 2, Spring 1985); "Lesbian Therapy" (3: 3, Fall 1985); "Femme and Butch" (2: 2, Fall 1986); "Sex" (2: 3, Summer 1987); and "Separatism" (3: 2, Fall 1988). Sex, as in "having sex," is just one among many topics receiving attention in *LE*, perhaps not discussed as frequently as color, class, and abuse, but not a topic that is avoided, either. *LE*'s range of topics can be gathered from a sampling of articles such as "Lesbian Nuns: Some Documents in the Case" (1: 3, Fall 1985); "Sado-Masochism: The Erotic Cult of Fascism" (Sheila Jeffreys, 2: 1, Spring 1986); "Found Goddesses" (Morgan Grey and Julia Penelope, 2: 2, Fall 1986); "Dyke Economics" (Joyce Trebilcot, 3: 1, Spring 1988); "If Looks Could Kill: Fat Oppression" (Bev Jo, 3: 1, Spring 1988); "Guerilla Feminism" (many authors, 3: 3, Summer 1989); "Lesbian Violence, Lesbian Victims: How to Identify Battering in Relationships" (Lee Evans and Shelley Bannister, 4: 1, Spring 1990); and "The Possibility of Lesbian Community" (Marilyn Frye, 4: 1, Spring 1990). Two installments (3: 3, Summer 1989, and 4: 1, Spring 1990) appeared in what was intended to be "a regular column on class" by JMax.

LE's announced "Readers' Forum" themes have frequently also elicited major non-forum essays with a focus related to that of the forum. Recently, a special focus for the whole issue has been announced in advance; next issue's focus (5: 1) is "Our Mothers." The two most recent issues are dedicated to JMax, Fox's beloved friend and partner, who ended her own life in November 1990. Both issues are focused on topics salient in JMax's life and death: "Class: How It Affects Our Lesbian Interactions" (4: 2, Spring 1991) and "Incest and Child Abuse: A Radical Lesbian Perspective" (4: 3, Spring 1992). I was unable to put down either of these issues until I had read the whole thing (not the first time *LE* has had this effect on me)—though these were exhausting experiences, especially the most recent issue. The editor's introduction to the latter forewarns the reader: "some pieces contain graphic descriptions of child rape and torture." The focus is less on what the perpetrator did than on how it felt and continues to feel to be such a victim or to be a survivor of major ongoing childhood sexual abuse, what kinds of damage it has done, challenges it presents to survivors and their partners, and how both survivors and partners are responding.

LE's guidelines for authors further state that "if the author agrees that her work can be used by non-lesbians for educational non-profit purposes, this is noted at the end of the article" and that "any other use must be cleared with the individual authors, who can be contacted through *LE*."[2] The issue on incest and child abuse contains many articles followed by the notice "This paper is for lesbians only and may be copied by them for non-profit, educational purposes" or "This paper is for women only and may be copied by them for non-profit, educational purposes." For those interested in ethical and political rationales of such separatism, there are extensive and helpful discussions by Marilyn Frye (1983, 95-109) and by Sarah Hoagland (1988, 24-68), and especially for lesbians in *LE* 3: 3 (Fall 1988) and in Sarah Lucia Hoagland and Julia Penelope (1988); a critical discussion of problems with separatism can be found in Kathleen Martindale and Martha Saunders (this issue).

In emphasizing "how lesbians behave with each other," *LE* interprets "lesbian ethics" in the spirit of Sarah Hoagland's book, *Lesbian Ethics: Toward New Value* (Hoagland 1988): more specific than ethics *by* or *about* lesbians in that it arises from reflection *by* lesbians on experience *with* lesbians, but also more general than ethics focused on lesbian sexuality or eroticism in that the relationships with which it is concerned may be primarily economic, domestic, spiritual, or other sorts. Critics sometimes object to both the specificity and the generality. Yet both have their roots in lesbian history.

In an era in which the very meanings of "lesbian" are in flux, in which such meanings can have vast implications for the interactions of real lesbians with educational institutions, health-care providers, and the law, and in which enforced ignorance of lesbian lives has been the lot of most nonlesbians (and many lesbians) for centuries, it is imperative that there be forums in which the meaning of "lesbian" takes shape from the self-concepts of lesbians formed in basically friendly and cooperative interaction with lesbians. Such lesbians ideally have what Sarah Hoagland calls "*autokoenony*"—the being of a self in community, "one among many," neither autonomous nor dissolved (Hoagland 1988, 12). To interpret lesbian ethics in this way is not to deny that many, perhaps most, who identify as lesbian interact in major parts of their lives with others who do not identify as lesbian and that major ethical issues are faced, and should be faced, by lesbians in such interactions. Many publications address such interactions in detail as *human* interactions. In contrast, *LE* highlights interactions and dialogues historically overlooked by those who have spoken in the name of humanity. Who lesbians are has been publicly defined too often by hostile parties. Public discussions of issues involving lesbians have focused on the dilemmas of *non*lesbian agents. "The lesbian" has been presented publically as interesting primarily as a problem for nonlesbians. *LE* reverses all this. In *LE*, the lesbian is interesting in her own right and as someone who interacts with lesbians, someone whose major ethical dilemmas tend to focus on interactions with lesbians. (Here men are apt to become interesting, if at all, primarily as a problem for lesbians).

It may seem that this understanding of "lesbian ethics" inevitably omits issues central to the lives of many lesbians who do not live in or identify themselves through lesbian communities—fighting court battles regarding child custody; some seeking court protection because they are stalked by men; some lesbians whose public political lives are centered on fighting poverty, illiteracy, or disease defined as human problems. Yet, in principle, none of these basic topics is excluded from discussion in LE, as the recent issues on class and child abuse illustrate. Although certain *aspects* of such issues and certain kinds of *approaches* will not be found here, one finds lesbians interacting around global as well as local issues and in relation to outside parties as well as in relation to each other.

In LE, "lesbian nation" has been supplanted by, or perhaps evolved into, "lesbian community," a community that is not meant to be geographically localized.[3] One way lesbians interact "in community" is *through* such journals as LE. In the words of Sarah Hoagland, "lesbian community is a context" making possible and created by "lesbians engaging and networking"; "it is a whole, not as an entity, but . . . as a ground of our lesbian be-ing"; "if there is an entity, it is not a state, an institution; it is our energy and the contextual reality that emerges from it" (Hoagland 1988, 290).

In an essay thought-provoking on many issues, Laurence Thomas hypothesized that a source of problematic interaction between Blacks and Jews is that as a group, Blacks are not "regarded by other groups as the foremost interpreters of [their] own history and experiences," whereas Jews as a group are so regarded, and that, further, among those regarded as foremost interpreters of the history and experiences of Blacks are Jewish historians (Thomas 1988, 112). A situation in some ways analogous may likewise problematize interactions between lesbians and nonlesbians in that nonlesbians (in former times, psychiatrists and criminologists; today, sometimes gay men) have long been publicly regarded as the foremost interpreters of lesbian experience and history. Interactions between lesbians and gay men, and between lesbian and nonlesbian feminists, may continue to be problematic, even when the latter mean to be friendly, until lesbians as a group come to be publicly recognized as the foremost interpreters of who we are, what we do, and where we have been. Journals like LE help lay the groundwork for that possibility.

NOTES

1. See the "Selected Bibliography of Lesbian and Related Works" at the end of this issue for past and present journals of lesbian culture. From some of these journals, special issues have been published separately as books—e.g., *Sinister Wisdom* 22/23 and 29/30 have been issued, respectively, as *A Gathering of Spirit: Writing and Art by North American Indian Women*, ed. Beth Brant (1984) and *The Tribe of Dina: A Jewish Women's Anthology*, ed. Irena Klepfisz and Melanie Kaye/Kantrowitz (1986). From others, articles from many issues have been published as books—e.g., *The Lesbian Reader*, ed. Gina Covina and Laurel Galana (1975); *Lesbiana: Book Reviews from The Ladder*, ed. Barbara Grier (1976); and the volumes of essays, stories, and biographies, ed. Barbara Grier and Coletta Reid (1976a, 1976b, 1976c).

2. LE Publications, P.O. Box 4723, Albuquerque, NM 87196.

3. On "lesbian nation," see Johnston (1973).

REFERENCES

Allen, Jeffner, ed. 1990. *Lesbian philosophies and cultures*. Albany, NY: SUNY Press.
Brant, Beth, ed. 1984. *A gathering of spirit: Writing and art by North American Indian women*. Ithaca, NY: Firebrand.
Covina, Gina, and Laurel Galana. 1975. *The lesbian reader: An amazon quarterly anthology*. Oakland, CA: Amazon Press.
Frye, Marilyn. 1983. *The politics of reality: Essays in feminist theory*. Trumansburg, NY: Crossing Press.
Grier, Barbara (a.k.a. Gene Damon). 1976. *Lesbiana: Book reviews from The Ladder, 1966-72*. Reno: Naiad Press.
Grier, Barbara, and Coletta Reid, eds. 1976a. *The lavender herring: Lesbian essays from The Ladder*. Baltimore, MD: Diana Press.
———, eds. 1976b. *The lesbians home journal: Stories from The Ladder*. Baltimore, MD: Diana Press.
———, eds. 1976c. *Lesbian lives: Biographies of women from The Ladder*. Baltimore, MD: Diana Press.
Hoagland, Sarah Lucia. 1988. *Lesbian ethics: Toward new value*. Palo Alto, CA: Institute of Lesbian Studies.
Hoagland, Sarah Lucia, and Julia Penelope, eds. 1988. *For lesbians only: A separatist anthology*. London: Onlywomen Press.
Johnston, Jill. 1973. *Lesbian nation*. New York: Simon and Schuster.
Klepfisz, Irena, and Melanie Kaye/Kantrowitz, eds. 1986. *The tribe of Dina: A Jewish women's anthology*. Montpelier, VT: Sinister Wisdom Books.
Penelope, Julia. 1992. *Call me lesbian: Lesbian lives, lesbian theory*. Freedom, CA: Crossing Press.
Thomas, Laurence. 1988. Liberalism and the Holocaust: An essay on trust and the Black-Jewish relationship. In *Echoes from the Holocaust: Philosophical reflections on a dark time*, eds. Alan Rosenberg and Gerald E. Myers. Philadelphia: Temple University Press.

Selected Bibliography of Lesbian Philosophy and Related Works

CLAUDIA CARD

I. REFERENCE WORKS

Daly, Mary with Jane Caputi. 1987. *Webster's first new intergalactic wickedary of the English language*. Boston: Beacon Press.

Grier, Barbara, ed. 1981. *The lesbian in literature*. 3d ed. Tallahassee, FL: Naiad Press. (Bibliography. Includes fiction, poetry, drama, nonfiction, and photographs. Dual-rating system separates degree of lesbian content from quality of work.)

Potter, Clare, ed. 1986. *Lesbian Periodicals Index*. Tallahassee, FL: Naiad Press.

Richards, Dell. 1990. *Lesbian lists: A look at lesbian culture, history, and personalities*. Boston: Alyson.

Roberts, JR, comp. and ed. 1981. *Black lesbians: An annotated bibliography*. Tallahaassee, FL: Naiad Press.

Wittig, Monique and Sande Zeig. 1979. *Lesbian peoples: Material for a dictionary*. NY: Avon. Originally published in France as *Brouillon pour un dictionnaire des amants*, 1976.

II. PERIODICALS, PAST AND PRESENT

Amazon Quarterly: A Lesbian Feminist Arts Journal. 1972-74. Gina Covina and Laurel Galana, eds. Amazon Press, Oakland, CA. Quarterly.

Azalea: Magazine by Third World Lesbians. 1977-?. New York City. Quarterly.

Canadian Journal of Feminist Ethics. 1986-89. Kathleen Martindale and Martha Saunders, eds. Montreal, Quebec, 1986-88. Calgary, Alberta, 1988-89. Title changed to *Feminist Ethics* in 1987.

Common Lives; Lesbian Lives: A Lesbian Feminist Quarterly. 1981-present. Lesbian Collective, ed. Iowa City.

Conditions: feminist magazine of writing by women with emphasis on writing by lesbians. 1977-90 (17 issues). Elly Bulkin, Jan Clausen, Irena Klepfisz, Rima Shore, founding eds. New York City.

Gossip: Journal of Lesbian Feminist Ethics. 1986-ca. 1988 (at least 5 issues). Onlywomen Press (38 Mount Pleasant, London WC1X OAP, U.K.).

Heresies: A Feminist Publication on Arts and Politics. Special issue: Lesbian Art and Artists. 3 (1977).

Hypatia vol. 7, no. 4 (Fall 1992) © by Claudia Card

Hypatia: A Journal of Feminist Philosophy. Special Issue: Lesbian Philosophy. 7(4), Fall, 1992.

Journal of Homosexuality. 1975-present. John P. De Cecco, ed. Center for Research and Education in Sexuality, San Francisco State University. Quarterly.

The Ladder. 1956-72. Originally published by Daughters of Bilitis, a lesbian organization founded in 1955 in San Francisco by Phyllis Lyon and Del Martin. Monthly. Reissued 1975 in 9 vols. Arno Press, New York City.

Lesbian and Gay Studies Newsletter. 1973-present. Margaret Morrison, current ed. (Dept. of English, North Carolina Wesleyan College, Rocky Mount, NC 27804.) Research newsletter of MLA Gay/Lesbian Caucus. 3x annually.

Lesbian Ethics. 1984-present. Fox (a.k.a. Jeanette Silveira), ed. (LE Publications, P.O. Box 4723, Albuquerque, NM 87196). Journal. 3x vol.

Matrices: Lesbian Feminist Resource & Research Newsletter. 1977-present. Jacqueline Zita, coordinating ed. (492 Ford Hall, University of Minnesota, Minneapolis, MN 55455.) 3x vol.

Signs: Journal of Women in Culture and Society. Special issue: The Lesbian Issue. 9(4), Summer 1984.

Sinister Wisdom: Journal for the Lesbian Imagination in the Arts and Politics. 1976-present (45 issues to date). Harriet Desmoines and Catherine Nicholson, founding eds. Elana Dykwomon, current ed. (P.O. Box 3252, Berkeley, CA 94703.)

Society for Lesbian and Gay Philosophy Newsletter. 1988-present. John Pugh, ed. (Dept. of Philosophy, John Carroll University, University Heights, OH 44881.) Semiannual.

Trivia: A Journal of Ideas. 1982-present (18 issues to date). Lise Weil and Linda Nelson, eds. (PO Box 606, No. Amherst, MA 01059).

III. ANTHOLOGIES: 1972-1992

Allen, Jeffner, ed. 1990. *Lesbian philosophies and cultures.* Albany, NY: SUNY Press.

Beck, Evelyn Torton, ed. 1982. *Nice Jewish girls: A lesbian anthology.* Watertown, MA: Persephone. Rev. and updated, 1989. Boston: Beacon Press.

Birkby, Phyllis, Bertha Harris, Jill Johnston, Esther Newton, and Jan O'Wyatt, eds. 1973. *Amazon expedition: A lesbian feminist anthology.* New York: Times Change Press.

Bunch, Charlotte and Nancy Myron, eds. 1974. *Class and feminism: A collection of essays from The Furies.* Baltimore, MD: Diana Press.

Card, Claudia, ed. 1991. *Feminist ethics.* Lawrence, KS: University Press of Kansas.

Chung, C., A. Kim, and A. K. Lemeshewsky, eds. 1987. *Between the lines: An anthology by Pacific/Asian lesbians of Santa Cruz, CA*. Santa Cruz: Dancing Bird Press.

Covina, Gina and Laurel Galana, eds. 1975. *The lesbian reader: An Amazon Quarterly anthology*. Oakland, CA: Amazon Press.

Cruikshank, Margaret, ed. 1982. *Lesbian studies: Present and future*. Old Westbury, NY: Feminist Press.

Curb, Rosemary and Nancy Manahan, eds. 1985. *Lesbian nuns: Breaking silence*. Tallahassee, FL: Naiad Press.

Darty, Trudy and Sandee Potter, eds. 1984. *Women-identified women*. Palo Alto, CA: Mayfield.

Faderman, Lillian, and Brigitte Eriksson, eds. 1980. *Lesbian-feminism in turn-of-the-century Germany*. Wetherby Lake, MO: Naiad Press. Reissued as *Lesbians in Germany: 1890s-1920s*. Tallahassee, FL: Naiad Press, 1990.

Fuss, Diana, ed. 1991. *Inside/out: Lesbian theories, gay theories*. New York: Routledge.

Grahn, Judy. 1989. *Really reading Gertrude Stein: A selected anthology with essays by Judy Grahn*. Freedom, CA: Crossing Press.

Grier, Barbara and Colette Reid, eds. 1976. *The lavender herring: Lesbian essays from The Ladder*. Baltimore, MD: Diana Press.

Hoagland, Sarah Lucia and Julia Penelope, eds. 1988. *For lesbians only: A separatist anthology*. London: Onlywomen Press.

Humphrey, Mary Ann, ed. 1990. *My country, my right to serve: Experiences of gay men and women in the military, World War II to the present*. New York: Harper and Row.

Jay, Karla and Allen Young, eds. 1979. *Lavender culture*. New York: Jove/HBJ.

Katz, Jonathan, ed. 1976. *Gay american history: Lesbians and gay men in the U.S.A.* New York: Crowell. (A documentary: 1566 to 1932.)

————, ed. 1983. *Gay/lesbian almanac: A new documentary*. New York: Harper and Row.

Kehoe, Monika, ed. 1986. *Historical, literary, and erotic aspects of lesbianism*. New York: Harrington Park Press.

Linden, Robin Ruth, Darlene R. Pagano, Diana E.H. Russell, and Susan Leigh Star, eds. 1982. *Against sadomasochism: A radical feminist analysis*. East Palo Alto, CA: Frog in the Well Press.

Lobel, Kerry, ed. 1986. *Naming the violence: Speaking out about lesbian battering*. Seattle: Seal Press.

Marcus, Eric, ed. 1992. *Making history: The struggle for gay and lesbian equal rights 1945-1990—An oral history*. New York: Harper and Row.

Myron, Nancy and Charlotte Bunch, eds. 1975. *Lesbianism and the women's movement*. Baltimore, MD: Diana Press.

Ramos, Juanita, ed. 1987. *Compañeras: Latina lesbians (an anthology)*. New York: Latina Lesbian History Project.

Stone, Sharon Dale. 1990. *Lesbians in Canada*. Toronto: Between the Lines.

Tobin, Kay and Randy Wicker, eds. 1972. *The gay crusaders*. New York: Paperback Library. (Includes interviews with Phyllis Lyon and Del Martin, Ruth Simpson, and Barbara Gittings.)

Trebilcot, Joyce, ed. 1984. *Mothering: Essays in feminist theory*. Totowa, NJ: Rowman and Allanheld.

Trujillo, Carla, ed. 1991. *Chicana lesbians: The girls our mothers warned us about*. Berkeley, CA: Third Woman Press.

IV. BOOKS: 1932-1992

Abbott, Sidney, and Barbara Love. 1973. *Sappho was a right-on woman: A liberated view of lesbianism*. New York: Stein and Day.

Allen, Jeffner. 1986. *Lesbian philosophy: Explorations*. Palo Alto, CA: Institute of Lesbian Studies.

Anzaldúa, Gloria. 1987. *Borderlands/la frontera: The new mestiza*. San Francisco: Spinsters/Aunt Lute Book Company.

Atkinson, Ti-Grace. 1974. *Amazon odyssey*. New York: Links Books.

Berube, Alan. 1990. *Coming out under fire: The history of gay men and women in World War Two*. New York: Free Press.

Butler, Judith. 1990. *Gender trouble: Feminism and the subversion of identity*. New York: Routledge.

Cavin, Susan. 1985. *Lesbian origins*. San Francisco: Ism Press.

Copper, Baba. 1988. *Over the hill: Reflections on ageism between women*. Freedom, CA: Crossing Press.

Cornwell, Anita. 1983. *Black lesbian in white America*. Tallahassee, FL: Naiad Press.

Daly, Mary. 1978. *Gyn/ecology: The metaethics of radical feminism*. Boston: Beacon Press.

————. 1984. *Pure lust: Elemental feminist philosophy*. Boston: Beacon Press.

Douglas, Carol Anne. 1990. *Love and politics: Radical feminist and lesbian theories*. San Francisco: Ism Press.

Faderman, Lillian. 1981. *Surpassing the love of men: Romantic friendship and love between women from the Renaissance to the present*. New York: Morrow.

————. 1983. *Scotch verdict: Miss Pirie and Miss Woods v. Dame Cumming Gordon*. New York: Quill.

————. 1991. *Odd girls and twilight lovers: A history of lesbian life in twentieth-century America*. New York: Columbia University Press.

Foster, Jeanette. 1956. *Sex-variant women in literature*. New York: Vantage.

Frye, Marilyn. 1983. *The politics of reality: Essays in feminist theory*. Trumansburg, NY: Crossing Press.

————. 1992. *Willful virgin: Essays in Feminism 1976-1992*. Freedom, CA: Crossing Press.

Fuss, Diana. 1989. *Essentially speaking: Feminism, nature, and difference*. New York: Routledge.

Gidlow, Elsa. 1975. *Ask no man pardon: The philosophical significance of being lesbian*. Mill Valley, CA: Druid Heights Books.

Grahn, Judy. 1978. *The work of a common woman: The collected poetry of Judy Grahn, 1964-1977*. New York: St. Martin's Press.

————. 1984. *Another mother tongue: Gay words, gay worlds*. Boston: Beacon Press.

————. 1985. *The highest apple: Sappho and the lesbian poetic tradition*. San Francisco: Spinsters, Ink.

Griffin, Susan. 1976. *Like the iris of an eye*. New York: Harper and Row. (Poems)

————. 1978. *Woman and nature: The roaring inside her*. New York: Harper and Row.

Heyward, Carter. 1989. *Touching our strength: The erotic as power and the love of God*. San Francisco: Harper and Row.

Hoagland, Sarah Lucia. 1988. *Lesbian ethics: Toward new value*. Palo Alto, CA: Institute of Lesbian Studies.

Jay, Karla. 1988. *The amazon and the page: Natalie Clifford Barney and Renee Vivien*. Bloomington: Indiana University Press.

Johnston, Jill. 1973. *Lesbian Nation: The feminist solution*. New York: Simon and Schuster.

Kitzinger, Celia. 1987. *Social construction of lesbianism*. London: Sage.

Lorde, Audre. 1980. *The Cancer Journals*. Argyle, NY: Spinsters, Ink.

————. 1982. *ZAMI: A new spelling of my name*. Trumansburg, NY: Crossing Press.

————. 1984. *Sister outsider: Essays and speeches*. Trumansburg, NY: Crossing Press.

————. 1988. *A burst of light: Essays*. Ithaca, NY: Firebrand.

Martin, Del, and Phyllis Lyon. 1972. *Lesbian/woman*. New York: Bantam.

McNaron, Toni. 1992. *I dwell in possibility: A memoir*. New York: Feminist Press.

Mohr, Richard D. 1988. *Gays/justice: A study of ethics, society, and law*. New York: Columbia University Press.

————. 1992. *Gay ideas: Outing and other controversies*. Boston: Beacon Press.

Nestle, Joan. 1987. *A restricted country*. Ithaca, NY: Firebrand.

Penelope, Julia. 1990. *Speaking freely: Unlearning the lies of the fathers' tongues*. New York: Pergamon.

————. 1992. *Call me lesbian: Lesbian lives, lesbian theory*. Freedom, CA: Crossing Press.

Pratt, Minnie Bruce. 1991. *Rebellion: Essays 1980-1991*. Ithaca, NY: Firebrand.

Raymond, Janice G. 1979. *The transsexual empire: The making of the she/male*. Boston: Beacon Press.

————. 1986. *A passion for friends: Toward a philosophy of female affection*. Boston: Beacon Press.

Rich, Adrienne. 1978. *The dream of a common language: Poems 1974-1977.* New York: Norton.

Robson, Ruthann. 1992. *Lesbian (out)law: Survival under the rule of law.* Ithaca, NY: Firebrand.

Roof, Judith. 1991. *A lure of knowledge: Lesbian sexuality and theory.* New York: Columbia University Press.

Sedgwick, Eve Kosofsky. 1990. *Epistemology of the closet.* Berkeley: University of California Press.

Wittig, Monique. 1992. *The straight mind and other essays.* Boston: Beacon Press.

V. ESSAYS, CHAPTERS, ETC.: 1952-1992

Allen, Jeffner. 1984. Women and food. *Journal of Social Philosophy* 15(2): 34-41.

―――. 1986. Lesbian economics. *Trivia* 8: 37-53.

―――. 1988. Poetic Politics: How the Amazons took the Acropolis. *Hypatia* 3(2): 107-22.

―――. 1989a. An introduction to patriarchal existentialism: A proposal for a way out of existential patriarchy. In *Thinking Muse: Feminism and modern French philosophy*, ed. Jeffner Allen and Iris Marion Young. Bloomington: Indiana University Press.

―――. 1989b. Women who beget women must thwart major sophisms. In *Women, knowledge, and reality: Explorations in feminist philosophy*, ed. Ann Garry and Marilyn Pearsall. Boston: Unwin Hyman.

―――. 1990. On the seashore, A writing of abundance. In *Lesbian philosophies and cultures*, ed. Jeffner Allen. Albany, NY: SUNY Press.

Allen, Paula Gunn. 1986. Hwame, Koshkalaka, and the rest: Lesbians in American Indian cultures. In *The sacred hoop: Recovering the feminine in American Indian traditions.* Boston: Beacon Press.

Anderson, Jacqueline. 1988. Separation in Black: A personal journey. *Lesbian Ethics* 3(2): 78-81.

Ayres, Tara and Lori Saxe. 1988. Politics, vision and play: Some thoughts on the lesbian separatist conference. *Lesbian Ethics* 3(2): 106-15.

Bar On, Bat-Ami. 1982. Feminism and sadomasochism: Self critical notes. In *Against sadomasochism*, ed. Robin Ruth Linden et al. East Palo Alto, CA: Frog in the Well Press.

Beauvoir, Simone de. 1952. The lesbian. Chap. 15 in *The second sex*, trans. H. M. Parshley. New York: Knopf.

Birke, Lynda I. A. 1981. Is homosexuality hormonally determined? In *Nature and causes of homosexuality: A philosophic and scientific inquiry*, ed. Noretta Koertge. New York: Haworth Press.

Blackwood, Evelyn. 1984. Sexuality and gender in certain Native American tribes: The case of cross-gender females. *Signs* 10(1): 27-42.

Bunch, Charlotte. 1987. Lesbian feminism. In *Passionate politics: Feminist theory in action.* New York: St. Martin's Press.

Card, Claudia. 1984. Sadomasochism and sexual preference. *Journal of Social Philosophy* 9(2): 42-52.

———. 1985. Lesbian attitudes and *The second sex. Hypatia* 3, published as *Women's Studies International Forum* 8(3): 209-14. Reprinted in *Hypatia Reborn.* Bloomington: Indiana University Press, 1990.

———. 1986. Oppression and resistance: Frye's politics of reality. *Hypatia* 1(1): 149-66.

———. 1988a. Female friendship: Separations and continua. *Hypatia* 3(2): 123-30.

———. 1988b. Lesbian battering. *APA Newsletter on Feminism and Philosophy* 88(1): 3-7.

———. 1989. Defusing the bomb: Lesbian ethics and horizontal violence. *Lesbian Ethics* 3(3): 91-100.

———. 1990a. Pluralist lesbian separatism. In *Lesbian philosophies and cultures,* ed. Jeffner Allen. Albany: SUNY Press.

———. 1990b. Why Homophobia? *Hypatia* 5(3): 110-17.

———. 1991a. The feistiness of feminism. In *Feminist ethics,* ed. Claudia Card. Lawrence, KS: University Press of Kansas.

———. 1991b. Intimacy and responsibility: What lesbians do. In *At the boundaries of law: Feminism and legal theory,* ed. Martha Albertson Fineman and Nancy Sweet Thomadsen. New York: Routledge.

———. 1992a. Fidelity. In *Encyclopedia of ethics,* Vol. 2, ed. Lawrence C. Becker with Charlotte B. Becker. New York: Garland.

———. 1992b. Lesbian ethics. In *Encyclopedia of ethics,* Vol. 2, ed. Lawrence C. Becker with Charlotte B. Becker. New York: Garland.

———. 1992c. Lesbianism and choice. *Journal of Homosexuality* 23(3): 39-51.

———. Forthcoming. Finding My voice: Reminiscence of an outlaw. In *Falling in love with wisdom,* ed. Robert Shoemaker and David D. Karnos. New York: Oxford University Press.

Colette. 1966. Chap. 5 (on Renee Vivien) and Chap. 7 (on the Ladies of Llangollen) in *The pure and the impure,* trans. Herma Briffault. New York: Farrar, Straus, & Giroux. Published in France as *Ces plaisirs* (1932) and as *Le pur et l'impur* (1941).

Cook, Blanche Wiesen. 1979. "Women only stir my imagination": Lesbianism and the cultural tradition. *Signs* 4(4): 718-39.

Cuomo, Chris. 1990. The wax problem. *Sinister Wisdom* 41: 114-15. (Poem)

———. 1991. Anna's eyes. *Common Lives; Lesbian Lives* 37: 53-56. (Story)

———. 1992. Ritual abuse: Making connections. *Lesbian Ethics* 4(3): 45-53.

Dworkin, Andrea. 1976. Lesbian Pride. Chap. 7 in *Our blood: Prophecies and discourses on sexual politics.* New York: Harper and Row.

Evans, Lee, and Shelley Bannister. 1990. Lesbian violence, lesbian victims: How to identify battering in relationships. *Lesbian Ethics* 4(1): 52-65.

Ferguson, Ann. 1989. Sexual identity: Lesbian and gay liberation. Chap. 9 in *Blood at the root: Motherhood, sexuality and male dominance*. London: Pandora.

————. 1991. Is There a lesbian culture? Chap. 7 in *Sexual democracy: Women, oppression, and revolution*. Boulder, CO: Westview Press.

Ferguson, Ann, Ilene Philipson, Irene Diamond, Lee Quinby, Carole S. Vance, and Ann Barr Snitow. 1984. Forum: The feminist sexuality debates. *Signs* 10(1): 106-35.

Freedman, Estelle and Barrie Thorne. 1984. Introduction to "The Feminist Sexuality Debates." *Signs* 10 (1): 102-105.

Frye, Marilyn. 1980. Lesbian perspectives on women's studies. *Sinister Wisdom* 14: 3-7.

————. 1985. History and responsibility. *Hypatia* 3, published as *Women's Studies International Forum* 8(3): 215-17. Reprinted in *Hypatia Reborn*. Bloomington: Indiana University Press, 1990.

————. 1988. Lesbian sex. *Sinister Wisdom* 35: 46-54.

————. 1990a. Do you have to be a lesbian to be a feminist? *off our backs* 20 (Aug/Sept).

————. 1990b. The possibility of feminist theory. In *Perspectives on sexual difference*, ed. Deborah Rhode. New Haven, CT: Yale University Press.

————. 1990c. The possibility of lesbian community. *Lesbian Ethics* 4(1): 84-87.

————. 1990d. A response to *Lesbian Ethics: Why ethics?* In *Feminist ethics*, ed. Claudia Card. Lawrence, KS: University Press of Kansas, 1991.

Garber, Eric. 1989. A spectacle in color: The lesbian and gay subculture of jazz age harlem. In *Hidden from history: Reclaiming the gay and lesbian past*, ed. Martin Bauml Duberman, Martha Vicinus, and George Chauncy, Jr. New York: New American Library.

Harding, Sandra. 1991. Thinking from the perspective of lesbian lives. Chap. 10 in *Whose science? Whose knowledge?* Ithaca, NY: Cornell University Press.

Harris, Bertha. 1977. What we mean to say: Notes toward defining the nature of lesbian literature. *Heresies* 3: 5-8.

Hoagland, Sarah Lucia. 1991. Some thoughts about "caring." In *Feminist ethics*, ed. Claudia Card. Lawrence, KS: University Press of Kansas.

Ketchum, Sara Ann. 1980. The good, the bad, and the perverted: Sexual paradigms revisited. In *The philosophy of sex: Contemporary readings*, ed. Alan Soble. Totowa, NJ: Littlefield, Adams, and Co.

Klepfisz, Irena. 1990. Anti-Semitism in the lesbian/feminist movement, Resisting and surviving America, and Jewish lesbians, the Jewish community, Jewish survival. In Part II of *Dreams of an insomniac: Jewish feminist essays, speeches, and diatribes*. Portland, OR: Eighth Mountain Press.

Koedt, Anne. 1973. Lesbianism and feminism. In *Radical Feminism*, ed. Anne Koedt, Ellen Levine, and Anita Rapone. New York: Quadrangle.

Koertge, Noretta. 1990. Constructing concepts of sexuality: A philosophical commentary. In *Homosexuality/heterosexuality: Concepts of sexual orientation*, ed. David P. McWhirter, Stephanie A. Sanders, and June Machover Reinisch. New York: Oxford University Press.

Lugones, María. 1987. Playfulness, 'world'-travelling, and loving perception. *Hypatia* 2(2): 3-19.

———. 1990a. Hablando cara a cara/speaking face to face: An exploration of ethnocentric racism. In *Making face, making soul/haciendo caras: Creative and critical perspectives by women of color*, ed. Gloria Anzaldúa. San Francisco: Aunt Lute Foundation.

———. 1990b. Hispaneando y lesbiando: On Sarah Hoagland's *Lesbian ethics*. *Hypatia* 5(3): 138-46.

———. 1990c. Structure/antiStructure and agency under oppression. *Journal of Philosophy* 87(10): 500-507.

Lugones, María, and Elizabeth V. Spelman. 1984. Have we got a theory for you! Feminist theory, cultural imperialism, and the demand for "the woman's voice." *Hypatia* 1, published as *Women's Studies International Forum* 6(6): 573-81. Reprinted in *Hypatia Reborn*. Bloomington: Indiana University Press, 1990.

———. 1987. Competition, compassion, and community: Models for a feminist ethos. In *Competition: A feminist taboo?* ed. Valerie Miner and Helen E. Longino. New York: Feminist Press.

Marks, Elaine. 1979. Lesbian intertextuality. In *Homosexualities and French literature*, ed. George Stambolian and Elaine Marks. Ithaca, NY: Cornell University Press.

Martin, Biddy. 1988. Lesbian identity and autobiographical difference(s). In *Life/lines: Theorizing women's autobiography*, ed. Bella Brodzki and Celeste Schenck. Ithaca, NY: Cornell University Press.

Midnight Sun. 1988. Sex/gender systems in Native North America. In *Living the spirit: A gay American Indian anthology*. New York: St. Martin's Press.

Penelope, Julia. 1984. The mystery of lesbians. *Lesbian Ethics* 1(1): 7-33.

———. 1985a. The mystery of lesbians: II. *Lesbian Ethics* 1(2): 3-28.

———. 1985b. The mystery of lesbians: III. *Lesbian Ethics* 1(3): 3-15.

Pierce, Christine and Sara Ann Ketchum. 1978. Separatism and sexual relationships. In *Philosophy and Women*, ed. Sharon Hill and Marjorie Weinzweig. Belmont, CA: Wadsworth.

Radicalesbians. 1973. The woman-identified woman. In *Radical Feminism*, eds. Anne Koedt, Ellen Levine, and Anita Rapone. New York: Quadrangle.

Rich, Adrienne. 1979a. "It's the lesbian in us. . . ." In *On lies, secrets, and silence: Selected prose 1966-1978*. New York: Norton.

———. 1979b. The meaning of our love for women is what we have constantly to expand. In *On lies, secrets, and silence: Selected prose 1966-1978*. New York: Norton.

———. 1979c. The problem of Lorraine Hansberry. *Freedomways* 19(4): 247-55.

———. 1980. Compulsory heterosexuality and lesbian existence. *Signs* 5(4): 631-60.

Roscoe, Will. 1988. Strange country this: Images of berdaches and warrior women. In *Living the spirit: A gay American Indian anthology*, ed. Will Roscoe. New York: St. Martin's Press.

San Francisco Lesbian and Gay History Project. 1989. "She even chewed tobacco": Pictorial narrative of passing women in America. In *Hidden from history*, ed. Martin Duberman et al. New York: New American Library.

Saxe, Lori and Tara Ayres. 1988. Politics, vision and play: Some thoughts on the lesbian separatist conference. *Lesbian Ethics* 3(2): 106-15.

Schockley, Ann Allen. 1979. The black lesbian in American literature. *Conditions* 5: 133-42.

Smith, Barbara. 1977. Towards a black feminist criticism. *Conditions* 2: 25-44.

Stimpson, Catharine R. 1977. The mind, the body, and Gertrude Stein. *Critical Inquiry* 3(3): 489-506.

———. 1981. Zero degree deviancy: The lesbian novel in English. *Critical Inquiry* 8(2): 363-79.

Trebilcot, Joyce. 1979. Conceiving women: Notes on the logic of feminism. *Sinister Wisdom* 11: 43-50.

———. 1984a. Notes on the meaning of life. *Lesbian Ethics* 1(1): 90-91.

———. 1984b. Taking responsibility for sexuality. In *Philosophy and sex*, 2d ed., ed. R. Baker and F. Elliston. Buffalo, NY: Prometheus.

———. 1985. Hortense and Gladys on dreams. *Lesbian Ethics* 1(2): 85-87.

———. 1986. Partial response to those who worry that separatism may be a political cop-out: Expanded definition of activism. *off our backs* (May). Reprinted in *Gossip* 3: 82-84.

———. 1988a. Dyke economics: Hortense and Gladys on money. *Lesbian Ethics* 3(1): 1-13.

———. 1988b. Dyke methods. *Hypatia* 3(2): 1-13.

———. 1990. More dyke methods. *Hypatia* 5(1): 140-44.

Van Kirk, Carol. 1990. Sarah Lucia Hoagland's *Lesbian ethics: Toward new value* and ablemindism. *Hypatia* 5(3): 147-52.

Williams, Walter L. 1986. Amazons of america: Female gender variance. Chap. 11 in *The spirit and the flesh: Sexual diversity in American Indian culture*. Boston: Beacon Press.

Wolfe, Susan J., and Julia Penelope Stanley. 1980. Linguistic problems with
    patriarchal reconstructions of Indo-European culture. *Women's Studies
    International Quarterly* 3: 227-37.
Zita, Jacqueline. 1980. Female bonding and sexual politics. *Sinister Wisdom* 14:
    8-16.
————. 1981. Historical amnesia and the lesbian continuum. *Signs* 7(1):
    172-87.
————. 1988. "Real girls" and lesbian resistance. *Lesbian Ethics* 3(1): 85-96.
————. 1990. Lesbian angels and other matters. *Hypatia* 5(1): 133-39.
    (Response to Joyce Trebilcot, Dyke Methods, 1988b.)

Notes on Contributors

TANGREN ALEXANDER teaches philosophy at Southern Oregon State College. She has published in *Teaching Philosophy*, and, under the name "Pearl Time's Child," in *WomanSpirit Magazine*, *Sinister Wisdom*, *SageWoman*, and in Tee Corinne's recent short story anthologies, *Intricate Passions* and *Riding Desire*. She's a founding member of the Southern Oregon Women Writers' Group, Gourmet Eating Society and Chorus, which for eleven years has been a focus for the creative women's community in her area. She's written a philosophical narrative, *The Auto Biography of Deborah Carr* (which proposes that God is actually a 1972 station wagon). And she is currently at work on a novel about Queen Christina of Sweden.

BAT-AMI BAR ON is associate professor of philosophy and director of women's studies at SUNY-Binghamton. She is currently working on a book of essays about everyday violence.

CLAUDIA CARD, a greying, vegetarian, cat-loving midwestern Sapphist of Celtic origins, professes lesbian culture, ethics, feminist theory, social philosophy, philosophy in literature, and environmental ethics in the Department of Philosophy and as a faculty affiliate in the Women's Studies Program and in the Institute for Environmental Studies at the University of Wisconsin-Madison. She received her Ph.D. in philosophy from Harvard in 1969 and has been teaching at Wisconsin since 1966, with visiting appointments at Dartmouth in 1978-79 and at the University of Pittsburgh in 1980.

ELISABETH DÄUMER was born in Berlin and moved to the United States in 1978 to attend Indiana University. She is now assistant professor of English at Eastern Michigan University where she teaches classes in Women's Studies and Literary Theory. She is also a member of the editorial collective of *Feminist Teacher*.

RUTH GINZBERG teaches philosophy at Wesleyan University. She has published articles in feminist ethics and feminist criticisms of philosophy of science. She is currently working on a book, *Flirting With Survival*, which examines foundationalism in feminist ethics.

SARAH LUCIA HOAGLAND is a Chicago dyke and a philosopher. She has been teaching philosophy and women's studies at Northeastern Illinois University in Chicago since 1977. She is the author of *Lesbian Ethics: Toward New Value* and, with Julia Penelope has edited an anthology *For Lesbians Only: A Separatist Anthology*.

BARBARA HOUSTON teaches philosophy, education, and women's studies at the University of New Hampshire. She writes on issues in ethics, feminist theory, and philosophy of education.

MARÍA LUGONES teaches at the Escuela Popular Norteña, a folk school for radical political education. She is devoted to the theoretico-practical project of fighting oppressions as interlocked.

KATHLEEN MARTINDALE is assistant professor of English at York University in Toronto where she teaches feminist literary theory, women's autobiography, and an introductory course on reading and writing about gender, race and class for students studying literature. She has written extensively about the relationship between ethics and literary theory. She is currently writing a book about lesbian literary theory in the upper and lower case.

RUTHANN ROBSON is an associate professor of Law at CUNY (City University of New York) Law School. She is the author of *Lesbian (Out)law* (Firebrand Books 1992). In addition to writing lesbian legal theory, Ruthann Robson writes lesbian theory in the form of fiction. *Eye of a Hurricane* received the 1990 Ferro-Grumley award for outstanding fiction on lesbian life and the recently released *Cecile* concentrates on lesbian daily life. She is presently working on a long fictional piece integrating theories of lesbianism, law, life and mothering.

MARTHA J. SAUNDERS has a Ph.D. in religion from Concordia University, Montreal, where she teaches religion and women's studies. She is interested in feminist and lesbian theory and ethics, particularly in relation to sexuality and to education and pedagogy.

LORENA LEIGH SAXE is completing her doctoral work in philosophy at the University of Wisconsin, Madison. She is writing her dissertation on friendship, concentrating on Lesbian-feminist and ecofeminist approaches to the topic. She is a lecturer on environmental ethics in the Philosophy Department. She was a co-creator and, for four years, co-organizer of an international Lesbian conference. She is white and of mixed (working/middle) class background.

NAOMI SCHEMAN is professor of philosophy and women's studies at the University of Minnesota. A collection of her essays in feminist epistemology, *Engenderings*, is forthcoming from Routledge, and she is currently working on a book entitled *Marginalities: Wittgenstein, Feminism, and the Problems of Philosophy*, which explores the intersections of marginality and privilege in relation to the activities of philosophy and theory.

JOYCE TREBILCOT was a founder of the Women's Studies Program at Washington University in St. Louis in the early seventies and the Program's coordinator for twelve years; she resigned that position in the spring of 1992. Since the late eighties she has been working on a book about (her) dyke ideas.

JACQUELYN N. ZITA has her Ph.D. in philosophy and is an associate professor in women's studies at the University of Minnesota. She is the executive secretary for the Midwestern Society for Women in Philosophy, the coordinating editor of *Matrices: A Lesbian Feminist Resource and Research Newsletter,* and faculty coordinator for lesbian area studies in the Center for Advanced Feminist Studies at University of Minnesota. She is currently finishing a book of essays on theorizing the body and is involved in the start-stop treacheries of "academizing" lesbian, gay, bisexual, transgender studies. She (currently) has a male lesbian kitten named Sunshine, her biting muse; and a long-standing relationship with Karen, her recurrently abiding muse.

Announcements

Society for Women in Philosophy. For information on membership in regional divisions, which includes receiving program announcements, the national SWIP newsletter, and a discount subscription to *Hypatia* contact:

Midwest SWIP: Executive Secretary, Jackie Zita, Women's Studies Program, University of Minnesota, Minneapolis, MN 55455. Treasurer: Carol Mickett, English & Philosophy Department, Central Missouri State University, Warrensburg, MO 64093.

Eastern SWIP: Executive Secretary: Patrice DiQuinzio, Philosophy Department, University of Scranton, Scranton, PA 18510; Treasurer: Linda Damico, Department of Philosophy, Kennesaw State College, Marietta, GA 30061.

Pacific SWIP: Executive Secretary, Rita Manning, Department of Philosophy, San Jose State University, San Jose, CA. 95192. Treasurer: Dianne Romain, Department of Philosophy, Sonoma State University, Rohnert Park, CA 94928.

Upcoming SWIP Meetings:

Midwest SWIP's Fall 1992 meeting will be held October 9-11, at Michigan State University in East Lansing, MI. Marilyn Frye is in charge of local arrangements. Contact her at Department of Philosophy, MSU, East Lansing, MI 48824. (517) 353-3981.

Eastern SWIP is turning, at least temporarily, into Southeastern SWIP this year. There will be no Fall meeting, but there will be a two-day meeting in Tampa, FL on March 20-21, 1993 with a keynote speaker (TBA) and a celebration of *Hypatia*'s 10th anniversary. Send papers and abstracts to: Donna Serniak, Department of Philosophy, Randolph-Macon College, Ashland, VA 23005. Deadline: December 1, 1992. Local arrangements chair is: Linda Lopez McAlister, Department of Women's Studies, University of South Florida, Tampa, FL 33620.

Announcing SWIP-L an electronic mail list for feminist philosophers. SWIP-L is an information and discussion list for members of the Society for Women in Philosophy and others who are interested in feminist philosophy. To subscribe to this list send the following one-line message to **LISTSERV@CFRVM** or to **LISTSERV@CFRVM.CFR.USF.EDU: SUBSCRIBE SWIP-L <YOUR FULL NAME>**. When you want to post messages on the list send them to **SWIP-L@CFRVM** or to **SWIP-L@CFRVM.CFR.USF.EDU**. The purpose of the list is to provide a place to share information about SWIP and other feminist philosophy meetings, calls for papers, jobs for feminist philosophers, etc., as well as to engage in more substantive discussions related to feminist philosophy. While the list is public and open to both SWIP members and non-members, it is meant for feminist philosophers and theorists. It is free of charge. The SWIP-L's home is in the *Hypatia* editorial office. If you have questions please e-mail, call, or write us at the addresses or telephone numbers listed on page ii of this issue.

An *International Network on Feminist Approaches to Bioethics* is being formed in conjunction with the Inaugural Congress of the International Association of Bioethics. The organizers, Anne Donchin and Helen Bequaert Holmes envision a more inclusive theory of bioethics, one that would encompass the experiences of women and other marginalized social groups, examine how the principles that dominate the prevailing discourse may favor those already empowered, create new methodologies, and look closely at the legitimizing function of mainstream bioethics. Plans are to meet at the Congress in Amsterdam (October 5-7, 1992) to determine the scope of future activities. The Congress Secretariat will forward to the organizers the names and addresses of those who circle this network when they register for the Congress. Those who cannot attend the Congress should contact Anne Donchin, Women's Studies, Indiana University, 425 University Blvd., Indianapolis, IN 46202 or Helen Bequaert Holmes, Center for Genetics, Ethics, and Women, 24 Berkshire Terrace, Amherst, MA 01002. Phone and FAX (413) 549-1226.

5th National Conference of the Concerned Philosophers for Peace will be held in Charlotte, NC on October 16-18, 1992. The theme of the conference is "Power and Domination." If you would like more information about the organization or the conference please call Laura Duhan Kaplan, Department of Philosophy, University of North Carolina at Charlotte, Charlotte, NC 28223. (704) 547-2780.

The Society for Analytical Feminism invites submissions for sessions at the 1993 Central Division APA meetings. The Society seeks papers that examine feminist issues by methods broadly construed as analytic, or that discuss the use of analytic methods as applied to feminist issues. Reading time should be about 20 minutes. Papers should be prepared for anonymous review and two copies submitted. Submissions should be postmarked no later than December 1, 1992 and sent to Virginia Klenk, Department of Philosophy, University of West Virginia, 252 Stansbury Hall, Morgantown, WV 26506. All members of the Society will be eligible to read papers. For information about membership in the Society, please contact Virginia Klenk at the address given above.

Call for Papers - Rereading the Canon: Feminist Interpretations of Simone De Beauvoir edited by Margaret A. Simons. Papers reflecting a diversity of philosophical methodologies and standpoints are sought for an anthology on Beauvoir's philosophy. Are Simone de Beauvoir's texts "out-of-date, male-identified, and just Sartrean anyway"? Is *The Second Sex* a modernist work rendered obsolete by the postmoderninst critique? Or does Beauvoir have relevance for contemporary feminist philosophy? Papers addressing these questions and others relating to Beauvoir's philosophy, inquiries, and abstracts should be sent to: Professor Margaret A. Simons, Dept. of Philosophical Studies, Southern Illinois University at Edwardsville, Edwardsville, IL 62026-1433. Deadline is November 15, 1992.

Call for Papers - Rereading the Canon: Feminist Interpretations of Descartes and Cartesianism. I am seeking feminist and other innovative perspectives on Descartes and Cartesianism. I welcome philosophical, literary, historical, sociological, and interdisciplinary papers, reflections on the impact of feminist studies on traditional readings, and explorations of gender, race, class, and culture. The collection will be part of a series, edited by Nancy Tuana, for Penn State Press. Send inquiries, proposals, papers, and suggestions to: Susan Bordo, Department of Philosophy, LeMoyne College, Syracuse, N.Y. 12314.

Call for papers for a collection entitled *Nexus: Writings on Location,* an interdisciplinary anthology drawing on the "New Subjectivity" or "personal," "narrative," or "autobiographical" criticism across a range of disciplines. If you are working in a autobiography—or you know others who are—we would love to hear from you. 15-25 page essays, double-spaced, in MLA parenthetical style with separate endnote and works-cited pages. Each critical/theoretical/autobiographical essay is to focus on the ethnicity, religion, gender, family, community, ability, discipline) to specific texts or current theoretical issues in her or his discipline. Deadline for submissions: February 15, 1983. Queries or submissions (in duplicate) to Olivia Frey, English, St. Olaf College, WordPerfect IBM-compatible files (on high-density diskettes) also appreciated.

"Women and Texts in Pre-revolutionary France" a conference sponsored by the Department of French, at the University of Waterloo, Waterloo, Ontario, Canada, will be held May 7-9, 1993. The conference will focus on questions related to the subject of French women as producers of texts in pre-revolutionary France. We understand the word text as referring to canonical as well as non-canonical works and genres. History, science and education are only a few areas in which women chose to express themselves textually. For information contact Hannah Fournier or Jean-Philippe Beaulieu, MARGOT Project, Dept. of French, University of Waterloo, Waterloo, Ont. Canada N2L 3G1. Phone (519) 885-1211, ext. 2249 or 3554.

The *Fifth International Interdisciplinary Congress on Women* will be held at the University of Costa Rica, February 22-26, 1993. For information write to Prof. Mirta González-Suárez, V Congreso Internacional e Interdisciplinario de la Mujer, PRIEG—Escuela de Psicología, Universidad de Costa Rica, Apdo. 2060, San Pedro, Costa Rica, América Central.

"Beyond the Boundaries," a conference sponsored by the Women's Caucus for Art will be held February 2-4, 1993 in Seattle, Washington. For further info: send stamped, self-addressed envelope to Jo Hockenhull, Box 897, Pullman, WA 99163; (509) 334-4137. FAX: (509)335-4171.

The Swarthmore College Peace Collection in conjunction with Swarthmore College and Friends Historical Library of Swarthmore College will be sponsoring an academic conference on the work of Lucretia Mott and other women in the nineteenth century peace movement in March, 1993 to celebrate the bicentennial of Mott's birth. The conference title is "Nineteenth Century Feminist Strategies for Non-Violence." For more information contact Dr. Wendy E. Chmielewski, Curator, Swarthmore College Peace Collection, 500 College Avenue, Swarthmore, PA 19081-1399.

Call for Manuscripts for an anthology on lesbians and the law and theory. Send manuscripts and inquiries to Ruthann Robson, CUNY Law School at Queens College, 65-21 Main Street, Flushing, New York 11367. (718) 575-4447.

Calls for Papers/
Guidelines for Contributors

Hypatia solicits papers on all topics in feminist philosophy. We publish two general issues and two special issues on selected themes or topics in feminist philosophy each year. All submissions should be in the format used in *Hypatia*—the *Chicago Manual of Style*'s Author/Date system of citing references. The author's name should appear on the title page only, to allow for anonymous reviewing. Please submit four copies of your paper. Authors of papers accepted for publication will be asked to submit the final version of their paper both in hard copy and on computer disk to facilitate the computerized typesetting process. Papers for all issues—general and special—should be sent to: Linda Lopez McAlister, Editor, *Hypatia*, Women's Studies Department, SOC 107, University of South Florida, Tampa, FL 33620-8100.

Call for Papers for a Special Issue on Feminist Philosophy of Religion, broadly defined as feminists reflecting philosophically on the phenomenon of religion. With this issue the editors seek to encourage potential authors to reshape the field of philosophy of religion along feminist lines of interest rather than to replicate the standard list of topics (e.g., the existence and attributes of God; the nature of religious belief; the problem of evil; immortality, etc.) or to produce further documentation of sexism or androcentric bias in the history of various religious traditions. Therefore, papers that deal with the following questions are most welcome:

(1) *Feminist Revisionings*: What would constitute the boundaries and problematics of a feminist philosophy of religion; what should be both the "feminist" and the "philosophical" aspects of this new field of feminist inquiry? Are the theories of "religion" that are currently presupposed or employed in feminist scholarship theoretically adequate either for feminist purposes or for understanding the phenomenon of religion? What new theoretical links need to be forged between an understanding of religious symbols, images, and concepts and the features of human embodiment and sexuality important to feminism? What politics does religion promote or impede in women's lives, e.g., in Latin American liberation struggles, South African anti-apartheid movement, African-American spirituality, Islamic fundamentalism, and the U.S. "civil religion" found among Christian groups? What do contemporary feminist spiritualities, particularly those with political and ecological concerns, suggest for refashioning philosophy of religion as a field?

(2) *Feminist Critiques*: What influential areas in current philosophy of religion require feminist critique, e.g., the "reformed epistemology" of A. Plantinga, et al. and other resurgences of classical Christian theism? Who are the neglected figures in the history of the philosophy of religion who might be reappropriated for contemporary feminist analysis, e.g., Alfred North White-head, Lao-Tzu, even Kierkegaard or Kant? What philosophical dimensions may have been omitted from existing feminist analyses of misogyny in the history of religious thought? What conceptual links illuminate the relationship between the Wholly Other of western religion and the male violence against women (the First Other) or between this god and religious sanctions for militarism?

(3) *Feminist Retrievals*: What are the speculative philosophical resources for articulating the connection between holistic worldviews and feminist meanings of the sacred? Who are the unsuspected foremothers for fashioning a contemporary feminist philosophy of religions, e.g., Charlotte Perkins Gilman, Simone Weil, Mathilda Joslyn Gage, Rebecca Jackson? What are the philosophical implications that feminists are finding in the comparative study of religion, especially for revising traditional notions of knowledge, truth, and the self?

Given the hope that this volume will break new ground and occupy a boundary between the two disciplines of philosophy and religion, the editors strongly encourage the submission of papers that are collaboratively authored by scholars in the study of religion and the field of philosophy. We especially invite papers from authors with expertise in African, Latin American, Asian, and indigenous religious philosophies as well as Jewish, Christian, and Islamic religious philosophies. Papers should be not longer than 30 pages double spaced and submitted in quadruplicate to the *Hypatia* editorial office (address above), with "Special Issue on Religion" clearly indicated on the envelope and the title page. Deadline: September 15, 1993.

Call for Papers for a Special Issue on Feminism and Peace. This volume will explore a range of issues concerning the interconnections between feminist philosophy and peace studies. Papers are welcome on a variety of topics, including (but not limited to) the following:

- The nature of a feminist peace politics or a feminist peace ethic;
- The relevance and implications of various feminist philosophies (e.g., liberal feminism, Marxist feminism, radical feminism, socialist feminism, ecological feminism, postmodernist feminism, pragmatist feminism) for an understanding of the just war and pacifist traditions;
- Feminist perspectives on the morality of war and the morality of violence;
- Feminist discussions of philosophical connections between the practices and ideologies of militarism, nuclearism, imperialism, and violence toward those perceived as "other";

- Feminist analyses of the relevance of race, gender, and class to discussions of war, peace, and various forms of institutional and interpersonal violence;
- Critical examinations of male gender-biased language in the contexts of discussions of war, peace, and violence toward women;
- Gendered conceptions of the body and sexuality as they relate to issues of war, peace, and "domestic violence";
- Feminist analyses of prostitution, rape, pornography, sexual harassment, and other forms of sexual abuse in the context of a feminist peace politics; ecofeminist perspectives on connections between women, peace, and the nonhuman natural environment; feminist explorations of the philosophical significance of women's peace camps and non-violent actions;
- Feminist analyses of Gandhian satygrahas as strategies of resistance.

Guest editors for this Special Issue are Karen J. Warren and Duane L. Cady. Submissions should be sent in quadruplicate to the *Hypatia* editorial office (address above) with "Special Issue on Peace" clearly indicated on the envelope and the title page. Deadline for submissions: March 15, 1993.

Book Review Guidelines. The *Hypatia* Book Review Section aims at increasing the visibility and readership of books in feminist philosophy. At present these general book review guidelines have been developed:

1. To promote dialogue between books, reviewers are asked to discuss, when possible, more than one book in feminist philosophy. Several books might be clustered around a theme, or a single book might be highlighted and its relation to other books in feminist philosophy might be mentioned in brief.

2. Book reviewers are asked to discuss the major claims of the book(s) reviewed and to present the reviewer's own reflections.

3. Reviews may be either Book Reviews (5 to 8 pages including notes and references) or Review Essays (10 to 15 pages including notes and references).

Books which will be the subject of any review should be proposed in advance to the Book Review Editor. For further information, contact the *Hypatia* Book Review Editor: Terry Winant, Department of Philosophy, California State University, Fresno, Fresno, CA 93740.

Books Received

Butler, Judith and Scott, Joan W., eds. 1992. *Feminists theorize the political*. New York: Routledge.

Caraway, Nancie. 1991. *Segregated sisterhood*. Knoxville: University of Tennessee Press.

Cornell, Drucilla. 1992. *The philosophy of the limit*. New York: Routledge.

Ellis, Carolyn and Michael G. Flaherty, eds. 1992. *Investigating subjectivity*. Newbury Park: Sage Publications.

Frye, Marilyn. 1992. *Willful virgin: Essays in feminism 1976-1992*. Freedom, CA: The Crossing Press.

Harth, Erica. 1992. *Cartesian women: Versions and subversions of rational discourse*. Ithaca, NY: Cornell Univ. Press.

Harvey, Elizabeth D. and Kathleen Okruhlik, eds. 1992. *Women and reason*. Ann Arbor: University of Michigan Press.

Helly, Dorothy O. and Susan M. Reverby, eds. *Gendered Domains*. Ithaca, NY: Cornell University Press.

Hirschmann, Nancy J. 1992. *Rethinking obligation*. Ithaca, NY: Cornell University Press.

Holmes, Helen Bequaert and Laura M. Purdy, eds. 1992. *Feminist perspectives in medical ethics*. Bloomington: Indiana University Press.

Kasl, Charlotte Davis. 1992. *Many roads, one journey*. New York: Harper Perennial.

Lotbinière-Harwood, Susanne de. 1991. *Re-belle et infidèle: La traduction comme practique de réécriture au féminin. The body bilingual: Translation as a rewriting in the feminine*. Québec: Les Éditions du remue-ménage and Toronto: Women's Press.

Manning, Rita C. 1992. *Speaking from the heart*. Lanham, MD: Rowman & Littlefield.

Monaghan, Patricia. 1992. *Seasons of the witch*. Oak Park, IL: Delphi Press.

Norton, Camille and Lou Robinson, eds. 1992. *Resurgent: New writing by women*. Chicago: University of Illinois Press.

O'Barr, Jean and Mary Weyr, eds. 1992. *Engaging feminism*. Charlottesville, VA: University Press.

Pardes, Ilana. 1992. *Countertraditions in the Bible*. Cambridge: Harvard University Press.

Ross, Stephen David. 1992. *The ring of representation*. Albany: State University of New York Press.

Schiesari, Juliana. 1992. *The gendering of melancholia*. Ithaca, NY: Cornell University Press.

Shiach, Morag. 1991. *Hélène Cixous: A politics of writing*. New York: Routledge.
Spretnak, Charlene. 1992. *Lost goddesses of early Greece*. Boston: Beacon Press.
Tuana, Nancy. 1992. *Woman and the history of philosophy*. New York: Paragon House.
Wartenberg, Thomas E., ed. 1992. *Rethinking power*. Albany: State University of New York Press.
Zalk, Sue Rosenberg and Janice Gordon-Kelter, eds. 1992. *Revolutions in knowledge: Feminism in the social sciences*. Boulder: Westview Press.

Recent Back Issues

Volume 6, Number 1, Spring 1991

Special Issue on Ecological Feminism: *Nature, Self, and Gender: Feminism, Environmental Philosophy, and the Critique of Rationalism*, by Val Plumwood, *Ecofeminist Theory and Grassroots Politics*, by Stephanie Lahar, *Loving Your Mother: On the Woman-Nature Relationship*, by Catherine Roach, *Toward An Ecological Ethic of Care*, by Deane Curtin, *Caring About Nature: Feminist Ethics and the Environment*, by Roger J. H. King, *Deep Ecology versus Ecofeminism: Healthy Differences or Incompatible Philosophies?*, by Robert Sessions, *Your Daughter or Your Dog?*, by Deborah Slicer, *Ecofeminism and the Eating of Animals*, by Carol J. Adams, *Ground, Pivot, Motion: Ecofeminist Theory, Dialogics, and Literary Practice*, by Patrick Murphy, *Feminism and Ecology: On the Domination of Nature*, by Patricia Jagentowicz Mills, *Ecological Feminism and Ecosystem Ecology*, by Karen J. Warren and Jim Cheney; Book Reviews: *Rape of the Wild* by Andrée Collard with Joyce Contrucci, *Healing the Wounds: The Promise of Ecofeminism* edited by Judith Plant, *Staying Alive: Women, Ecology and Development* by Vandana Shiva

Volume 6, Number 2, Summer 1991

Where Are All the Pragmatist Feminists? by Charlene Haddock Seigfried, *Remaking the She-Devil: A Critical Look at Feminist Approaches to Beauty* by Kathy Davis, *Reconstructing the Subject: Feminism, Modernism, and Postmodernism* by Susan Hekman, *Irigaray on Subjectivity* by Ofelia Schutte, *Gendered Reason: Sex Metaphor and Conceptions of Reason* by Phyllis Rooney, *Feminist Philosophy and the Genetic Fallacy* by Margaret A. Crouch, *Toward A Value-Laden Theory: Feminism and Social Science* by Susan E. Bernick, *An Ethical Justification of Women's Studies, Or What's a Nice Girl Like You Doing in a Place like This?* by Lynette McGrath, *"Double Trouble": An Introduction* by Nancy Fraser, *The Subject in Feminism* by Rosi Braidotti, *The Morality of Feminism* by Selma Sevenhuijsen, *Her Terrain is Outside His "Domain"* by S. Elise Peeples, *The Science of Caring* by Bill Puka, *In Praise of Clutter as a Necessary Part of the Feminist Perspective* by Maryann Ayim, *Reply to Maryann Ayim* by Susan Wendell, *Open Letter to the Editors and Advisors of* Hypatia by Jo Trigilio, Book Reviews by Carole Boyce Davies, Susan Hekman, Patricia S. Mann, Andrea Nye, and Jo-Ann Pilardi

Volume 6, Number 3, Fall 1991

Special Issue on Feminism and the Body with an Introduction by Elizabeth Grosz; *Corporeal Habits: Addressing Essentialism Differently* by Vicki Kirby, *Women and the Knife. Cosmetic Surgery and the Colonization of Women's Bodies* by Kathryn Morgan, *Renaturalizing the Body (With a Little Help from Merleau-Ponty)* by Carol Bigwood, *Plastic Actions: Linguistic Strategies and Le Corps Lesbien* by Karin Cope, *Irigaray's Body Symbolic* by Margaret Whitford, *This Body Which is Not One: Technologizing an Embodied Self* by Elspeth Probyn, *The Foucauldian Body and the Exclusion of Experience* by Lois McNay, *The Face Before the Mirror Stage* by Cathryn Vasseleu, *In Excess: The Body and the Habit of Sexual Difference* by Rosalyn Diprose, *The Passion of the Signifier and the Body in Theory* by Robyn Ferrell, *Writing the Mystic Body: Sexuality and Textuality in the* Écriture feminine *of Saint Catherine of Genoa*, by Anna Antonopoulos, Review Essay by Eléanor Kuykendall, Book Reviews by Kelly Oliver and Eloise Buker, *Feminism in Cuba: Report on the 3rd Conference of North American and Cuban Philosophers* by Julien S. Murphy, Ofelia Schutte, Jan Slagter and Linda Lopez McAlister

Volume 7, Number 1, Winter 1992

The Logic of the Development of Feminism; or, Is MacKinnon to Feminism as Parmenides is to Greek Philosophy?, by Susan Bernick, *Trust, Distrust, and Feminist Theory*, by Trudy Govier, *Moral "I": The Feminist Subject and the Grammar of Self-Reference*, by Wendy Lee-Lampshire, *Toward a Feminist Conception of Self-Respect*, by Robin Dillon, *Aristotle on Necessary Verticality,*

Body Heat, and Gendered Proper Places in the Polis: A Feminist Critique, by Judith Green, *Relativism/There is No Given/On Liberation,* by Joyce Trebilcot, Review Essays by Nancy Tuana and Helen J. John, *Personal Autonomy or the Deconstructed Subject? A Reply to Hekman,* by Diana T. Meyers, *On the Compatibility of Pacifism and Care,* by Laura Duhan Kaplan, *Caring and Violence,* by Victoria Davion, Book Reviews by Rosemarie Tong, Samantha Brennan, Sherri Paris, Arlene Dallery, Jane Rineheart, and Carol Le Masters

Volume 7, Number 2, Spring 1992

Special Issue on Philosophy and Language with an Introduction by Dale M. Bauer and Kelly Oliver; *Discourse Competence; or, How to Theorize Strong Women Speakers,* by Sara Mills, *Frege's Metaphors,* by Andrea Nye, *Surviving to Speak New Language: Mary Daly and Adrienne Rich,* by Jane Hedley, *The Ideology of Fair Use: Xeroxing and Reproductive Rights,* by Judith Roof, *Blood Relations: Feminist Theory Meets the Uncanny Alien Bug Mother,* by Lynda Zwinger, *At the Limits of Discourse: Tracing the Maternal Body with Kristeva,* by Ewa Ziarek, *Headaches of Headless: Who is Poet Enough?,* by Teri Stratton, *What's "I" Got To Do With It?,* by Susan David Bernstein, *Disarticulating Voices: Feminism and Philomela,* by Elissa Marder, *Presence of Mind, Presence of Body: Embodying Positionality in the Classroom,* by Ann Ardis, Review Essays by Natalie Alexander, Sangeeta Ray, Beth A. Boehm, and Diane Shoos, Book Review by Dianne Rothleder

Volume 7, Number 3, Summer 1992

Philosophy: A Woman's Thought or a Man's Discipline? The Letters of Abelard and Heloise by Andrea Nye, *Feminism, Ethics, and the Question of Theory* by Margaret Urban Walker, *Corporeal Archetypes and Power: Preliminary Clarifications and Considerations of Sex* by Maxine Sheets-Johnstone, *Antigone's Mirrors: Reflections on Moral Madness* by Annie Pritchard, *The Pornography/Civil Rights Ordinance v. The BOG: And the Winner Is. . . ?* by Melinda Vadas, *Male Friendship and Intimacy* by Larry May and Robert Strikwerda, *Virtue Without Gender in Socrates* by Patricia Ward Scaltas, *Thinking About Gender* by Julie Nelson, Symposium on Susan Bordo's "Feminist Skepticism and the 'Maleness' of Philosophy" including, *Why Care About Gender?* by Anne Garry, *Response to Bordo's "Feminist Skepticism and the 'Maleness' of Philosophy"* by Judith Butler, *Reflections on Feminist Scepticism, the "Maleness" of Philosophy and Postmodernism* by Maureen Milligan, *Gender and Other Categories* by Linda Fisher, *Applying the Concept of Gender: Unsettled Questions* by Jane Upin, *Philosophy and Feminism: The Case of Susan Bordo* by Susan Bernick, *"Maleness" Revisited* by Susan Bordo, Book Reviews by Amanda Leslie-Spinks, Amy Morgan, Lori Gruen, and S. Elise Peeples and A. D. Miller

Back issues each: individuals $10.00, institutions $20. Journals Manager, Indiana University Press, 601 North Morton Street, Bloomington, IN 47404.

PSYCHOLOGY OF WOMEN QUARTERLY

Published on behalf of Division 35 of the American Psychological Association

EDITOR:
Judith Worell, *University of Kentucky*

Psychology of Women Quarterly publishes empirical studies, critical reviews, theoretical papers, and book and media reviews addressing a wide range of issues aimed at establishing a greater understanding of women's issues and sex roles in society. The intent of the journal is to present current research, theory and application and to influence the development of the field through maintenance of rigorous standards.

Recent Special Issue (Vol. 15, No. 4, Dec. 1991) Available at the special price of $13.95 each

WOMEN'S HERITAGE IN PSYCHOLOGY Origins, Development, and Future Directions

Agnes N. O'Connell and Nancy Felipe Russo *Guest Editors*

Articles Include . . .

Social Psychology: Humanist Roots and Feminist Future, *by B. Lott*

The Impact of the Feminist Critique on Tests, Assessment, and Methodology, *by M. Lewin and C.L. Wild*

Feminism and Diversity in Psychology: The Case of Women of Color, *by L. Comas-Díaz*

. . . and many other contributions

Call toll free 1-800-431-1580, ext. 175 for MasterCard or Visa orders, or for information about discounts on multiple copies for classroom use.

Send mail orders to:
Journals Department
Cambridge University Press
40 West 20th Street, New York, NY 10011, USA; or
The Edinburgh Building, Cambridge CB2 2RU, UK

Psychology of Women Quarterly (ISSN 0361-6843) is published quarterly. Subscriptions to Volume 16, 1992 (US, Canada and Mexico only): $96.00 for institutions; $37.00 for individuals; single parts $26.00.

ROUTLEDGE

lesbian philosophies and cultures
jeffner allen, editor

"I urge everyone to read it."
— Carol Anne Douglas, *Off Our Backs*

"Happily, this collection is as diverse in style and form as it is in Lesbian perspective."
— Carla Flanagan,
The Lesbian and Gay News-Telegraph

"Bound together, these many voices—of pain, hope, resistance, and dissent—reflect the diversity in modern lesbian experience: its connections as well as its ambiguities, dissonances, dislocations, and separations. The text is generally optimistic for, as [Nicole] Brossard reminds us, 'all reading, every reading is a desire for image, an intention to re/present which gives us hope.'"
— Elizabeth Wood, *New Directions for Women*
410 pages • $14.95/T paperback • ISBN 7914-0384-X

State University of New York Press
c/o CUP Services, PO Box 6525, Ithaca, NY 14851
VISA, MasterCard, American Express
1-800-666-2211 (orders)
Please add $3 for shipping.

a feminist quarterly

Multicultural essay, creative prose, poetry and art

Special Issues:
Writing Women's Stories
Feminist Considerations of music
Women and Violence
In Honor of Meridel LeSueur

Subscription $9
207 Lind Hall, 207 Church St. S.E., Minneapolis, MN 55455

Writing by women of color especially welcome

Faculty of Arts
Department of Philosophy

—— *Applications are invited for the following positions, which are subject to budgetary approval.*

1) One or more tenure-stream positions at a junior level. An appointment at the assistant professor level is expected, but more senior scholars may also apply. Successful candidates will have a strong scholarly record in addition to a PhD in any area of philosophy, but preference will be given to those whose areas of specialization include history of modern philosophy, contemporary existentialism, contemporary phenomenology, philosophy of language and mind, or logic.

2) A tenure-track position at the assistant professor level, beginning July 1, 1993. The successful candidate will be cross-appointed between the Department of Philosophy and the Division of Humanities. Candidates should have a PhD, or equivalent, with a strong scholarly record in practical ethics or a related field. The successful candidate will participate in graduate and undergraduate teaching. Those with experience in designing and teaching interdisciplinary courses are encouraged to apply.

3) A tenure-track position at the assistant professor level, beginning July 1, 1993. The successful candidate will be cross-appointed between the Department of Philosophy and the Interdisciplinary Progràmme in Law and Society in the Division of Social Science. Candidates should have a PhD and a strong scholarly record in any area of ethics, practical ethics, medical ethics, and any area of specialization linking philosophy, law and society. Graduate and undergraduate teaching may be required of the appointee.

—— *Applications with curriculum vitae and names of three referees should be sent to:*

Prof. J.N. Hattiangadi, Chair, Department of Philosophy, Faculty of Arts, York University, North York (Toronto), Ontario, Canada M3J 1P3.

Candidates should request their referees to send letters of reference directly to the Chair. Deadline for applications is October 31, 1992.

York University is implementing a policy of employment equity, including affirmative action for women faculty. In accordance with Canadian immigration requirements, priority will be given to Canadian citizens and permanent residents of Canada.

Abortion and Dialogue
*Pro-Choice, Pro-Life, and
American Law*

Ruth Colker

"The issues she takes on are crucial . . . she brings a
strong, evolving and distinctive perspective to the
discussion." —Emily Fowler Hartigan
Ruth Colker argues that when the state intervenes
in decisions regarding pregnancies, it falsely views
the woman and the fetus as having conflicting
needs. Her feminist-theological perspective on
reproductive health issues encourages both pro-
choice and pro-life advocates to consider how
the value of life is implicated in discussions of
reproduction. Colker examines effective and
respectful family-planning strategies that truly help
women in making reproductive choices.
Available September 1992
cloth $29.95 paper $12.95

Living Laboratories
*Women and Reproductive
Technology*

Robyn Rowland

" . . . convincing and terrifying." —Fay Weldon
In the last ten years, women have been
specifically targeted as "living laboratories" for
experimentation, whether to limit their fertility or to
end their infertility. Rowland explores the use of
women as raw material in the drive for profit and
power. In her investigation, the effect of new
reproductive technologies is clear: the increasing
alienation of people from reproduction and the
increased control by medical science and the
state over the "quality" of children born.
cloth $35.00 paper $14.95

The Publication Committed to the
Research and Concerns of Women Around the World

WOMEN'S STUDIES INTERNATIONAL FORUM

African and European Editor: **Claire Duchen,** England
Australian and Asian Editor: **Robyn Rowland,** Australia
Irish and British Co-Editors: **Ailbhe Smyth,** Ireland; **Pat Mahony,** England
Latin and North American Co-Editors: **Sue V. Rosser & Charlotte Hogsett,** USA
Feminist Forum Editor and Managing Editor: **Christine Zmroczek,** England
Consulting Editor: **Renate Klein**
Founding Editor: **Dale Spender**

WOMEN'S STUDIES INTERNATIONAL FORUM is a bi-monthly journal designed to aid the distribution and exchange of Women's Studies research from many disciplines and from around the world. The policy of the journal is to establish a feminist forum for discussion and debate and to account for and value cultural and political differences. The journal seeks to critique and reconceptualize existing knowledge, and to examine, and re-evaluate the manner in which knowlege is produced and distributed, and the implications this has for women's lives.

Subscribers to **WSIF** also receive *Feminist Forum,* a news and views supplement which appears in each issue with information on forthcoming and recent conferences, current research, new Women's Studies publications and Women's Studies centers.

RECENT ARTICLES

Judy Nolte Lensink (USA); Strategies for integrating material in the introductory Women's Studies course.

Somer Brodribb (Canada); Discarnate desires: Thoughts on sexuality and poststructuralist discourse.

Tobe Levin (Germany); Jelinek's radical radio: Deconstructing the women in context.

Ursula Streckeisen (Switzerland); "More and More Women Work": Inquires into the work patterns of adult Swiss women.

Ruth Parkin-Gounelas (Greece); Charlotte Bronte's *Villette* and the textuality of selfhood.

SUBSCRIPTION INFORMATION

Volume 15, 1992	ISSN: 0277-5395	Published 6 issues per annum
Annual Institution Subscription Rate (1992)		*£ 115.00/US$ 210.00
Two-year Institution Rate (1992/93)		*£ 218.50/US$ 399.00
Profesional Rate (1992)		*£ 37.00/US$ 59.00

A special rate is available to NWSA members upon request.

*Sterling prices quoted are definitive and apply worldwide with the exception of Japan. US dollar prices are quoted for convenience only and are subject to exchange rate fluctuation. Prices include postage and insurance.

FREE SAMPLE COPY AVAILABLE UPON REQUEST

 PERGAMON PRESS
US: 660 White Plains Road, Tarrytown, NY 10591-5153
UK: Headington Hill Hall, Oxford OX3 0BW, England

🐾 NWSA Journal
The National Women's Studies Association's
tri-annual journal of interdisciplinary, multicultural, feminist research

EDITOR:	ASSOCIATE EDITORS:	BOOK REVIEW EDITOR:
Patrocinio Schweickart	Susan Franzosa	Barbara White
	Mary Beth Rhiel	

MANAGING EDITOR:
Lili Ellison

NWSA NATIONALDIRECTOR:
Debbie Louis

EDITORIAL BOARD:
Nupur Chaudhuri • Sandra Coyner • Carole Boyce Davies • Tucker P. Farley • Maria C. Gonzalez
Veena P. Kasbekar • Elinor Lerner • Helen A. Moore • Vivien W. Ng • Barbara Corrado Pope
Vicki Ruiz • Charol Shakeshaft • Caryn McTighe Musil

Reflecting two decades of feminist scholarship emerging from and supporting the women's movement, the *NWSA Journal* will publish scholarship which continues to link feminist theory with teaching and activism. The *Journal* will raise critical and challenging questions in women's studies for the decades ahead.

A selection of articles from Vols. 1-3 include:

Ruth Bleier, "The Cultural Price of Social Exclusion: Gender and Science"
Minrose Gwin, "A Theory of Black Women's Texts and White Women's Readings"
Donna R. Kaufman and Frances J. Perry, "Institutionalized Sexism in Universities:
    The Case of Geographically Bound Academic Women"
Judith A. Baer, "What We Know as Women: A New Look at *Roe v. Wade*"
Autumn Stanley, "Gender Segregation in the Workplace"
Linda Gordon, "The Peaceful Sex? On Feminism and the Peace Movement"
Lori A. Goetsch, "Feminist Pedagogy: A SelectiveAnnotated Bibliography"
Betty LaDuke, "Egyptian Painter Inji Efflatoun: The Merging of Art, Feminism, and Politics"
Patricia Hill Collins, "On Our Own Terms: Subjugated Standpoints and Curriculum Transformation"
Marcia Westkott and Gay Victoria, "A Survey of the Women's Studies Major"

INFORMATION FOR AUTHORS — Manuscripts, 25-35 pages long, an abstract, and separate cover sheet with the author's name and institutional affiliation, should be submitted to Patrocinio Schweickart, Editor, English Department, University of New Hampshire, Durham, N.H. 03824; phone: 603-862-3976, fax: 603-862-2030. We cannot consider material previously published or that which is under consideration elsewhere. Manuscripts, including endnotes, must be double-spaced and submitted in duplicate. Style should be in accordance with that for the humanities; see *A Manual of Style*, 13th ed. (Chicago: University of Chicago Press, 1982). Submissions will be returned to authors who include a self-addressed, stamped envelope.

CALL FOR PAPERS — Readers are encouraged to submit manuscripts written from an interdisciplinary perspective or that which, although specific to a single discipline, retains broad implications. The *Journal* particularly encourages articles by and about women of color, research analyzing class issues, scholarship examining non-Western cultures, and research focusing on feminist pedagogy. Articles must be written from a feminist perspective and in accessible language and style.

NWSA JOURNAL Order Form

_____ Please send me a personal subscription at the
    special NWSA member rate beginning with
    Volume 4, No. 1 @ $24.00

_____ Please send me a non-member personal
    subscription @ $39.50

_____ Please send me an institutional subscription at
    the special NWSA group member rate @$45.00

_____ Please send me an institutional subscription
    @$105.00

_____ Please send me a sample issue for my review

_____ Please send me Information for Authors

(Note: All subscriptions must be prepaid. For subscriptions outside the U.S. and Canada, please add $15.00 for postage and handling. Payment must be made in U.S. currency.)

Name_____

Address_____

_____

City _____

State/Zip _____

Return coupon to Ablex Publishing Corporation • 355 Chestnut St. • Norwood, NJ 07648

University of South Florida

Degrees in Communication - B.A., M.A., Ph.D.

Communication Theory
Cultural Studies
Feminist Studies
Health Communication
Marital and Family Communication
Media Studies
Organizational Communication
Performance Studies
Rhetorical Theory and Criticism

Faculty: _____

Arthur P. Bochner
Communication Theory

Kenneth N. Cissna
Interpersonal Communication

Bernard F. Downs
Performance of Literature

Michael G. Garko
Persuasion

Carol J. Jablonski
Rhetoric & Social Change

Navita Cummings James
Media Studies

Mark Neumann
Cultural Studies

P. Judson Newcombe
Speech Education

A. David Payne
Rhetorical Studies

Loyd S. Pettegrew
Organizational Communication

Raymond J. Schneider
Communication Aesthetics

David H. Smith
Health Communication

Marsha L. Vanderford
Rhetorical Criticism

*Graduate assistantships are
available for qualified students*

For more information contact:
Kenneth N. Cissna
Director of Graduate Studies
Department of Communication
University of South Florida
Tampa, FL 33620-5550
813-974-2146

Recent courses include "Rhetoric of the
19th Century Feminist Movement" and
"Gender and Communication"

DIALOGUE

Canadian Philosophical Review/Revue canadienne de philosophie

Dialogue est la revue trimestrielle de l'Association canadienne de philosophie. Des contributions représentant les domaines principaux de la philosophie y sont publiées. Certains des articles du volume 28 sont mentionnés ci-dessous.

Dialogue is the quarterly journal of the Canadian Philosophical Association. Most of the main areas of philosophy are represented in its pages. Articles from Volume 28 are listed below.

Les manuscrits d'articles, d'études critiques et de comptes rendus rédigés en français ainsi que les livres pour recension doivent être adressés à : François Duchesneau, Département de philosophie, Université de Montréal, C.P. 6128, succ. A, Montréal, Québec, H3C 3J7, Canada.

English-language manuscripts and books for review should be sent to Professor Steven Davis, *Dialogue*, CC8311 Simon Fraser University, Burnaby, BC, V5A 1S6, Canada.

Les cotisations de membres (65 $; philosophes à la retraite, sans emploi ou détenant un emploi à temps partiel, 40 $; étudiants, 15 $) et les abonnements individuels à l'étranger (45 $) doivent être adressés à l'Association canadienne de philosophie, Pavillon Morisset, Université d'Ottawa, Ottawa, Ontario, K1N 6N5, Canada. Les abonnements institutionnels (au Canada, 60 $; à l'étranger, 65 $) doivent parvenir à Wilfrid Laurier University Press, Waterloo, Ontario, N2L 3C5, Canada.

Memberships ($65.00 regular; $40,00 retired, unemployed, and part-time philosophers; students $15.00) and foreign individual subscriptions ($45.00) should be addressed to the Canadian Philosophical Association, Morisset Hall, University of Ottawa, Ottawa, Ontario, K1N 6N5, Canada. Institutional subscriptions ($60.00 Canadian; $65.00 foreign) should be sent to Wilfrid Laurier University Press, Waterloo, Ontario, N2L 3C5, Canada.

Hypatia
TOTE BAGS!

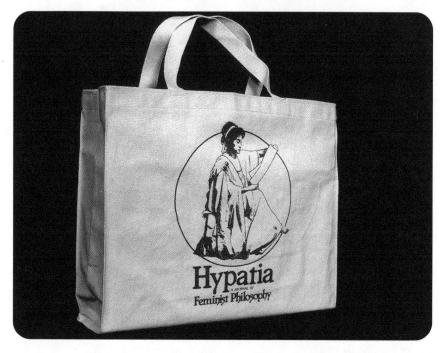

Please send me _____ Hypatia Tote Bags at $8.00 each including postage and handling. (Florida residents add 6% tax).
Make checks payable to: Hypatia, Inc.

Total $_____

Name_____

Address_____

City_____State_____Zip_____

Mail orders to: Hypatia
University of South Florida
4202 East Fowler Avenue, SOC 107
Tampa, Florida 33620